D0534122

THE EVERYTHING®

GROWTH FUND

MUTUAL FUNDS BOOK

How to pick, buy, and sell mutual funds
and watch your money grow!

Rich Mintzer

Adams Media Corporation
Holbrook, Massachusetts

An Everything® Series Book.
Everything® is a registered trademark of Adams Media Corporation.

Published by Adams Media Corporation
260 Center Street, Holbrook, MA 02343. U.S.A.
www.adamsmedia.com

ISBN: 1-58062-419-7

Printed in the United States of America.

J I H G F E D C B A

Library of Congress Cataloging-in-Publication Data
available upon request from the publisher.

This publication is designed to provide accurate and authoritative information with regard to the subject matter covered. It is sold with the understanding that the publisher is not engaged in rendering legal, accounting, or other professional advice. If legal advice or other expert assistance is required, the services of a competent professional person should be sought.
— From a *Declaration of Principles* jointly adopted by a Committee of the American Bar Association and a Committee of Publishers and Associations

Many of the designations used by manufacturers and sellers to distinguish their products are claimed as trademarks. Where those designations appear in this book and Adams Media was aware of a trademark claim, the designations have been printed in initial capital letters.

Illustrations by Barry Littmann

This book is available at quantity discounts for bulk purchases.
For information, call 1-800-872-5627.

Visit our home page: www.adamsmedia.com
Visit our exciting small business Web site: www.businesstown.com

TABLE OF CONTENTS

CHAPTER FOUR: FUND SIZE: THE LARGE AND SMALL OF IT / 87

CHAPTER FIVE: THE NAME IS BOND, BOND FUNDS / 99

CHAPTER SIX: MONEY MARKET FUNDS / 115

CHAPTER SEVEN: MUTUAL FUND FAMILIES / 123

CHAPTER EIGHT: CLOSED-END MUTUAL FUNDS / 133

CHAPTER NINE: LOADS OR NO LOADS, A LOADED QUESTION, PLUS FEES AND EXPENSES / 141

CHAPTER FIFTEEN: MUTUAL FUNDS AND RETIREMENT PLANS / 213

CHAPTER SIXTEEN: BUYING, HOLDING, AND SELLING YOUR MUTUAL FUND SHARES / 225

CHAPTER SEVENTEEN: ASSET ALLOCATION: SOME PLANS OF ACTION / 245

CHAPTER EIGHTEEN: CONCLUSION: SOME POSITIVES AND NEGATIVES / 261

INDEX / 271

ACKNOWLEDGMENTS

There were quite a number of sources used and people who answered questions in the research of this book. I'd like to thank in particular Greg Knopf of HighMark Funds, Max Jonas Ferris of MaxFunds.com, and Tara McDonough. I want to thank Pam Liflander for the opportunity to do the book, Bob Adams, Sarah Larson just for being so damn nice, and the folks at Adams Media. Interestingly enough, the crash of the stock market on Friday, April 14th paled in comparison to the crash of my computer on Friday, April 21st. Probably the biggest thank you goes to my brother-in-law Dave Lipschitz who diligently helped me survive by getting me up and running again from the brink of disaster. I should probably thank the makers of computer disks as well as my wife, Carol, for being calm, even at 6 A.M. when I sat wide awake after the computer nightmare earlier in the evening—and also for reminding me many times to "back up your files on disk." Thank you, Carol.

INTRODUCTION

As the 1990s unfolded, the world of investing became open to the masses. As the final decade of the century played out, the hot conversation at parties, and not just lavish cocktail parties, was mutual funds. From family picnics to PTA meetings, people were talking about the mutual funds that they just bought for their goals and the future needs of their families. Television commercials for mutual funds began to appear between advertisements for Burger King and Mentos. Their appeal was neatly tied to significant financial goals of Americans: saving money for college, buying a new home, and retirement. But it was more than marketing that launched the age of the mutual fund. Mutual funds provided a vehicle for investing that took away the need for mastering the stock market or understanding the jargon behind bonds. They became the "mom and pop" investment tool of the baby boomer generation, expected to provide for the American dream. Mutual funds offered a chance to achieve that dream and were cost and risk effective for the average investor. As the '90s played out with a bull market charging forward, mutual funds evolved as a practical investment that was now easy to research and easy to buy via an 800 number phone call or a few clicks of the mouse. And it didn't hurt that mutual funds soared in the '90s, producing stunning results.

Much of the success of mutual funds has been linked to the emergence of technology. The rapid development of financial software for brokers and for home users, along with the proliferation of the Internet and online investing, opened up the door to a wider potential market than ever before. Global technology linked markets worldwide, put a wealth of data just a click away, and allowed the average investor to become more sophisticated about investing. Thanks to magazine interviews and publicity, mutual fund managers suddenly became as popular in financial circles as ballplayers in the sports bars. Analysts had more than their share of data to analyze with 3-, 5-, and 10-year returns, sectors, global markets, and much more. The information highway put more substantial data in the hands of the media at local levels as well, so those without PCs and Internet access were not left out in the cold. Local newspapers carried stock market returns, and financial networks emerged, thanks to the growth of cable television and numerous financial magazines such as *Kipplingers, Money, Barons, Morningstar,* and *Your Money;* and *Business Week* enjoyed broader distribution. Tracking investments became as common an activity in the American household as breakfasting in the kitchen, mowing the lawn, or watching Monday Night Football.

In this book we'll give you all the basic information you will need to know about mutual funds: how to research and study them, select, buy, monitor, and sell them. We'll even give you the fund families, some strategies for allocating your money, listings of brokers, and more. We'll discuss goals, risks, diversification, volatility, derivatives, and the psychology of investing. The one thing you won't find, however, are "Best Mutual Fund Picks" since, in the few months that it takes to put this book together, the hottest funds can change several times over. There are examples of 1-, 5-, and 10-year listings, however, to give you an idea of how much funds can move over those time periods. There is also a breakdown of the types of funds, including the various sectors and what to look at when selecting a mutual fund. First we will look at some of the basics, as we look at what mutual funds are, and discuss some of the steps in determining whether you are ready to invest.

Keep in mind that this book is designed to help you learn about and understand mutual funds. It is not in any way designed as an endorsement for any fund, fund family, or fund selecting strategy. In other words, this is a book designed to teach you about mutual funds in general terms. The market, the economic picture, and the economic trends will change frequently. In the end, however, investors who do their homework and invest in what is best for their own personal goals and needs will flourish. Be self-motivated, know yourself, and don't be guided by marketing, salesmanship, or popular trends.

CHAPTER ONE

MUTUAL FUND BASICS: WHAT ARE MUTUAL FUNDS AND HOW DO THEY WORK?

Ten Reasons to Invest in Mutual Funds

1. You can get greater diversification across sectors.
2. You can get a broader range of companies within a single sector.
3. You can track a few funds more easily than a wide range of stocks.
4. There are fund possibilities to cover all goals and needs.
5. Your investment is in the hands of a competent professional.
6. You can have a fund that mirrors the S&P 500 or another significant benchmark.
7. You can get your money back in a short amount of time without penalties.
8. You are able to stretch your investment further through greater purchasing power.
9. You can choose a fund that is appropriate for level of risk.
10. The better funds in recent years have shown excellent returns.

A mutual fund is an investment vehicle that pools the money of many investors and buys stocks, bonds, or other securities, depending on the type of fund. It is a way for a single investor to own pieces of many different securities at one time for less money than if he or she were to go out and buy each security individually. Furthermore, it is also a way of achieving great diversity. Since funds own anywhere from 25 stocks to thousands, you have a diversified investment from the start, meaning you do not have all of your eggs in one basket and have not invested in the future of just one company as you would if you owned a stock. Obviously, the more stocks the fund owns, the less impact one single stock will have on the fund, which can be good or bad, depending on the stock. Thus, one advantage to owning a mutual fund is that it minimizes the risk brought on by having one bad apple.

In mutual funds, you can own stocks in the financial services, transportation, and technology fields with one fund. You can own IBM, Lucent, Disney plus smaller companies you've never heard of. You can own a variety of stocks in companies in Thailand, Singapore, and China. Your money can be spread around the country or around the world in numerous types of companies. On the other hand, you can have a fund that specializes in one area, or one industry. This can be more risky, but if the industry is thriving, you'll own a small piece of all the key players for one investment price. Should a single company be in a downswing, a fund can withstand that decline. However, if the entire market is down, funds investing in that market will follow suit.

Funds are handled by fund managers, or teams of managers, who are buying and selling securities to meet the goals of the fund, which can be growth or income or both. Fund managers generally have advanced degrees in business and financial analyst certification. They work with research analysts and others to create strategies and plot a successful course for the fund. The paths to reaching the goals of a fund can be followed aggressively or more conservatively, depending on the nature of the fund and the fund style. The most basic goal of any fund is to make money, in either the short term or the long term.

Mutual funds are created to meet a wide range of goals and financial plans. Mutual funds can provide a steady flow of income

or can be engineered for short-term or long-term growth. There are numerous categories of funds designed to meet a variety of goals. The success of the fund depends on the sum of its parts, which are the individual stocks, bonds, and other securities within the fund's portfolio plus the management team heading it.

Each mutual fund is in essence its own management company within the framework of the larger brokerage firm or "fund family." Each fund is also registered individually with the Securities and Exchange Commission. The sponsor of the fund, which is the brokerage house or a bank or even a wealthy individual, starts the fund with its own money. The sponsor then issues shares and promotes the fund to the public, which buys into it. Naturally it's much easier for a huge fund family like Fidelity to spread the word than it is for a small fund group. *It doesn't mean the small fund family won't have a successful fund. It just may be harder to find out about it and riskier to invest in it because you may not know the reputation of the smaller fund family.* Shareholders of a fund can later sell their shares, which are redeemed by the company. Assets in the company grow by the number of investors adding money to the overall pool. This allows the fund to purchase more securities, which in a good market is a positive factor. A fund can close to new investors if the asset pool becomes unmanageable for meeting the goals of the fund. Very large funds, like a huge tractor trailer truck, are sometimes harder to maneuver. Don't forget, a fund is set up to invest all, or nearly all of the pooled assets that come into the fund into various securities. Therefore, the more money that comes pouring in, the more good investments the fund manager has to find. And, no, they can't just dump it all into a few favorite stocks. The SEC has regulations that say a fund cannot invest too heavily in any one company. Therefore, they have to spread the assets around, but this is why you buy a fund in the first place.

The success of a mutual fund is measured by calculating the value of all the securities in the portfolio plus all the assets minus all liabilities. This provides the total net assets, which is then divided by the number of shares outstanding to produce the *net asset value,* or NAV, which is the number you will look at in the financial pages or online to see how your mutual fund is doing. The latest NAV (an overall share price for the fund, like a stock

Open or Closed End

Mutual funds are either open- or closed-end funds. Unlike an open-end mutual fund that is simply closed to new business, a *closed-end fund* issues only a certain number of shares from the start. The money is invested in securities, but the fund company is not obligated to redeem the shares or offer new ones. Closed-end funds trade in an entirely different manner; buyers and sellers deal with one another similar to the way bond buyers and sellers trade. Far more common are the open-end mutual funds that are constantly growing as new shares are offered to the public and outstanding shares are redeemed by the company. Some of these funds grow to be quite huge in terms of assets and securities held.

The Fund Craze

The latest technological advances have gone hand in hand with the success of the mutual fund market as buyers have simply gone online to make their purchases. Convenience and a wealth of readily available information have also fueled the mutual fund phenomenon. Much of this ties into the Internet and those who use it. People are accessing more and more information from their PC's. Front and center on many Web servers is the latest in mutual fund news. Like most trends, information feeds on itself. People are buying mutual funds; therefore, more fund related news is being posted on Web sites. The more news posted, the more new investors are attracted to mutual funds, and so on. It's an ongoing growth cycle.

price) is calculated at the end of each day. Unlike a stock price, the NAV deducts the operating expenses of the mutual fund, since it is a business and the expenses of running that business are passed onto the customers, in this case the investors.

Currently, the number of mutual funds in the United States is just over 11,000. Consider that as recently as 1991 the number was just over 3,000, and at the end of 1996 it was listed at around 6,000. Mutual funds have become extremely popular. Stock funds, also called equity funds, are growing as a way to play the market without having to make all the choices of what to buy and when to sell. However, bond funds are also growing, partly because of the complexities associated with understanding individual bonds and also as a way to hold more bonds than the average investor could afford to purchase on an individual basis. Since bond funds invest in debt instruments, usually corporate bonds or government bonds, they are generally exposed to less risk than stock funds. There are also money market mutual funds, which offer a safe alternative to bank accounts, providing higher interest rates, but also providing much lower returns than most stock funds. They are a safe place to keep your cash reserve.

Every financial institution worth its weight in earnings offers a variety of mutual funds to choose from, and many business school graduates with MBAs from top universities are now working their way up the ladder to positions as fund managers. As we enter the new millennium, funds now total over $4 trillion in investments with nearly one quarter of American households owning at least one mutual fund. The number of accounts keeps growing, and there are now nearly 100 million individual accounts in mutual funds.

Following are a few reasons funds are so popular.

1. Very solid rates of return in recent years
2. Ease of purchasing
3. More purchasing power for your dollar
4. Liquidity
5. Lower risk than individual stocks
6. Diversification
7. Good way to meet long-term goals

8. Professionally managed
9. Excellent investments for retirement plans
10. Great cocktail party conversation

Some funds have seen returns of 30%, 60%, or 150% and higher in recent years. And while this trend may not last, over the 3-year period of 1996 through 1998, the average domestic stock fund produced an annualized rate of return of 18.5%. Over 5 years from 1994 through 1998, the average annualized return rate was 15.5%, which, compared to other types of investments, is hard to beat. Even domestic bond funds over the same period have averaged 5.5% to 6%.

Purchasing a mutual fund is now as easy as making a phone call or a trip to your PC. Fund families, which are part of major investment firms such as Fidelity, Dreyfus, Janus, and AIM, have responded to the surge of interest in mutual funds. They have tried to make funds easily accessible to all investors with 800 numbers and Web sites that allow easy buying, selling, and switching mutual funds. Most fund families offer automated reinvestment programs whereby money feeds into the fund from your bank account at regular intervals. There are also payments, or distributions, on a periodic basis for those who want ongoing income. Since there is so much demand for funds, fund managers are trying to think up new ways to make their funds the most attractive and easiest to obtain. Fund supermarkets are relatively new places to go online and look at funds from different fund families and take one from aisle one, and two from aisle two, and so on. There's a whole new world of easy fund shopping. However, homework is strongly recommended before you jump in.

Compounding Interest

Keep in mind the rule of 72 that says that if you divide the number 72 by the interest rate, you'll know how long it will take for your money to double. Therefore a $10,000 investment paying at 9% (without reinvesting the interest) would double in 8 years. Because 72 divided by 9 is 8, that is the number of years until you would have $20,000.

THE GROWTH (AND BRIEF HISTORY) OF MUTUAL FUNDS

Many modern investors assume that mutual funds emerged as the result of technological advances. Why not create a product to share, since we now have the ways and means to communicate with such a broad cross section of the American public? That is not, however, how it came about. Mutual funds have been around for quite a while. In fact, they came into being over 75 years ago. The first funds, organized in 1924, were the Massachusetts Investors Trust and State Street Investors Trust. These, and subsequent funds, were created to provide investors with a means of playing the stock market without having to analyze and select individual stocks. The basic concept holds true today, only the marketing has changed dramatically. In fact, the modern mutual fund is the result of fund creators and financial planners who lived decades ago. Despite what many people would believe, the first no-load fund was actually introduced by Scudder, Stevens and Clark back in 1928.

Within 5 years after the dawn of "the fund," the market crash sent stocks and mutual funds reeling. No one wanted anything to do with such investments in the early 1930s, no matter what they promised. The Securities and Exchange Commission was created in 1933 to reform the securities industry. This would be no small undertaking, considering the state of the economy in the 1930s. The first order of business was to find a way to protect the consumer from fraudulent practices and to prevent anything like the great crash from ever occurring again. With many struggling companies and numerous dissatisfied investors, it took the commission and the government many years before they once again gained the trust of the American public. It took a while before the public ventured back to investment vehicles. At first mutual funds grew slowly, reaching a total of 70 in the early 1940s.

The Investment Company Act of 1940 defined mutual funds as open-ended management companies and set up more definitive parameters under which these companies would operate. The new regulations, however, would concern only a few, as interest in mutual funds did not grow quickly. By the early 1950s less than 1% of Americans owned funds. The public didn't quite understand the concept of buying shares of a fund that owned many stocks, and fund information was buried deep inside the *Wall Street Journal* and other financial papers. Nonetheless, the first international fund was introduced.

At the start of the 1970s, although still far from "the rage," mutual funds were increasing in number, with nearly 400 available to the public. Corporate retirement plans known as 401k's and tax exempt municipal bond funds were introduced, both encouraging people to save money while avoiding the tax bite. The 401k plan

afforded companies an opportunity to assist their employees in a savings program. Ongoing monthly investments were introduced in the 1950s, but it was something an individual had to commit to on his or her own. Since there was far more concern about the communist menace than investment portfolios, the idea of regular investing in such new vehicles was still fairly minimal. The 401k, however, made investing more attractive, particularly when companies matched a portion of each employee's contribution to the plan. Slowly but surely, people joined 401k plans, but they had little idea of where the money was actually being invested. Many others hooked up directly with the Treasury Department and ordered Treasury bills, which were paying double-digit interest and were as safe as an investment could be. The demand was so great that the government raised the minimum to $10,000 to stem the tide. While T-bills were the rage, the index mutual fund was introduced by Vanguard in the mid '70s, with an eye toward the future. But it was another new favorite investment option that took over as the '80s began.

At the start of the 1980s, money market mutual funds, which had first been introduced in 1972, suddenly caught on. They invested in CDs and Treasury bills; when the interest rates were high, returns of 7% or 8% were not uncommon. Money market funds offered decent returns, liquidity, and check writing privileges. Furthermore, they sought to maintain a net asset value of $1 per share, so they remained a very safe investment. But as the interest rates of these high quality, short-term obligations began to drop, the public needed a new place to turn.

Finally, as computers and technology created a burgeoning new industry rich with jobs and great potential, the 1990s ushered in the age of the mutual fund. In 1990 the public invested less than $13 billion in stock funds. By 1993, funds were on the rise with a bullish economy, and the number of funds surpassed the number of stocks. The surge continued. In 1996 nearly $30 billion poured into just stock funds alone in the first month of the year. Mutual funds had finally come of age. Technology stocks soared and led the way as numerous companies flourished. In an age of quick fixes, fast food, and rapid information, the public needed a way to build a portfolio of stocks without having to take the risk (and chart) individual stocks.

Funds Offer Greater Affordability Than Individual Stocks

It is often easier to select an amount of money you are willing to invest and find a fund with that minimum investment amount than it is to find stocks that fit your budget. Many of the best-performing stocks and the biggest companies will have high per share prices. A stock price at $100 per share means your $5,000 investment will buy you 50 shares. The same $5,000 in a $20 NAV mutual fund will buy you 250 shares and the stock you wanted that was priced so high may be one of the stocks in the fund. Additionally, you will own hundreds of stocks for the same investment.

CHAPTER TWO

MUTUAL FUND INVESTING: THE FIRST STEPS

So, what do you do first? Before selecting a mutual fund, it's important to determine your goals and your time frame for reaching those goals. The first question you need to ask yourself is where you stand financially. If you are in debt or are not covering your current expenses, the risk of even the safest investments is not generally worth taking. Borrowing money to invest in a "sure thing" is not a way to get out of debt. The mutual fund investor should have a cushion, money in cash reserve that you can turn to beyond that which is needed to cover your daily, weekly, monthly, and annual expenses. Once you determine that you have some money to invest in mutual funds, even if it's $500, you need to ask yourself when you are looking to reach your goals. Are you putting money away for your retirement in 25 years? For your children's college tuition in 17 years? For buying a house in 5 years? Is this your only savings plan or do you have one at work? If you already have a retirement plan in place, perhaps you can use the mutual fund to meet other needs.

Along with retirement planning, one of the biggest reasons for the increase in fund buying is to put money aside for children. Results of long-range investing have shown time and time again that mutual funds are an ideal way to build a college tuition fund.

Whether or not your children opt to go to college, saving money for their future is something you should consider when they are in diapers, or shortly thereafter. An initial investment of a few thousand dollars can grow into substantial savings as your youngster goes from preschool to driver's ed. There is even a new wave of kid-oriented funds that are buying into companies that deal in kid products and services such as Disney, Johnson & Johnson, Coca-Cola, or one of the toy manufacturers. Funds such as American Express New Dimensions, USAA First Start Growth, and Stein Roe Young Investor are targeting this huge market by investing a good portion of their portfolio in kid familiar/kid friendly companies and even sending educational materials to children and quarterly newsletters about money and investing. While it may be regarded as yet another marketing ploy, the idea is to teach kids about investing.

Saving money for retirement and saving money for college have one important factor in common. They are both goals that are down the road. Saving for such goals works because time is on your side. Traditionally, the theory is that if you won't be touching the capital for 10 or more years, you should go with stocks, which can be riskier investments in the short term but have a great upside. According to history, the market over time will show a good return, and no 10-year period has seen an overall loss in the stock market. So why not use dividend reinvesting and compounding in your favor if you have several years to watch the money grow. If, however, you are looking at a short-term goal and will need the money in a few years, two or three perhaps, you should keep a good portion of your money in more conservative investments, including bond funds and money markets.

Opponents to this more aggressive long-term investing approach say "Why go the riskier route at first when you could also lose a portion of the principal investment and spend much of your time just trying to catch up or break even?" There are those who feel you should start off with a middle of the road stance, making sure you are protecting your principal investment. Once you are showing profits, you then take some of the profits and invest in more high-risk/potentially high-growth funds, since you are now investing money from your income and not playing with the principal. It's similar to the gambling philosophy of playing with the house's money. In gambling, however, you have to get lucky and win early in the game. In the world of investing, you can set up a winning portfolio that gives you enough in returns to start building toward more exciting, aggressive investments. Then as your goal approaches, you go back to the more conservative route.

There are many theories and variations thereof, and advisors will vary widely in their opinions. Of course, since it's your money going into the fund(s), it's your decision that ultimately matters most. We'll get to the very important topic of allocating your assets shortly.

Short Term Versus Long Term

Short-term investing usually means more volatility or more ups and downs and more risk. Long term usually means volatility along the way, but a less rocky road overall and lower risk. Mutual funds are generally thought of as long-term investments unless you have short-term goals and are "sure" you've got a winner. Remember that it's risky to invest for the short term.

THE SLOW AND STEADY APPROACH TO INVESTING

Don't forget, many of the mutual fund publications are written by people who are quite bored with the slower, safer approach and prefer to see people hitting long home runs; it makes for more interesting stories. Mark McGwire hitting one 450-foot home run garners more attention on the sports pages than four singles in a game by a great hitter like Tony Gwynn. Yet after they retire, both will end up in the Hall of Fame. You can similarly take the slower and steadier approach with mutual fund investing. If you want to build savings for your future, let time take its course. In short, your asset allocation will depend less on what some 31-year-old MBA Wall Streeter with no family or children to support tells you to do and more on what risks you feel comfortable taking financially. When it comes to your investments, you're the coach giving the bunt sign or deciding whether it's time to swing for the fences. Remember that flashy returns make great headlines, but you are not in it for the headlines. There is no blueprint for mutual fund investing. In fact, financial advisors have varied opinions on all areas of investing—*which also explains why there are so many publications and investment books and Web sites*. With that said, let's look at the area of risk and tolerance, which, along with your goals, will help determine your asset allocation and which funds to buy.

RISK VERSUS TOLERANCE

You can secure your money in a bank vault, earning low interest, but safely insured by the FDIC. On the other hand, you can put down $50 a day betting on the horses or playing the lottery. How risky you choose to be with your money is part of your personality. If you are going to invest in a high-risk fund and spend all of your profits on medical bills thanks to the high level of stress associated with your investment choice, then you're defeating the purpose. Investing is a way of building money for a better quality of life.

In life, most activities involve some degree of risk, no matter how minimal; you can slip and get injured taking a shower. Financially, you can lose money in the wrong stock or in the

wrong fund. Tolerance is how comfortable you will feel with an unfavorable outcome. When you take greater risks, you will need to know from the onset that the chance of losing money increases along with the chance of making money.

Risk versus tolerance is one of the first determinants of which funds you will buy and how you will allocate your assets. Some investors will take much bigger risks looking for large gains while others are content just having their money earn them a steady income. There are plenty of levels in between.

Following are a few sample risk tolerance questions that often appear on investment company questionnaires. It is a good idea to look these over and think about your answers. If you can determine where you stand on the risk tolerance scale, you will better be able to make your own decisions based on the information presented to you via the Internet or by a broker. It's not a broker's call where you should stand on the risk tolerance scale, it's your call. Therefore, what you should do at any point is contingent on your judgment and comfort level.

1. Suppose you invest $20,000 in an index fund (rather conservative) that boasts a 25% return the first year (we'll call it fund A). The next year you learn about a more aggressive fund that earned 89% the same year, but the previous year, during a down market had dropped by 30% (fund B). You do not have additional money to invest in both funds at present so you:
   A. Do nothing and just stay put.
   B. Take your 25% profit in fund A ($5,000) and invest it in fund B.
   C. Take 50% of your money from fund A ($12,500) and move it into fund B.
   D. Take the entire $25,000 from fund A and invest it in fund B.
2. Which of the following concerns you the most when you consider buying a mutual fund?
   A. The potential for loss.
   B. Primarily the potential for loss, with some concern for the potential for gain.

Risk Factors

Remember, factors in determining risk include:

- How long you have to reach your goals; a rule of thumb says the longer the time frame the more risk you can take.
- Your own personal comfort level. We are all brought up with certain attitudes about money, about spending it, earning it, and saving it. Now we need to determine how comfortable we feel investing it.
- What you are looking for from your investments. Do you want capital gains, a steady source of income, or a little of both?

C. An equal concern for the potential for loss and gain.

D. Mostly the potential for gain, with a minor concern for the potential for loss.

E. The potential for gain.

3. Experts predicts a potential downturn in the market. You have three stock funds. Do you:

A. Hold onto your funds and ride out the down market.

B. Sell off some of your shares.

C. Move all of the money into bond and money market mutual (safer) funds.

4. Inflation can affect your mutual fund returns. Higher returns will override higher inflation but will generally come with more risk attached. Which philosophy would describe your investment strategy?

A. I want investments that are expected to keep pace with inflation. These types of investments generally have a lower chance of short-term losses and lower returns.

B. I want investments that are expected to moderately out-pace inflation. These types of investments generally have a moderate chance of short-term losses and potentially greater returns.

C. I want investments that are expected to significantly out-pace inflation. These types of investments generally have a greater chance of short-term losses and much greater returns.

The four preceding questions are designed to determine where you are on the risk tolerance scale. If you answered A to all of them, you would prefer taking the conservative route and would therefore look for funds of a more conservative nature. The middle answers put you in the middle of the road, which is a wide ranging place to be; you will have to allocate your fund investments accordingly. Whether you choose a 50–50 split between conservative and aggressive funds or a 65–35 split in either direction, your decision will come from looking over the funds carefully, studying the returns, looking at how they fared when the market went through down periods (a bear market), plus your own gut feeling about how you will handle the potential risk. If you took the last answer (highest letter) for each question, then you are willing to throw caution to the winds and invest aggressively. Just as one gambler will let it ride on the craps table and another will just play the slots, it's your call. Only in this case, there is a lot more information available, and with the right approach, you have significantly better odds than gambling (which has odds that are stacked against you). Investing correctly is stacked in your favor.

THE OTHER RISKS

The term *risk* generally refers to the overall risk of losing your principal investment. While this fundamental risk is of primary concern, there are other important risks associated with investing. They are also worth considering, especially technical risk.

TECHNICAL RISK

Economic factors such as changes in interest rate, unemployment rate, inflation, the global economy, the budget deficit, and other indicators will affect your investment. Technical risk, also known as *market risk*, is how well your investment will react to any and all of these factors. The best way to manage technical risk is to allocate your assets in different market classifications, spreading your money around in bond funds, stock funds, and cash accounts such as CDs and money markets. This way, if one market gets affected by external factors, the others (and your other investments) will be safe. You can spread your assets out in many different ways, including larger and smaller cap funds (funds investing in larger or in smaller companies) and even diversify by putting money into foreign markets. Generally, the theory that "A rising tide affects all ships" holds true for investing, meaning that all stocks or funds within a single market will be affected by the same factors. Therefore, you want to diversify among markets to lower your exposure to technical risk.

Risk Level

The highest level of potential risk to the lowest level of potential risk (in general) among several types of funds.

Aggressive growth funds

Specialty stock funds

International stock funds and global stock funds

Growth stock funds

Growth and income stock funds

Large-cap stock index funds

Balanced funds and asset allocation funds

Long-term bond funds

Intermediate-term bond funds

Short-term bond funds

Money market funds

Bearing with the Bear

The 1998 bear market showed that some funds stood up better than others did when the market sank. The fund categories hit hardest by the bear market were: small-cap, micro-cap, and mid-cap stock funds. On the other hand, only a very small percentage of the growth, growth and income, or large-cap funds were in the negative column by the end of that bear market. S&P index funds were all on the plus side when it was all over.

INTEREST RATE RISK

Interest rate risk is how well your investment will fare over time in comparison to the changing interest rate. The strongest correlation to the interest rate falls within the bond market. Bond values have an inverse reaction to the interest rate. In other words, if the interest rate drops, your bonds are more valuable on the bond market and vice versa. If you have a bond paying at 7% and the interest rate drops to 5%, your 7% bond will sell for more money because it's more valuable. Conversely, if you have a bond paying 7% and interest rates go up to 9%, your bond drops in value because who wants a bond paying only 7% when you can get one at 9%? To manage interest rate risk, you would lean toward short-term bond funds. This way the bonds will come due before the interest rates can change too often or too drastically. Conversely, the risk is greater in bond funds holding long-term securities.

INFLATION RISK

Inflation risk is the possibility that the rate of inflation will rise faster than your investment. An investment paying you interest at a rate of 5% is fine as long as the inflation rate remains around 3%. However, if the inflation rate jumps to 5.1%, your 5% rate of interest is behind rising inflation and you are now coming out .1% below inflation. To best combat inflation risk, look toward investing in large-cap stock funds for the long term (10 years or more). If you look at the stock market over the span of any 10 years since the depression of 1929, you will see that, on average, stocks have gone up by at least 10%. As long as inflation is below 10% (and at the start of 2000, it was below 4%), you should almost always come out ahead with stock funds (if you hold onto them) even after paying fees, expenses, and even taxes.

LIQUIDITY RISK

Not really a risk of the investment itself, but more of a personal risk, or concern, liquidity risk pertains to having your money tied up in investments that you can get your money out of should you

need to. Mutual funds can be sold rather easily, and your money can be moved into a money market account in most fund families very quickly. Even though you may sell at a loss, you can still turn a stock or mutual fund into cash fairly quickly in open-end funds (which are most funds). Closed-end funds are less liquid because you cannot redeem (or sell) your shares back to the investment company but need to find a buyer, much like selling a bond on the bond market.

TAX RISK

Like liquidity risk, this is more of a personal risk than an investment risk.

If you are in a high tax bracket or simply want some investments that are outside of the reach of Uncle Sam, you can use retirement vehicles such as a 401k plan or IRA, or you can invest in tax-free municipal bonds. You can also look for stock funds that have a low turnover, meaning they do not do a great deal of trading but exercise a buy and hold philosophy. This will keep the tax bite lower (more on this in Chapter 14).

STYLE DRIFT RISK

A separate risk you will take on when you buy mutual funds is the risk of style drift, which means that the fund, as guided by a fund manager, does not stick to the style it was designed to follow. This can be partly the fault of the fund manager (taking a different course) or the fault of the companies owned by the fund. As small caps grow into mid caps or mergers and acquisitions cause larger companies to grow even larger, the holdings of a fund can change. Industries can change as well.

The best way to avoid style drift is to keep a close eye on the key holdings of the fund and read the latest fund information to see if your conservative fund is becoming more aggressive or vice versa. Sometimes funds are forced to move into other types of securities when they grow too large (in terms of assets) too quickly. This is more a problem of the fund becoming too cumbersome for

Bear Markets

The stock market crash of 1929 saw the market drop by nearly 48%. It took years before the market rebounded. Another significant bear market was in 1987 when the market took a 22.61% hit in just one day. The 1998 bear market is the most recent one to look at to see how well your fund fared. In 1998 the market plunged over 500 points in one day (a 6.37% drop). Although over time the market has always rebounded and made money, these can be hard times to endure. Long-term strategy, however, says that once the bear market ends, and history shows that they always do, you will usually come out ahead if you hold stocks or stock funds for 10 or more years.

the fund manager to manage. Watch out for funds that are growing too quickly. You can also avoid style drift with an index fund.

In the end, the levels of risk you take will all tie in with the returns you will gain. Greater risks can mean greater returns, but can also mean greater losses. Assess your own level of risk and your goals, then allocate your assets accordingly.

DIVERSIFICATION

You hear it mentioned time and time again, but why is it important to *diversify?* By diversifying you lower your risks, all types of investment risks. The commuter who owns three cars lowers her risk of not being able to get to work one day when her car breaks down. She has two other cars ready to go. Investors with 10 stocks can have three losers or even four or five and not be losing money in their overall portfolios. In fact, one big winner can offset nine losers. But buying several different stocks does not mean you are diversifying if you are buying the same type of stock. Within an asset class, you can spread your money around. There are numerous types of stocks and various types of stock funds. Diversifying means having a minivan for the family, a sports car for yourself on weekends, and a practical everyday car for the weekly drive to work. Diverse investments could include a large-cap growth fund, a sector fund, and a small-cap fund. The don't-put-all-of-your-eggs-in-one-basket theory works well for investing; you are covered if one type of fund, one stock, or a particular industry is not doing well.

Down Markets Are Hard to "Bear"

When the market is down it is called a bear market. While the market has had greater highs in recent years than ever before, there has also been greater volatility in the climb to the top.

A true bear market isn't just a daily dip but a longer period of down time. It still doesn't mean you need to panic. If your assets are well diversified and you are invested for the long term, you should be able to ride out the bear. It's comforting to know that only once between 1980 and 2000 was there a bear market that lasted as long as 3 months.

You can take note of statistical averages. An average takes into account many highs and lows. For example, between 1930 and 2000, small companies averaged an annualized return of around 12%. This average includes a wide range from over 140% in gains to over 50% in losses. The +12% also includes bear markets that the market went through along the way.

You may also want to use certain averages as benchmarks to guide you.

It is in your best interest to look at how the fund you are interested in fared against a down market. Did the fund manager buckle under the pressure to keep the fund afloat or were the losses rather minor? Recent stock funds are measured against the market downswing of 1998, which saw the S&P 500 Stock Index drop by 18.8% and the average U.S. stock fund fall off by 23.1%. If your stock fell only 12% during that bear market, then the fund manager apparently did his or her best to position the fund to withstand the downswing. This is usually done by moving funds into safer securities.

Approaching bear markets do not mean it's time to panic. As when facing an approaching storm, you want to have investments to come back to when the storm has passed. It is therefore up to you to assess your position and take necessary precautions to board up your portfolio. Make sure you are diversified and leaning toward conservative investments.

ALLOCATING YOUR ASSETS

Like diversifying, *asset allocation* means spreading your investment around. However, it means spreading your investment across various markets and buying different types of securities, including stocks, bonds, and cash instruments. This means having three cars plus easy access to the train in case the snow makes it impossible to get any car out of the driveway. Likewise, one entire market could be struggling.

Financial experts may disagree on many things, but it is widely agreed that asset allocation may be the most important aspect of investing. Allocating assets means how you slice up your financial investment pie. Do you slice it in quarters? Does half of the pie go into growth mutual funds? How much goes into bonds or bond funds?

How you allocate your assets will be as important as your choices of investment vehicles, even more so. You can build an entire portfolio around mutual funds if you choose (since there are mutual funds to fit every need), then put some cash reserve in a money market account. You can also invest in stocks, bonds, mutual funds and, if you're daring, the futures market. There are numerous scenarios. It is estimated that more than 80% of investors spend too little time in this area and could do better if they allocated their money to meet their own needs, taking into account their own level of risk tolerance.

Allocating assets is not a one-time financial project. As your goals, needs, and the time frame to meet such goals change, you will need to reallocate your investments. The funds you choose now may be for the long term, however, you may sell off shares and invest in less risky ventures as your capital grows inside the fund. You may find a need for income at a certain point in life and allocate more money to an income-generating fund. On the other hand, you may inherit a great amount of money and want to play the market more aggressively with aggressive growth funds. Too often investors put their money into a fund and let it sit there. This is fine in a long-term growth fund, but look out if it's a volatile fund that produced big returns last year but doesn't look so good this year.

The need to reallocate applies especially to 401k plans and IRAs. For some reason, people tend to forget that they can move their money into other investment vehicles offered within the retirement plan.

ASSET ALLOCATION PLANNING

Rule number one, don't listen to everyone else. Make your own investment plan and follow it. The steps for planning asset allocation are very simple, but they may take some time.

1. Determine how much money you are allocating. If you are covering your expenses, not in debt with your credit cards or anywhere else, and have savings put aside that are in cash reserve accounts, you can determine how much money to invest.
2. Your next step is to decide how much goes into mutual funds and how much you plan to invest directly into stocks or bonds. Many new investors are not yet comfortable taking on the task of choosing individual stocks beyond perhaps a couple of long-term, sure-fire blue chip favorites with household names. Bonds are also often tricky; so bond funds can make life much simpler. There's nothing wrong with purchasing mutual funds along with some individual stocks and bonds or making up your portfolio strictly with funds. The key is breaking down your allocation by levels of risk and by expected returns that meet your estimated time frame.
3. Think about long-term "projected" goals. It's worth noting that you do not have to have your whole life planned out to start investing. Many financial planners and brokers want details including exactly at what age you plan to retire and where you're planning to settle down some 30 years from now. This is their way of drawing up a plan for you that in most cases won't be realized since life changes. Yes, the part where they punch up numbers that says if you put away x amount of dollars a month at $x\%$ return, you will have so many dollars after 20 or 30 years

Remember, Investing Is Not for Everyone

Investing, particularly riskier investing, is not for people in debt or for anyone who is living from paycheck to paycheck. To invest in the stock market or in mutual funds, you should first have some savings tucked away in cash instruments, be it $10,000 or $20,000. If you have a 401k or similar retirement plan, you are already investing to some degree and your company is putting in money to help build a retirement plan for you. Like the sign at the racetrack "Bet with your head, not over it," investing follows the same principle. You should not be risking or playing the stock market with money you cannot afford to spend. Invest money you do not need for daily expenses and cash flow.

is valid. The problem is you can only estimate what your needs will be.

Why? Because things change. You may start your own business at the age of 59 and decide to keep on working. On the other hand, you may be forced to retire early. You could come into unexpected money by selling an antique, receiving an inheritance, or hitting the lottery. You could save for your daughter's tuition, and she could get a full scholarship. The point is, while you want to invest for the future, you do not know where life will take you over the next 30 years. It's hard to know for sure what is coming up. All you really know is where you are at present and that you want to build savings toward future projected goals. Although there is no data on hand, it's a safe assumption that over 50% of people who predict at age 25 where they will be financially at the age of 50 and what their life will be like are incorrect when they reach the half century mark. They may be far richer than they ever dreamed of or their needs and goals may be completely different. On the other hand, financial emergencies may have forced them to use much of their money earmarked for retirement.

4. Do the numbers game. Look for a fund that shows the kind of success over the long term that will meet your need. Will $10,000 in a fund with a 5-year return of 12% get you where you want to be? Do you have a longer time, say 15 years until college? Look at past performance of funds, but remember that past performance is no surefire indication of future results. Although long-term performance is more likely to be a better gauge than the short-term numbers. Before returning to allocating your assets and considering some examples of ways in which you can divide up your own pie, let's look at the objectives of the mutual funds. This will make your choices easier. You might also look ahead at the types of funds offered in the "Selecting a Fund Section." It's easier to play the game when you understand the different players.

INVESTMENT OBJECTIVES AND YOU!

Just as you have goals, your mutual funds have objectives. Now all you need to do is match the two accordingly. As you become more familiar with the wide variety of mutual fund categories, you will determine which types of funds will help you achieve your goals.

Fund objectives include the following:

Preservation of Capital and Liquidity   This is achieved by investing in short-term bonds or bond funds, also known as fixed income funds.

Income   An income fund seeks preservation of capital, is less concerned with growth, and is a steady source of income achieved through bond funds, which is why these funds are called *fixed income funds*.

Growth   A growth fund aggressively seeks greater returns and an increase on your principal, while accepting higher risks, generally through stock funds.

Income and Growth   An income and growth fund has a middle of the road approach utilizing stocks and bonds for steady income and potential growth.

There are numerous types of funds, including value funds and so on, but these are the principal goals that funds have for you as an investor. Fund goals are outlined in the fund prospectus and funds are mandated by the SEC to follow such objectives.

Legal stipulations state that diversified funds can buy only up to *x* amount in one industry and that funds can buy no more than 5% of shares in any one company. Sector funds, on the other hand, can hold shares exclusively in one industry, but there are still stipulations regarding how much of any one company they can own. The fund objective will state clearly how the fund manager intends to guide the fund, by seeking out undervalued companies in a value fund or looking for long-term growth through large-cap funds, or any of a number of plans of action.

You must match your own goals to those of a fund, and, just as your time parameters change, you may need to reassess whether the goals of a particular fund are still your goals. Funds change too,

sometimes because of their size and sometimes because of the nature of the market and other external factors.

Matching a fund with your objectives is very important. If you are looking for steady income, look for a fund that is designed to produce income. If you are looking to cut your tax expense, look for a tax exempt municipal fund. If you are looking at a long-range goal, you can build toward that goal by owning growth funds. Carefully find the right fund(s) for you by matching your goals with the objectives of the funds.

Remember to invest with the understanding that you will reassess as you go forward; investing is an ongoing process. It's not like buying a 30-year savings bond that you can stick in the drawer; this is a hands-on process.

THE PSYCHOLOGY OF INVESTING

There are psychological reasons why we choose certain investments—if we choose to invest at all. Our asset allocation, risk tolerance, and how we choose funds and other investments hinge directly on the type of person we are. Hence the following section is devoted to investment psychology (a much broader area than we have room to cover) and emotional and rational investing.

From a practical perspective, investing is a means whereby you are looking to use some of your current funds to build up more money in the future. Psychologically, investing means different things to different people. For some, investing means working toward a future goal. This can be motivating or at least puts a light at the end of the investment tunnel. You may see yourself in a different place in later life and investing is a means to getting there. A future goal gives you a focal point to look down the road. There's a built-in investing incentive—your future. If you are putting money away for your retirement, you are building up a cushion so that you won't have to worry when you decide to stop working. The reality is that you might never retire in the sense of not working at some job. However, there is comfort in knowing that you have money set aside so that you could retire if you wanted to.

Although you'll read it and hear time and time again, that you need to set your goals to invest in mutual funds, the reality is that

you might not have a specific goal in mind. Sure, you might want to retire someday or buy a house. On the other hand, you might own your own business, which you will eventually sell. You might be living in a rental apartment or townhouse that you love and not be planning to move into that dream house any longer. A goal for some investors is to simply have more money for whatever the future holds. You need not have specific future plans to be an investor. Saving for a rainy day is still the philosophy of many people, and mutual funds are a way to save while letting your money work for you. The liquidity in mutual funds makes them particularly attractive investments. Even if you don't plan to touch the money for 10 years, it's comforting to know you could sell off your shares if you needed to. While bonds can be sold (it's not always easy), people often feel that it's a long-term commitment when they purchase an individual bond since bonds are bought for 5, 10, 15, 20, or more years until they mature.

Psychology also affects your manner of investing. Choosing investments is a way of controlling your assets, and being in control is important to many people, particularly when it concerns money. This is another reason why the home computer has led to so much more mutual fund activity. People are able to sit at home, learn about investments, and do something about them on their own. Buying funds through the Internet or 800 numbers basically means you are making financial decisions by yourself. This is comforting to investors who enjoy that degree of control. It also provides a new area of interest, investing, which broadens one's horizons.

On the other hand, full service brokers can be helpful to people who are not as confident in their own investment abilities and want a second opinion. There's nothing wrong with seeking professional advice. In fact, we seek out medical advice and then even look for second opinions. Even the President of the United States has advisors. Whether he follows their advice is another story. Simply stated, one philosophy says "If you want something done right do it yourself," while another is "If you don't know something well, hire someone who does."

There's also a psychological issue in taking advice. Some investors are so hungry to make their next move that they listen to the wrong people or take the first advice that comes their way. While experts and advisors can be very helpful, as can a knowledgeable friend who is familiar with the activities of the market, a problem can arise when someone seeks out advice and is overwhelmed by a financial planner or full service broker who either intimidates the investor or overloads the investor with tons of options.

Brokers or planners can be intimidating if they are condescending or act like they know it all and you don't. There is a level of confidence necessary even when you go to see a planner or a broker. On your part it's a matter of being prepared. On their part, it is a matter of respecting you and understanding that you are not as well versed in the field but are not totally ignorant about your financial picture either.

Let's not forget risk! Risk tolerance is related to the psychological makeup of the investor. Some people will invest with the mindset of "I don't want to lose" while others will invest with the "I want to win" strategy. Beyond practical money concerns, there is the basic psychological makeup of individuals; some want to play it safe and others want to take risks. One person will buy a sports car and drive at 90 MPH, while another will buy a four-door practical vehicle and never exceed 65 MPH. There are very wealthy investors with plenty of money to play high-risk games, who will invest very conservatively while other investors with only $3,000 to invest will pick a high-risk, aggressive fund. It's as much personality type as anything else.

But, Dr. Freud, why mutual funds? What makes funds so attractive? Do they remind me of my mother? From a psychological point of view, people simply feel that funds offer more for less. Who doesn't want that? They also provide a manner of not putting all of your eggs in one basket. If a fund says you can own a piece of 500 stocks for one price, do you not feel that you are getting more for less? The idea of diversity is also a welcome feeling for anyone who is worried about buying one and only one stock. People then buy a second fund when they realize they only have that one fund to follow and need somewhere else to turn.

The Emotional Investor

Behavioral finance is the phrase for a new field of study that delves into how people's emotions affect their investment behavior. How people react to market news, how they handle risk, and whether they follow a herd mentality are all areas of study. A mindset held by many people, whether it's panic or greed, can move the market in a big way.

What are some of the results of this new field of study? For one thing, it has shown that more confident investors, usually those who are initially successful, will be more active in trading. This will often cause them to become overconfident and even cocky, resulting in diminished success. Frequently online investors fall into this category.

INVESTING ONLINE + EARLY SUCCESS + GAINED CONFIDENCE + VERY ACTIVE TRADING = LESS SUCCESS OR EVEN LOSSES

The key to breaking this equation is to stop and enjoy the early success for a while before proceeding.

Another behavioral pattern is that of investors who chase high returns and buy into an industry in an overly aggressive manner. This results in inflated prices in the industry and a high potential for a major downfall. These investors, who are guided by greed, do not diversify and protect some of their money in safer places. Jumping on the bandwagon is not necessarily wrong, especially when the bull market is running for a long stretch of time.

BULL MARKET + CHASING HIGH RETURNS + AGGRESSIVE INVESTING = LARGE DOWNSIDE RISK AND POTENTIAL DISASTER

Then there is the panic behavior that has sent the market on a roller-coaster ride on many occasions since the new millennium began. This is where investors see a small drop in the market and through impatience react by selling. This panic is magnified by the ease in which people can make a transaction. It is also magnified by the marketing that constantly promotes a better choice (whatever it is) waiting for you. In this case it's a better, new fund. Why hold onto anything for very long in an age when there's something new on the market the next day?

DROP IN THE MARKET + PANIC + SELLING = LARGER DROP IN THE MARKET, FOLLOWED BY RECOVERY EVERY TIME (WITH YOU LEFT OUT IN THE COLD IF YOU PANICKED)

Smart investors respond in the opposite manner and wait while others panic. Then, when the market has dropped, they swoop in and get some good buys at low per share prices.

Another psychological reason why people are turning to mutual funds is to be a part of the latest cultural phenomenon; and mutual funds (besides showing solid returns) are certainly in vogue. When you see your neighbors pull into their driveway in a brand new car that they purchased from the shares they sold of their mutual fund, it's an encouraging sign pointing you in the direction of fund investing.

A lot more can be written about the psychology of investing. When you are making investment decisions, you should think through your general attitudes about investing. You should determine how you feel about the following questions:

Are you comfortable seeking out investment advice
    if necessary?
Do you feel intimidated by investment professionals?
Do you feel confident in your investment abilities, and
    able to motivate yourself to learn about investments and
    make the proper decisions?
Are you investing for certain goals or just to have money
    for the future?
Can you sleep at night with your money in a potentially
    higher risk investment?
Are you investing the amount of money that you feel
    comfortable investing or are you feeling pressured to
    invest more by a broker, planner, or
    even your spouse?
Are you following parental invest-
    ment advice or forging
    your own? *Many people
    invest based on prin-
    ciples passed down
    from their par-
    ents, whether
    they realize it
    or not.*

PSYCHOLOGICAL PROFILES

Mr. or Ms. Instant Gratification   These investors want their money to go to work for them immediately—and do overtime! They look for the action scenes but do not stick around for the end of the movie. If their fund is going well they're happy, but if the fund drops they're on to another one. This is more of a gambling philosophy than it is an investment philosophy. You'll often find these investors complaining that the fund they bought last week dropped and right after they sold it the fund went up. They have no patience for the long term or even for waiting a couple of months. These individuals often have money come easily to them via gifts, trust funds, inheritance, or having a relative give them a cushy job. Instant gratification does not correspond well with any investment formula.

Mr. or Ms. Slow but Steady   The opposite of instant gratification, these are the investors who believe in winning the race the way the tortoise did, with a slow and steady approach. When it comes to investing, this includes low-risk investments that pay reasonable returns and possibly income. It's a psychology that many people have, especially those who've worked long and hard to get enough money to invest. On the bright side, these investors are usually relatively successful. There's nothing wrong with their approach, but they could see greater returns if they moved over to the middle lane occasionally and didn't just stay in the right lane.

Mr. or Ms. Indecisive   Investors who follow a fund and can't decide whether to buy shares, investors who own a fund and can't decide whether to put more money into it, and the investors who can't decide which of numerous funds to purchase, all fall under this heading. While decision making can be difficult, at some point a successful investor has to act. Often indecisive investors are people looking for the market to make decisions for them. What happens is the market goes up and they complain, "I should have bought," or the market drops and they complain, "I should have sold." Passivity doesn't generally work as a mutual fund strategy. It only gives someone carte blanche to complain a lot when they could have done something differently.

Three Key Questions

1. Is your portfolio properly diversified? You should allocate your assets into different investment vehicles and diversify within each to avoid the negative effects of a market decline.

2. Have you determined the level of risk you can handle? Know yourself and invest depending on your age, timetable for meeting your goals, and comfort level with risk.

3. Are your financial goals realistic and attainable? Calculate what could happen through proper ongoing investing over time. There are plenty of online calculators to help you. Do not expect to make windfall profits in stocks or funds in the short term, meaning months or even a year or two.

Mr. or Ms. Mom and Pop These are investors who are following a particular strategy, usually more conservative, because it is what they have been taught and what has been ingrained in their subconscious from childhood. Perhaps the family needed to watch their money closely as they were living hand to mouth. Perhaps the grandparents, often immigrants, passed on to the parents and they passed it on to you, the young investor. The personality of investing and attitudes regarding money are often learned at a very young age. The teenager who has summer jobs and the teenager whose parents pay for everything so he can take his summers off and relax have different attitudes about money, spending, and saving. It doesn't mean that one is right and one is wrong, only that investment personalities come from somewhere, and that somewhere is often parents and even grandparents. Mutual funds were never as popular as they are today. Many new and would-be investors are the first in their family to utilize the wealth of knowledge now available to learn about investments. For these investors it's a battle of breaking with traditional teaching and stepping into the modern world of investing. Some will take the big steps, even if they start out more gingerly, while others will shy away from online investing completely—after all, Dad always called his broker.

Mr. or Ms. Online Obsessed This is someone who should be playing video poker or another game but has discovered how easy and fun it is to buy and sell stocks and funds on the Internet. Usually they are not dealing with great sums of money (they don't have a lot to play with because they were so recently obsessed with the idea of buying everything they could by credit card). Sometimes it's just too easy to feed money into your E*TRADE or Ameritrade account and hit the buttons to buy (and sell). This is not unlike the instant gratification investor, except it's less a matter of making the quick buck than it is of having fun playing at investing. Since investing isn't a craze or a fad, these people will generally burn out, sometimes before they blow too much money on impulse investments.

The Rational Investor

What is the opposite of the emotional investor? The rational investor. Rational investing takes a degree of confidence, not in what you know, or think you know, but in who you are. Reading fund literature and being confident that you know all about the fund and believe in it and then allocating 99% of your assets into one fund is having confidence in what you know. Reading and learning all about a fund and investing 50% of your investment assets into the fund, and 50% into other funds that balance your portfolio is having confidence that you believe in a strong, well balanced portfolio that suits your needs and goals.

Investing is a very personal thing. For one thing, it's your money. But it's also your own personal goals, your own personal dreams and needs that are factored in. Chasing a hot tech fund may be a reasonable course of action for a 29-year-old, single high earner, but for a married family man or woman with three kids to send to college it's certainly not the most rational approach.

Investing is only one aspect of life and should be treated as such. After all, keep in mind that for every millionaire who is enjoying his or her life, there are several thousand middle income earners who are also enjoying their lives. Sure, they might like to have a million dollars, but lifestyle priorities and expectations vary greatly among people. Someone who grew up in poverty may make $50,000 in the market and it will be more than he or she ever dreamed of. Someone who grew up in great wealth may invest that much in a fund in a single afternoon and be miserable if it only goes to $75,000. Money, how much it means, and how it affects your enjoyment of life, is something only you can know. Rational investing, therefore, is investing in a manner that suits you, your family, and your goals and needs.

The rational investor does the following:

- Decides on an investment plan of action that is focused on goals and needs and sticks with it.
- Allocates assets according to set plan.
- Stays away from getting suckered onto a ride on the investment roller coaster and doesn't react from greed or panic when the market makes its moves.
- Looks at his or her position relative to the past and future, not just the present.
- Understands that information and technology is to be used wisely, not abused or overused.
- Stays patient.
- Plays computer solitaire in the evenings rather than the buying and selling online game.

Mr. or Ms. For the Future These folks are living today but thinking about tomorrow, at least from an investment point of view. This can be a relatively healthy attitude, unless they become so preoccupied with the future that they don't pull out some of that money for vacations and plain old fun. Planning for the future, as noted earlier, is a strong incentive to build your investment portfolio. Mutual funds are investments in the future, and they can provide that security in a more positive manner than life insurance. Keeping an eye toward the future (with realistic goals), while living in the present is healthy from a psychological standpoint.

CHAPTER THREE

DIFFERENT TYPES OF MUTUAL FUNDS: HOW TO CHOOSE THE FUND THAT IS RIGHT FOR YOU

Mutual funds come in all styles, various asset sizes, and with a wide variety of securities that are also quite diverse. There are multimillion and multibillion dollar mutual funds holding hundreds or thousands of stocks in their portfolios. Sector funds may be smaller, holding the cream of the crop (or trying to) in a specific industry, while an index fund may mirror the Wilshire 5000, which, despite the name, holds over 7,000 common stocks. Just to confuse matters, there are also funds that are made up of various funds. A fund of funds owns several mutual funds, each of which owns stocks and/or bonds. More on funds of funds later.

CAP SIZES

As you are deciding which funds to purchase from any of 15 to 25 categories or more (there are variations on old categories emerging constantly), you will see the terms large cap, mid cap, small cap and micro cap. *Cap* is short for market capitalization. The market value of all outstanding shares of a particular stock is synonymous with the market capitalization of the company. Market capitalization is calculated by multiplying the market price by the number of outstanding shares. Therefore, a company with 40 million outstanding shares trading at $20 each would have a market capitalization of $800 million dollars.

The breakdown is different depending where you look, but the range is generally as follows:

Large cap—over $5 billion
Mid cap—$1 billion to $5 billion
Small cap—$250 million to $1 billion
Micro cap—under $250 million (In some places you'll see this
    raised to $300 million or even $500 million.)

The cap size indicates the size of the companies. While some funds and indexes span different size companies, many invest in large or small companies with some overlap into that mid-cap area. In general, large-cap companies are less risky than small-cap

companies, and in recent years the big industries have been going strong. Small caps have, over the years, very often performed better than the larger companies. Trends change, however, and it's worth your while to diversify between larger and smaller companies.

Large-cap funds have the built-in safety feature of holding more stable, well known companies. Such companies may be industry leaders and have the manpower and technology to withstand down markets and rebuild their foundation when necessary. They may not have as much growth potential as a smaller company, but they offer stability because the vast majority of large-cap companies have been around awhile.

Small caps may be undervalued, especially with such attention in recent years given to the big blue chippers. This may serve as a value investment of sorts whereby a fund finds good small-cap companies with plenty of growth potential. Small companies have a higher risk/reward ratio than larger companies, which is often because they are more volatile. They may be largely dependent on one product or service while a large company can have many subdivisions making various products. If the one service is something that catches on, like FedEx, it can make for a successful company.

Meanwhile, micro-cap companies are the smallest of the lot, still building and growing. They are generally not household names and don't have the benefit of huge advertising budgets as do the large-cap companies. But the right micro cap can yield high returns (although at a greater risk). One plus of micro-cap funds is that there is less concern about the constant fluctuations in foreign markets than there is with the larger companies since the micro caps do far less overseas business.

Your asset allocation, in conjunction with your own personal goals, needs, and level of risk will determine how much of your portfolio will be heading into large- and small-cap funds. You will also look at the objectives and risk associated with each style of fund. By combining the various aspects of a fund, you will determine if the fund style is right for your portfolio.

Mid Cap Rising

Mid-cap funds are a result of growing corporations that haven't yet joined the upper echelon of biggies, but are no longer small companies. From fewer than 70 mid-cap funds in the early '90s, there are now nearly 400 as the number of midsized companies has grown with the successful economy of recent years. It is certainly worthwhile to consider a mid-cap fund, perhaps one tracking the S&P Midcap 400 Index.

CATEGORIES AND YOU

Fund categories—aggressive growth, long-term growth, growth and income, and so on—dictate the path that they will take and the securities their managers will buy to meet their objectives. Are you seeking healthy returns now? Are you looking for steady returns over time? Are you looking for income-producing funds? Are you looking for a fixed asset fund that protects your principal while providing you with income? Each of these objectives can be reached with the right category fund. Each of these categories involves a degree of risk. The faster you want to see returns, the riskier the fund will be.

Keep in mind that the approach to meeting a single goal can take on different forms; with so many funds out there, it's unlikely that any two funds, outside of an index fund, are alike. Funds fall into categories but they do cross lines. Small-cap funds often have mid-cap companies, growth funds have some value stocks, and so on. There are SEC regulations and guidelines, but even they cannot always prevent funds from changing their style, sometimes because of new management but often because the management (new or old) have too many assets on their hands and need to find other places to invest them. Also, a small-cap company may grow quite large and still remain in a fund that it has outgrown. Many small-cap funds held onto Internet stocks like Yahoo! and AOL even when they outgrew the small-cap label.

There is no foolproof technique for selecting mutual funds, which explains why there is such a wealth of information available to help you make your choices.

In accompanying sidebars, we will look at some of the many categories that funds fall into, but first it's important to take a quick look at the indices used as the benchmarks by which funds measure their success or failure. Then we'll move to the index funds, which are based on the indices and have (as of early 2000) become the most popular type of stock fund in America.

Large-cap Diversification and Strategy

Not all large-cap companies are created alike. While they are big in terms of market capitalization, they are diverse in what they make, services they provide, and which industry they are a part of. Large-cap mutual funds can be significantly different in what they are seeking out when looking at companies. There are large-cap growth funds that focus on leaders in their respective industries. They often seek out the best known companies that have established themselves as frontrunners with great potential to continue to grow. On the other hand, there are the giants that for whatever reason are lagging behind and are now undervalued in their respective industries. With good management and a definite plan of action, these companies may soon become competitive. Large-cap value funds seek out big companies that have fallen behind. Motorola and the toy manufacturer Mattel, among other large-cap corporations, have found themselves in the value category as they were undervalued and shares could be purchased for lower prices.

An investor looking for diversification among the giants will seek a mix of all of the above, established winners, fast-rising super stocks, and veterans on the comeback trail. Looking for large-cap funds to span a variety of economic sectors will add diversity to the large-cap portion of your portfolio as well as the growth and value portions.

Of late, the Goliaths have been on a winning streak, which isn't to say the Davids of the stock world won't rise again. This means you should have a lesser amount of your assets (but something) in small caps. At present (early 2000), the giant companies keep on merging, growing, and acquiring, then growing some more. Therefore, large caps are very much in favor, but spread your large-cap investment around. Look for diverse industries or sectors; look for growth; look for value; look for a fund or funds that cover the large-caps thoroughly, which might simply mean a large-cap index fund.

INDICES

It would be convenient if the stock market had one index to use as a benchmark, but, like everything else these days, there is specialization. A stock market index is defined as a hypothetical, often weighted, grouping of securities used as a benchmark to measure a larger group of securities. The most popular indices are the S&P 500 and the Dow Jones Industrial Average. Others include the Russell 2000, the Wilshire 5000, and the Domini 400 Social Index. Like the Neilson ratings for television or Media Metrix, which charts Internet users, each index serves as a barometer of a certain size or type of company. Naturally, there are stocks within each index that go against the grain; when the Dow is down, you may have a blue chip stock on the Dow that is doing just fine. An index measures overall trends.

THE DOW JONES INDUSTRIAL AVERAGE

The Dow Jones Industrial Average is nearly 105 years old. For many years and for long-time stockholders of blue chip, large-company stocks, this is the benchmark of benchmarks. Thirty stocks made up the DJIA at the turn of its second century, while only 12 made up the list at the turn of its first century. General Electric is the only one that was there for both turns (and even GE was dropped and brought back a couple of times).

The current Dow Jones Industrial Average, as of April 2000, is made up of the following stocks:

Alcoa Inc. (AA)
American Express Co. (AXP)
AT&T Corp. (T)
Boeing Co. (BA)
Caterpillar Inc. (CAT)
Citigroup Inc. (C)
Coca-Cola Co. (KO)
DuPont Co. (DD)
Eastman Kodak Co. (EK)
Exxon Corp. (XON)
General Electric Corp. (GM)

Hewlett-Packard Co. (HWP)
Home Depot Inc. (HD)
Honeywell International, Inc. (HON)
Intel Corp. (INTC)
International Business Machines Corp. (IBM)
International Paper Co. (IP)
J.P. Morgan and Co. (JPM)
Johnson & Johnson (JNJ)
McDonald's Corp. (MCD)

Merck & Co. (MRK)
Microsoft Corp. (MSFT)
Minnesota Mining and
    Manufacturing Co. (3M)
    (MMM)
Phillip Morris Cos. (MO)

Procter & Gamble Co. (PG)
SBC Communications Inc.
    (SBC)
United Technologies (UTX)
Wal-Mart Stores Inc. (WMT)
Walt Disney Company (DIS)

The Dow, originally founded by Charles Dow, cofounder of the *Wall Street Journal,* has stayed in the *Journal* family and is run by Paul Steiger, Managing Editor of the *Wall Street Journal* and John Presbo, who owns it.

Unlike some of the newer indices, which have utilized more sophisticated means of weighing and measuring larger companies versus smaller ones, the Dow measures each stock's performance based on its price. And while all the companies listed in the Dow are fairly well known, some have a higher market value than others. A $500-billion company is larger and carries more clout than a $10-billion enterprise. However, the stock price of the larger company may be 70 and the smaller company 100. Therefore, the smaller company would have a greater impact on the Dow because it is based on the stock process only and not the size and scope of the company.

The Dow has been criticized for lagging behind the times and not including many of the hot tech stocks. But it does represent a cross section of American business, and, for that reason, even experts and analysts who lean toward the S&P and NASDAQ Composite still respect the Dow. Financial consultants and fund managers still look at how the Dow is doing and often hang onto a few of the Dow's blue chips as a safety cushion, especially when the market gets volatile or when an industry has run its course. The American public still pays attention to the Dow as well, having heard the term forever.

STANDARD & POOR'S 500 STOCK INDEX

The Standard & Poor 500 came into being in 1957, just 61 years after the debut of the Dow. The S&P, as it's widely known, includes 500 stocks. This, one of several S&P indices, features large-cap stocks that together amount to 80% of the total value of the U.S. stock

Point/Counterpoint

Point The market has been doing well of late, but what if it falls? Then the index funds are monitoring a sinking ship with no experienced fund manager making changes to protect their investments by moving them to safer areas like bond funds.

Counterpoint But if the market is in trouble, you can move your money into a money market account and sit on the sidelines until the worst is over. You can also ride it out since the market will bounce back. If you go to an actively managed fund, how do you know the money manager will choose the right securities in a down market—or in any market for that matter?

market. Because it includes such a significant portion of large companies, the S&P is considered the premier benchmark by much of the financial industry. Mutual fund companies measure their funds against the success of the S&P, and index funds use it as a guide. The S&P is run by a nine-member panel who decide which 500 stocks to include. They also use a system that weights the stocks so that they are not all represented equally, as in the Dow. For this reason, the index can do one thing, while individual stocks in the index may produce different returns. You would have to have the same proportionate amount of shares in each company as the index to get the same results. Nonetheless, the S&P has taken over as the favorite among mutual fund managers.

THE RUSSELL 2000

The Russell 2000 is, to a degree, the opposite of the S&P 500, focusing attention on the little guy. Small companies or small-cap funds are represented in the Russell 2000. Formed around 1984 by the Frank Russell Company, an investment consulting firm, the index has become the place to look for emerging small companies. Each May, Russell's team ranks the top 3,000 companies in the United States, based on their market value, and then sets the top 1,000 aside and takes number 1,001 through number 3,000 to form the index. The companies included generally fall between $175 million and just over $1 billion in market value. While these numbers may not sound that small, consider that Microsoft, as of 1999 had a market value of nearly $600 billion.

While many of the companies remain the same, there are companies that outgrow the Russell 2000, and new companies formed every year that make the list. Since the system is set in advance it is less subjective than the Dow or even the S&P. The small companies, however, trying to succeed in a world of giants, can be very volatile. Many investors, investment advisors, and fund managers follow the Russell 2000 with a cautious eye, ready to pounce on a few hot commodities but not willing to embrace the whole index.

S&P Indices

The S&P 500 is the most widely used benchmark of U.S. stocks and features 500 stocks in a weighted index representing the stock price times the number of outstanding shares for each company. As of March 2000, the S&P was 75% industrial while utilities, financial, and transportation companies made up the other 25%. The total market value of the S&P 500 was over $11.5 billion. Standard and Poor's other indices worldwide, include the following:

The S&P Euro Index representing European markets
The S&P/TSE 60 Index (TSE, Toronto Stock Exchange), which is a
    large-cap benchmark of Canadian companies
The S&P/TSE Canadian Midcap Index
The S&P/TSE Canadian SmallCap Index
The S&P/TOPIX 150, covering major sectors of the Tokyo market
The S&P Asia Pacific 100 Index, which includes companies in Australia,
    Hong Kong, Malaysia, New Zealand, Singapore, and Taiwan
The S&P Latin America 40 Index, which includes companies in Mexico,
    Brazil, Argentina, and Chile
The S&P United Kingdom 150 Index
The S&P Global 100 Index, combining 100 companies from
    around the globe

This is in addition to the Domestic 500, Midcap 400, Small Cap 600, Supercomposite 1500, 100, REIT, Barra Growth Index, and the Barra Value Index.

THE WILSHIRE 5000

Formed by the Wilshire Association in Santa Monica, California, the Wilshire 5000 is essentially an index that follows all domestic stocks. When it was founded it had 5,000 stocks, but the number has risen as companies have been divided, merged, new IPOs have been issued, and so on. The companies are weighted by their market value and not by their stock prices, which means the larger corporations have a greater impact on the overall index. In fact, nearly half of the stocks included (the larger companies) make up 97% of the total earnings.

There has been less talk about the Wilshire than the S&P partly because the S&P is a selected grouping that indicates analysis and sparks debate as to what is and isn't included. Everyone loves to question the system and the choices. The Wilshire and the S&P generally perform similarly, with the larger cap companies having a stronger impact on the results.

THE DOMINI 400

In this time of increased social awareness, those who want to invest while easing their conscience have found that socially responsible funds serve both purposes. Socially responsible funds are those that take a positive and responsible stance from an environmental standpoint. An argument about what is and isn't socially responsible would be a lengthy one that would encompass many points of view. While a company may be using environmentally sensitive materials rather than plastics, they might also be printing up an excessive number of glossy marketing materials, not to mention the prospectus, thus using more paper from trees. And what about companies that advertise on, and thus support, television programs that promote violence to a young audience? In other words, it's almost impossible to find companies that are not going to offend someone's sense of what is right from a social and environmental standpoint. The guidelines that are most commonly followed include, among the things, protection of the environment and natural resources, occupational health and safety, as well as life supportive goods and services. Companies not included are those manufacturing or selling liquor, firearms, or tobacco products.

These socially responsible funds have their own index. The Domini 400 Social Index, composed of 400 stocks, is the result of the efforts of Amy Domini, an author and money manager for private clients for a Boston firm. Reviewing the investments of her own church in the 70s, she found the church was investing in companies that made weapons and realized that they, like most of us, do not know all the branches, divisions, and practices of major companies. She set out to enhance the public's awareness of the practices and policies of large corporations.

In 1990 Amy Domini started the Domini 400 as a way of screening stocks with socially redeeming features. Companies in her listing must have a clean record concerning the environment, provide fair treatment to women and minorities, and not be involved with alcohol, tobacco, gambling, or manufacturing weapons. There are not many socially responsible funds, but there is a growing demand from a cross section of the American public who are watching companies more closely, looking for them to get their act together. The trend toward this type of investing is expected to grow in the future with the baby-boomer and post–baby-boomer generations looking at more than just the bottom line of financial figures and investing with their minds and their consciences.

Many hardened, bottom line analysts and brokers don't turn to the Domini 400. While many investors appear to be more socially conscious, as evidenced by certain industries falling out of favor, others are only guided by profit potential. Nonetheless, there is certainly plenty of room for a conscience in the financial community. And, by the way, the Domini and other social indices have done well.

THE BARRA GROWTH/VALUE INDICES

Subsets of the S&P 500, the Barra indices are separate value and growth stock benchmarks. For someone looking to find value or growth investments, this is a good place to start. Vanguard Growth Index and Vanguard Value Index are among the funds that follow these indices.

There are other indices, but these are the most widely known in the United States.

Love Those Tax Advantages

Whenever a fund manager sells a security in the fund, you get hit for capital gains taxes. This won't happen nearly as often with index funds since there is a much lower turnover ratio. Yes, some stocks will be added and others banished from the S&P 500 or even the Dow, but it is far less than a manager will buy and sell in an actively managed fund. For those who want to avoid high capital gains taxes, index funds are attractive, especially over long periods of time— especially those that are specifically tax managed index funds.

NASDAQ

The NASDAQ was developed in the late 1960s as the first electronic stock market. The first day of trading was February 8, 1971, when the NASDAQ officially began trading with more than 2,500 over-the-counter securities. All trading was, and still is done electronically. In 1990 the NASDAQ officially became the NASDAQ Stock Market and surpassed the New York Stock Exchange in annual share volume. By 1989 the NASDAQ had reached a share volume of 202 billion in trading. In 1998, the NASDAQ and American Stock Exchanges merged creating the NASDAQ-Amex Market Group. Over the years the NASDAQ has also grown as a leader in trading technology and computer related industries. Today it is side by side with the New York Stock Exchange as the two largest exchanges in the United States.

SOME OF THE OTHER INDICES

Beyond the NASDAQ Composite, the Dow Jones Industrial Average, the Wilshire 5000, the Russell 2000, and the S&P 500, there are many other indices, including these:

- *NASDAQ 100*—Comprises the top 100 largest nonfinancial companies listed on the NASDAQ Stock Market, based on market capitalization.
- *NASDAQ Financial 100*—Comprises the top 100 financial companies on the NASDAQ market, based on market capitalization.
- *NASDAQ Bank Index*—Comprises all banking and savings institutions plus others related to the banking industry.
- *NASDAQ Biotechnology Index*—Features over 100 companies in biomedical research.
- *NASDAQ Computer Index*—Made up of over 600 companies (both hardware and software) that have something to do with computers.
- *NASDAQ Insurance Index*—Features over 100 insurance companies. The NASDAQ also has a National Market Industrial Index, an Industrial Index, a Telecommunications Index, Transportation Index, and other industry-specific indices.

- *Dow Jones Average*—20 Transportation—Comprises 20 companies in the railroad, airline, shipping, and trucking businesses.
- *Dow Jones Average*—15 Utilities—Features gas and electric companies plus utilities from different sections of the country.
- *Russell 3000 Index*—Measures the 3,000 largest U.S. companies based on market capitalization.
- *Russell 1000 Index*—Measures the top 1,000 of the Russell top 3,000!
- *Russell Midcap Index*—Measures the bottom 800 in the top 1,000 of the Russell 3,000!
- *NYSE Composite Index*—Actually four composite indices of all the stocks on the NYSE, divided into Transportation, Financial, Industrial, and Utilities.
- *S&P Midcap 400 Index*—Measures the performance of 400 midsized companies.
- *S&P 100 Index*—Made up of 100 large, blue chip companies.
- *S&P 600 Index*—Made up of 600 small-cap companies.

INDEX FUNDS

From 1994 through 1999, the S&P 500 Index performed better overall than 80% of general equity funds. In 1993, '94, and '95, actively managed funds outperformed the S&P by 68%, 59%, and 61%, respectively. Before this and since, the S&P 500 has outpaced the majority of the funds. In 1997, it outpaced 90% of actively managed funds. Why is the S&P getting harder to beat? Three theories try to explain the increased volatility in the market that makes it harder to select the right stocks: the Internet and technology boom; the sudden massive growth in the number of funds, which gives fund managers too many choices; and the competition among leading fund managers to try to best one another by discovering the next Intel or AOL.

Managers for numerous funds still may make claims to the contrary, but the numbers don't back them up. Who hasn't heard claim after claim of beating the S&P in recent years? Even the pretzel vendors on Wall Street claim to beat the S&P. The stats show, however, that less than 30% beat the S&P. S&P index funds have been

Some Positives about Index Funds

1. It's easy to determine an index fund's objective: to replicate the returns of a particular benchmark.
2. You need not worry about the fund manager drifting away from the style of the fund or leaving; you don't have to worry about ongoing managerial turnover.
3. The turnover ratios are very low since the only securities purchased or sold are those that the index fund adds or drops from the index. Expense ratios are also low.
4. Since index funds do little buying and selling, capital gains distributions are minimal, which is a tax benefit to investors.
5. Index funds are very easy to follow, since you can look at the index itself and have a pretty close approximation of how the fund is doing.

dependable, although not breathtaking, places in which to invest over the past decade.

Index funds, as a rule, are designed to match the performance of a specific index. They will closely emulate that index. This includes buying stock in the same companies and with the same weight as the index. Index funds will have lower costs since there are not a lot of transactions going on and there is not much of a fee being paid to the management of the fund, as they are not actively managed funds.

The theory behind the index funds is to capitalize on the brains behind the funds and the significant research that is being used as a way of measuring the market or a section thereof. It basically allows those who run the index to create the fund. Index funds, such as those monitoring the S&P or those monitoring the Dow, are popular with new investors because they are easy to follow and they offer an instant cross section of securities while providing great diversification across sectors. More seasoned investors will hang onto an index fund as a dependable, safe fund, should their more aggressively managed funds not pan out. It allows them to be in a broader cross section than would a more focused sector fund.

While it is not actually an index, the NASDAQ Composite is set up to mirror the entire NASDAQ. Many funds are jumping on the lead set by the NASDAQ Composite since it has produced tremendous gains in recent years, around 70% in 1999. The emphasis on the technology stocks has been the biggest attraction of the NASDAQ as of the start of 2000.

Mirroring Closely

Here is an example of how closely an index fund will match the index it represents, using the very popular Vanguard 500 Index Fund.

AVERAGE ANNUAL RETURNS (THROUGH DECEMBER 1999)

	5 years	3 years	1 year
Vanguard 500 Index Fund	28.46%	27.50%	21.04%
S&P 500 Index	28.56%	27.56%	21.04%

There are over 150 index funds; the number of such funds is growing. Their popularity is growing because many individuals would prefer to bet on the big boards as opposed to the success of a single fund manager. The funds are highly attractive for many reasons and have become a very common first fund for new investors. In fact, it is estimated that nearly one third of the money invested in mutual funds is now going into index funds.

More savvy investors looking for the big windfall can and will find actively managed funds that will outperform the index. Only about 25% fall into this category. Tech funds, for example, have outperformed everything in recent years. The bottom line is that if you do your homework and know which actively managed funds have been consistently outperforming the index in recent years, and we emphasize *years*, then you can opt to go with those funds. It still does not mean that you cannot also be in an index fund to provide greater diversity and some security.

CHOOSING AN INDEX FUND

It sounds simple: you pick an S&P 500 index and you're in the market. Whew, that was easy. But guess what? Nothing in the world of investing is that simple. Therefore, new segmented indices have been created from the indices to add that much more specialization to a category that was refreshingly free of it. The Wilshire 4500, for example, is essentially the Wilshire 5000 without the S&P 500 stocks in it; you'll also see the S&P 400, which is an index of stocks of midsized companies, or the NASDAQ 100, which reflects the NASDAQ's 100 largest companies across industry groups. There are numerous subcategories being created that reflect an index of a certain grouping of stocks; there is even an index of stocks reflecting stock car racing!

As a new investor, however, it is more common to start with an index fund that covers the broader S&P 500. But what about all those other index funds? Index funds, like any funds, need to suit your portfolio. If you have funds that are loaded with large-cap companies, then you will want a small-cap fund to balance your portfolio. The Russell 2000 is the place to go if you believe

Size Is Good

Index funds are often very large, but since there is very little turnover in the index, there is very little turnover in the fund. This minimizes capital gains tax distributions because an index fund simply mirrors the index as closely as possible, so the decisions are already made. Indices don't change the stocks held as much as a managed fund. The fact that an index fund holds a large number of different equities is a benefit because, if one stock is dropped from the index or is doing poorly, it won't have a great impact on the index or the fund as a whole. One stock out of 500 is not going to make a significant impact, even if it is a major company. On the other side, and in investing there is always the other side, a very strong stock cannot make a big impact if it is one of 500.

Index Funds = Lower Expense Ratios

Since there are fewer transactions and these funds are not actively managed, index funds have a lower expense ratio than other funds. The Vanguard Index 500 Fund, for example, has an expense ratio of 0.18, which is significantly lower than most actively managed funds, which have expense ratios around 1.20 or 1.25.

strongly that David will rise and beat Goliath again. However, the results have not been as favorable; over 60% of actively managed funds beat the Russell 2000 over the past five years (up through the end of 1999). What this tells investors is to put a higher percentage in the S&P and a lower percentage of their investment (perhaps a 75%/25% breakdown) into the Russell 2000 index. Others opt to go with an S&P fund and then cover smaller companies more selectively in the actively managed funds, possibly in an area like technology.

You can use an index fund to have a cross section of stocks in whichever area you are looking to cover, whether it's domestic mid caps or international funds. Index funds are a good starting point.

If you really want to take the long-term approach and achieve maximum diversification, you can invest in an index fund that mirrors the Wilshire 5000 (7,100 stocks as of early 2000) which basically says if it's a stock, you own it. Large-, small-, and mid-cap companies—you've got a tiny piece of all of them. You need only to be concerned with the market as a whole; over time (15, 20, or 30 years) being in the market has always been a good investment.

The more expert you become as an investor, the more you can look at other indices, including those that cover socially responsible stocks and specific industries. Funds mirroring less widespread indices, such as an Internet sector index fund, will be more risky than going with those that cover the broader grouping of companies.

In fact, surveys indicate that more than 80% of S&P index funds will produce results within 4% of the S&P index, and many will be within 1% or 2%. The difference is primarily due to expense ratio (which should be under .40) and how the fund is managed. While these funds are largely "unmanaged," there is some leeway for the fund manager to

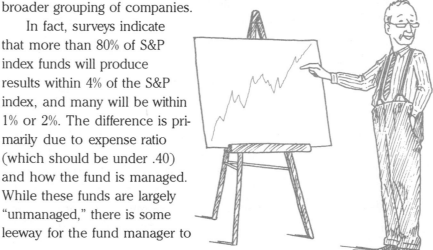

Index Funds

Dow Jones Industrial Average
Waterhouse DJIA

Wilshire 4500
E*TRADE Extended Market
Fidelity Spartan Extended Market
T. Rowe Price Extended Market
Vanguard Extended Market

Wilshire 5000
Fidelity Spartan Total Market
T. Rowe Price Total Equity Market
Vanguard Total Stock Market

Domini Social Index
Domini Social Equity Fund
Green Century Equity Fund

NASDAQ 100
Rydex OTC

S&P Large Cap 100
Principal Preservation S&P 100 Plus

S&P Midcap 400
Dreyfus Midcap Index
Federated Mid Cap
Gateway Mid Cap Index
Vanguard Mid-Cap

S&P 500
American Century S&P 500
Aon S&P 500
BT Investment Equity 500
Dreyfus Basic S&P 500
Dreyfus S&P 500
E*TRADE S&P 500
Fidelity Spartan Market Index
INVESCO S&P 500 Index II
Merrill Lynch S&P 500 Index D
Schwab S&P 500 Inv.
Scudder S&P 500 Index
SSGA S&P 500 Index
Strong Index 500
T. Rowe Price Equity Index 500
USAA S&P 500 Index
Vanguard 500
Vanguard Tax Managed Growth
    and Income

S&P Small Cap 600
California Investment Trust S&P
    Small Cap Index
Dreyfus Small Cap Index
Galaxy Small Cap Index
Vanguard Tax Managed Small-Cap

tip the balance sheets slightly by purchasing more or fewer shares in a certain stock that is in the index. There is also the cash factor. Generally, no more than 3% or 4% of the assets are in cash, but this, too, will result in a slightly lower return. Nonetheless, the index fund will usually be very close to the index. Since most actively managed funds fall short (75% or more), if you're a couple of percentage points behind the index, you're not in bad shape and you are usually in better shape than the average fund.

OTHER INDEX FUND CHOICES

While most often index funds are unmanaged, or managed in a passive manner, meaning they primarily follow the lead set by the index, there are index funds that are quite actively managed (also known as enhanced index funds). An actively managed index fund is managed to try to beat the index it is mirroring. Generally this is done by actively shifting the amount of assets or the weight in some of the securities or even sectors held in the fund. The funds manager also can buy some stocks that are similar to those in the index, which he or she feels will outperform the stocks in the index.

Enhanced index funds will generally end up slightly ahead or behind the benchmark index, so the difference is usually minimal. In fact, if the fund deviates by more than 2% from the index, it is no longer considered an index fund. Other than bragging rights for the fund manager who can say he or she beat the index, there isn't really any great advantage to having an actively managed index fund unless there is a sharp downturn in the market and the more active manager or management team shifts more assets to safer places like cash accounts. If, however, the fund simply outperforms the index by 1% and you are paying 1% more in fund fees because of the active management, then the whole concept is a wash. If the fund beats the index by 1% and you are paying 1.25% in fees, you'll be kicking yourself for bothering. Also keep in mind that if the actively managed index fund does more trading, you may be paying more in capital gains taxes. The best of these enhanced index funds may be ones that are not following the most widely tracked indices but perhaps those tracking a small-cap index where the fund manager might be able to swing the index fund more in your favor.

There are also index funds covering the foreign markets, such as the Dreyfus Index International Stock Fund and the Vanguard International Index. Mutual funds dealing in the international markets are riskier than those dealing primarily with domestic funds and are usually better selections for the more experienced investor. The Morgan Stanley EAFE index is one among several international indices monitoring international stocks. International index funds generally have higher fees than domestic index funds.

Sector funds mirroring sector indices can also be found. The Galaxy II Utility Fund, for example, mirrors the S&P Utility Index. There are other indices popping up to follow various sectors and to allow for the creation of more sector funds. Internet index funds started the year 2000 as a hot ticket.

And finally, all the major brokerage houses also handle bond index funds, which will be discussed in Chapter 5.

SECTOR FUNDS

Sector funds are mutual funds that invest in one specific industry, or sector, of the overall market. For example, a fund might buy stocks in only the financial services industry or only in technology, transportation, health, or real estate. There is little or no diversification in these funds, other than large and small companies. What this means to you is that there is potential for greater highs or greater lows, depending on the specific industry and how it fares in the overall economy. Tech stocks and funds investing in the technical sector were flying high in recent years. There are even more specific sub-categories, such as sector mutual funds that invest in only Internet-related stocks. The risks are obviously greater, so you have to be very knowledgeable and very confident in your industry of choice.

The idea behind sector funds is to let you capitalize on the hottest industries. It is a chance to cash in on what is sweeping the business world or the world in general. Computer software, hardware, and the Internet led the charge out of the 1990s. Telecommunications and the new world of wireless communications also sparked great enthusiasm coming into the new century, and there has been a lot of attention focused on the biotechnology segment of the medical field.

Mirroring the S&P Closely

The S&P 500 over the past three years (up to the end of 1999) had returns of 27.56%. Most of the S&P 500 stock funds listed above had returns between 26.5% and 27.5%, which means they did their jobs, or mirrored the index quite closely.

Spiders and Diamonds
(Exchange Traded Index Funds)

No, these are not mutual funds that invest in spiders and diamonds, although the latter could be profitable. The 1990s saw index funds take off. So, as one might expect, variations on the theme have arisen. The American Stock Exchange and its partner, the very popular NASDAQ, in an effort to benefit from the wealth of assets being poured into such index funds, introduced Exchange Traded Index Funds (ETFs).

Spiders is the nickname for ETFs that track the price performance and dividend yields of the Standard & Poor 500 Index. The new spiders are based on Standard & Poor's Depository Receipts (SPDRS). Hence the name *spiders* (and symbol: Spy). Diamonds, meanwhile, track the Dow Jones Industrial Average (DIA), which follows 30 blue chip stocks. The SPDR or DIA trust is a unit investment trust that holds shares of all the companies in the index and closely tracks the price performance and dividend yield of the index. Many other ETFs have since

emerged including Qubes (QQQ), which track the S&P 100. Qubes are popular because the S&P 100 includes a lot of the hot Internet companies. There are also mid-cap spiders and sector spiders.

What's unique about ETFs is that they trade on the exchanges like stocks, meaning you can easily buy and sell shares at any time during the day without the details of a mutual fund application. You can benefit from a jump in the share price, whereas with a mutual fund you have to wait until the NAV is calculated at the end of the trading day. This is not much of an advantage to buy and hold investors, who are more common, particularly in these days of market volatility.

Spiders trade at one tenth the value of the S&P 500, which as of the spring of 2000 has been around the 4,000 mark, and diamonds trade at one one-hundredth the value of the DOW, which as of spring 2000 was bouncing back and forth around the 10,000 mark.

Spiders and Diamonds
(Exchange Traded Index Funds) *(continued)*

Operating a lot like index funds, ETFs are not actively managed, meaning low expense ratios and not much turnover. Like index funds, these new exchange traded index funds offer investors a broad range of investments, which are easy to follow with the one listed price. They do, however, require you to pay a commission every time you buy or sell shares of an ETF. Spiders and diamonds do not have the option to reinvest; owners can receive quarterly cash dividends, which represent the accumulated dividends of the underlying stocks held in the trust.

In short, ETFs:

- Are similar to index funds except they trade on the stock market, making it easier to buy and sell them quickly during the day
- Have low expense ratios
- Have low turnover, meaning less capital gains
- Are very easy to follow since they track an index closely
- Offer the same diversification as an index fund
- Do not yet offer no-loads, which are funds bought without paying a commission to a broker
- Do not have reinvestment plans yet

For the long-term investor or the no-load enthusiast (which is a great portion of investors who'd prefer to get something for nothing), there is no particular advantage to buying a spider or diamond over an index fund. For the investor who likes to buy and sell often and even time the market (good luck), this is a way to play the market game with mutual funds. You'd better know what you're doing, as all short-term stock investing is higher risk. The risk in these funds is essentially based on your buy and sell philosophy. If you buy and hold, you'll have less risk, but then you need not buy a spider or a diamond, at least not this kind of diamond.

There are several approaches to make the riskier sector funds a little safer. One is to go with funds that invest primarily in industry leaders. Dell Computer is less likely to struggle than a small, start-up computer company. Also, if at some point the industry does reach its saturation level, the bigger companies will stand tall and, in many cases, buy up the smaller ones, making them even stronger. No industry can grow at the current rate of the Internet without some fall off. When the automobile first came upon the scene, several hundred automobile companies sprang up; everyone with sufficient tools thought he could build a car. In time, the big companies, Ford, General Motors, and others, survived. Likewise, Yahoo!, AOL, Netscape, and other well established Internet or Internet-related companies will be going strong for years to come. But the market will not handle every small player that joins the fray. The same holds true with e-commerce and other Web sites. An example of oversaturation could be found in real estate; there are nearly 25,000 Internet sites dealing with real estate. They won't all last.

It is also worthwhile to have a sector fund holding a fair amount of assets in the major players of the industry because when the market slumps, they will still remain stronger. Yahoo! and AOL may drop, but they have a better chance to rebound faster than a smaller company that is just out of the starting gate.

Another theory regarding sector funds says to lean toward industries that can't go out of fashion. If the economy takes a turn for the worse, areas like the electronics or the automobile industry could fall off. Other industries will be less volatile, however, such as companies that deal in the food industry or utilities because people need to eat and they need gas and electricity.

POSITIVES ABOUT SECTOR FUNDS

One of the best aspects of a sector fund is that it saves you the trouble of deciding between five tech stocks or 12 financial services companies. You can have a piece of all of them. If the industry is on the rise, the prospering companies will outweigh the few bad apples.

Following is a closer look at eight of the key sectors or industries: technology, communications, health/biotechnology, financial services, and utilities. Other categories include natural resources, transportation, precious metals, and real estate (which has struggled in recent years). Some fund families have broken the industries into subcategories, for example, Fidelity offers sector funds such as Fidelity Select Home Finance, Fidelity Select Gold, or Fidelity Select Computers. You can get as subdivided as you like. Remember, however, that the more you put into a very specified fund, the more you lose in diversification. You then run a higher risk if that specialty market falls off.

A Look at Several Key Sectors
Electronic Technology

Yes, this has been a hot area, but you still need a road map. Not all tech stocks are alike. The tech industry features computer and computer-related technology including hardware, software, e-commerce, Internet companies, and telecommunications. Whereas many of these companies are growing rapidly and producing big returns, the technology industry is constantly evolving. Twenty years ago answering machines and VCRs were the latest items in new technology, then came computers featuring DOS, and soon it was Windows. The laptop, the Internet, and the mass evolution of cellular phone rounded out the 20th century. Soon broadband technology and conversion between television and the Internet will emerge as the new wave of the new media. The trick is to be invested in each technological improvement that you believe will flourish. Remember, if the market goes to the bears, all bets are off when it comes to items people can do without. Look forward with technology, see what the next must-have items are for home and for business use. Will DVD players take off? Will video streaming be the manner of meetings and conferences of the future, or will people still prefer getting on a plane and meeting face to face?

Health Care/Biotechnology

Advances in medical science, new drugs, and people living longer contribute to the strength of this industry, which has fared well in recent years after struggling in the mid 90s. The major drug

Get the Guys Who Make the Nuts and Bolts

Cisco has attracted a lot of investors, as one of the more stable companies in an unstable sector. They make the switches that route the data that travel over the telecommunications systems. Other companies that make the hardware behind technology, like semiconductors and other fun little trinkets are worth looking at since they interface with a wide range of other tech companies.

companies, medical research firms, and companies making products used in the medical industry are all part of the health sector funds.

The biotech companies are the riskier investments. While there is great promise for these companies in the future, many have yet to show profits or even get the patents they need to be successful. These companies sit on the cutting edge with new medications and amazing medical advances, however, they are in a highly competitive field where one patent and FDA approval can mean everything. The larger drug companies can withstand the competition and wait for FDA approval on a particular product. They are already making and selling enough successful medications to remain industry leaders. In many instances, however, investments are being made in a company that does not yet have a tangible product (new medication), but are in the process of developing one. This can be a more volatile investment, which is why fund managers need to include the Pfizers, Mercks, and other mega pharmaceutical companies along with the new biotechs. It's difficult to pick the winners in the drug market since many of the biotech companies, like the Internet companies, are in their infancy, and many have yet to show a profit. Some biotech funds, like the one offered by Fidelity, have shown good long-term performance. Otherwise, you might lean toward an overall health care fund that is less risky and will react favorably if and when the hot new biotech companies do create a hot sector. Funds like Vanguard Health Care Fund and Eaton Vance Worldwide Health Sciences Fund are broader health care funds.

Financial Services

When the economy is good and everyone is investing, why not invest in the investment industry? A growing segment of the population is putting money away for retirement plans, for college, and for other future goals. Many more companies are also now offering 401k's and other investment plans to attract prospective employees at a time when unemployment is low and job hunters can enjoy being selective. Besides investing in banks, brokerage houses, and mortgage lenders, the financial services industry includes online investment firms and financial service companies such as American Express.

The financial sector funds are more volatile than the S&P but won't bounce around as much as a technology fund. Often they will mirror the overall economy, which means, should the booming

The Internet

Technically speaking, this is a sector within a sector. The tech funds have relied heavily on the Internet to bolster their three-digit gains. Since early 1999, Internet fund families have put the development of Internet funds as one of their top priorities. In fact, there were only four such funds at the start of 1999, and there are now nearly 40. As of early 2000, the Internet Fund and Munder's NetNet combined for over $10 billion, and, needless to say, neither has been around very long. There are new Web sites popping up all over the place offering everything from business-to-business solutions to pet care products. You can't watch television for more than 10 minutes without seeing at least one ad for a dot com company.

Investing in an Internet fund is a "now" investment, meaning you are investing in the future without much, if any, past data to look at. You won't find 5- and 10-year returns or any long-term history. You also won't have fund managers who have 5 years' experience managing Internet funds. These are funds of the future, but for how long into the future remains to be seen. The bright side of Internet funds has been the Internet stocks like Yahoo! and AOL. You needed only look at some of the Internet stock activity over the past couple of years to be ready to jump on the bandwagon. However, there is another side.

You must consider that for every Internet giant, be it a search engine, e-commerce site, or service provider in some field, there are 20 more on the way. It is therefore a very speculative and shaky area since many Internet companies are pre-IPO and struggling to get off the ground. The market has also been very volatile, and new and unproven funds can be the first ones hit by panic.

As of January 2000, Internet and tech stocks and funds were going strong, but by the spring the NASDAQ was dropping like a lead balloon and investors were fleeing this area. What this means is that if the tech and Internet funds are back in favor as you are reading this, they are a place to go with caution: step carefully. The tech and Internet "can do no wrong" days of 1998 and 1999 are behind us.

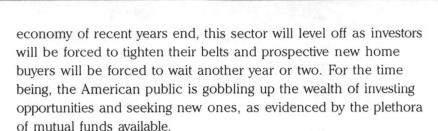

Price Earnings Ratio

Price Earnings Ratio is the stock price divided by the earnings per share. It tells you how much investors are willing to pay for one dollar of the company's earnings. Some companies sell at inflated prices that are much higher than their actual earnings. It's a good idea to compare P/E ratios of stocks similar to those in the fund to see if certain companies are valued higher than others. One of the concerns about many of the Internet companies is that they are overvalued, based on speculation, and not on actual earnings.

economy of recent years end, this sector will level off as investors will be forced to tighten their belts and prospective new home buyers will be forced to wait another year or two. For the time being, the American public is gobbling up the wealth of investing opportunities and seeking new ones, as evidenced by the plethora of mutual funds available.

Communications

The communications industry overlaps heavily with the technology industry, however, rather than including the computer software and hardware companies, you'll find AT&T, Lucent, and other such giants.

The communications industry has cashed in heavily on the fact that everyone is walking around, riding buses, and driving while talking on their cellular phones. Telephone companies are now at the center of the information age holding the key to high-speed Internet service, as well as video transmission. Cable operators are also entering the area of telecommunications; on the global front, many countries are upgrading their communications networks to meet worldwide needs. Companies that are providing and servicing the integral technology that makes up wireless transmissions are also a big part of these new telecommunications funds.

Like all funds, communications and telecommunications funds will have their share of volatility and risk attached. The industry is subject to greater changes in government regulation than other industries.

International regulations may also factor into the volatility of the fund. Like the technology industry, telecommunications is an ever-changing field where new developments can occur overnight and suddenly create a new industry giant.

Utilities

Needless to say, utility mutual funds are not the talk of the town. In fact, finding an article on them in a financial magazine will take quite a bit of searching. Their returns pale in comparison to the recent returns of the flashy technology and communications funds. However, if and when the economy takes a prolonged down-turn, these are safe places to be.

Electricity, gas, and water are essentials that keep such funds relatively steady in all economic climates. Also, because they are not the most popular funds, many utility funds pay dividends. For a safe, long-term investment or to balance an otherwise more high-risk portfolio, a utility fund can be attractive.

OTHER SECTORS

Energy

These are funds that buy stocks in companies involved in anything used as a power source or energy source, including oil or natural gas plus energy-based services. Supply and demand affects the prices of these energy sources which, as anyone who drives a car can vouch for, do change. Emerging markets often directly affect this sector, based on their own natural resources that they are selling to the United States and other global markets.

Precious Metals

Gold, silver, copper, and other precious metals are the resources behind the companies in this category. Funds look at the stock of companies that mine, process, or distribute these precious metals. Since these funds are based on the market value of the metals, they can be highly volatile. These funds, however, can still be far safer than investing in precious-metal stocks or in the futures market, which is quite risky, particularly for new investors. Fund managers may be looking at mining companies in Africa, Australia, and other parts of the world or may be more concentrated on North America. The value of precious-metal stocks depends largely on the anticipated value of gold and silver.

Real Estate

One of the most cyclical of industries, the real estate market can be the place to be or the place to steer clear of without much middle ground. Funds investing in real estate companies are investing in any businesses that deal with real estate, which includes selling it, managing it, or dealing in related services. Often when interest rates are low the real estate industry will be doing well. Determine where the overall real estate market is as a whole before even looking into real estate mutual funds. Look at current interest rates, the latest home buying statistics, and other data that indicate whether real estate is the place to be now. You

Dot.Wow

Despite the stock market turnaround regarding tech and Internet stocks and funds, there is still a tremendous, growing e-commerce business. Much of the spring decline in the tech stocks was due to overvaluation of these companies and widespread panic whereby everyone followed everyone else and jumped ship.

Nonetheless, e-commerce is still growing. It is estimated that retail dollars spent over the Internet will go from nearly $20 million in 1999 to over $100 million by 2003. Wow! It's important that you look closely at which dot coms, if any, are part of your Internet or tech sector mutual fund. Be prepared to weather the volatility of this market.

Moving On Up!

Did you know that if you invested $10,000 in an index mirroring the S&P at the start of 1979, by the end of 1999 you would have had over $268,000—in just 20 years. Not bad!

can also consider REITs if you are interested in real estate investing (see page 63).

The following tables show 3-year returns for some successful sector mutual funds in five major industries.

Communications	3-Year Returns Through 1999
AIM Global Telecommunications A	40.60*
Fidelity Select Developing Communications	57.90
Fidelity Select Multimedia	37.38
Fidelity Select Global Telecommunications	44.03
Flag Investors Communications A	54.70
Flag Investors Communications B	53.57
Gabelli Global Telecommunications	47.41
Gabelli Global Interactive Couch Potato	58.04
Invesco Telecommunications	64.94
Montgomery Global Communications	54.14
Smith Barney Telecommunications Income	35.45
T. Rowe Price Media & Telecommunications	49.50
Warburg Pincus Global Telecommunications	78.29

*Indicates fund returns were rounded off.

Financial Services	3-Year Returns Through 1999
AIM Global Financial Services Adv.	22.95
AIM Global Financial Services A	22.35
AIM Global Financial Services B	21.76
Davis Financial A	17.83
Davis Financial B	16.82
Fidelity Advisor Financial Services A	16.82
Fidelity Advisor Financial Services T	16.58
Fidelity Advisor Financial Services Institutional	16.15
Fidelity Select Brokerage & Investment	31.00
Fidelity Select Financial Services	18.85
Fidelity Select Insurance	17.75
INVESCO Financial Services	18.28
T. Rowe Price Financial Services	17.07
Titan Financial Services	18.73

While the 3-year and 5-year returns were strong for financial services funds, many of these funds took a beating in 1999 because of the international market, Y2K, and numerous other economic factors. Nonetheless, whether people are investing more conservatively or more aggressively, there is still a wealth of investing going on, and these are the places where investing is done. It does seem awkward to some people, however, to invest in an investment company.

Health Care	3-Year Returns Through 1999
Dresdner RCM Global Health Care	28.08
Eaton Vance Worldwide Health Science A	19.12
Eaton Vance Worldwide Health Science B	18.46
Fidelity Advisor Health Care Institutional	23.35
Fidelity Select Biotechnology	38.98
Fidelity Select Health Care	21.87
Fidelity Select Health Care A	23.02
Fidelity Select Health Care T	22.72
INVESCO Health Sciences	19.55
John Hancock Global Health Sciences A	15.48
John Hancock Global Health Sciences B	14.68
Merrill Lynch Health Care A	23.57
Merrill Lynch Health Care B	22.34
Merrill Lynch Health Care C	22.27
Merrill Lynch Health Care D	23.19
Munder Framlington Healthcare Y	17.92
Putnam Health Sciences A	17.16
Putnam Health Sciences B	16.19
Putnam Health Sciences M	16.58
T. Rowe Price Health Sciences	16.42
Vanguard Health Care	24.67

While these were some of the funds in the health care sector that fared well over a 3-year period, you have to look more closely at the securities held by the fund and learn more about them. The 1999 returns (1-year returns) for these funds ranged from losses of around 5% to gains in the 20% to 30% range. There is greater disparity among these funds on a year-to-year basis because of patents, mergers, legislation, competition, the FDA, and numerous other factors.

A New "Remodeling" Sector?

It's only a matter of time before a mutual fund features, and reflects, the popular trend for homeowners to upgrade and remodel their homes. Home Depot, Linens 'n Things, and Bed Bath & Beyond are among the stocks that might be included in this unique group, all of which have been picked by (various) strategists to do well in the coming years. There are plenty of potential new sectors with the growing variety of companies being publicly traded.

Technology	3-Year Returns Through 1999
Alliance Technology A	43.10*
Amerindo Technology D	74.08
Dresdner RCM Global Technology I	79.58
Fidelity Advisor Technology A	51.93
Fidelity Advisor Technology Institutional	52.32
Fidelity Select Electronics	52.74
Fidelity Select Technology	64.52
First American Technology Y	60.91
First American Technology A	60.48
First American Technology B	59.32
Internet	119.43
John Hancock Global Technology A	54.63
John Hancock Global Technology B	53.55
MSDW Information B	63.97
MSDW Institutional Technology A	76.63
Munder NetNet A	92.34
Northern Technology	71.10
PBHG Technology & Communications	64.82
PIMCO Innovation A	67.31
PIMCO Innovation B	66.22
PIMCO Innovation C	66.21
WWW Internet	66.04

*Indicates fund returns were rounded off.

Most of the tech stocks listed gained between 130% and 240% in 1999, and many stayed at that level into 2000. But in the early spring of 2000, the tech industry hit the skids, and many investors started getting out and heading back to big, blue chip favorites. You'll know the direction this sector is taking at any given time by looking at the NASDAQ.

REIT—Real Estate Investment Trust

A REIT, or real estate investment trust (pronounced REET), offers investors a way to invest in commercial real estate without having to actually buy property or land. There are over 200 REITs to choose from, and shares of REITs are traded in much the same manner as shares of a stock. In fact you can find REITs listed on the stock exchanges.

REITs are not actually mutual funds, but they do share some of the same characteristics. They were created by an act of Congress in 1960: the idea was to allow small investors to invest directly in income-producing real estate, by pooling their investment resources to acquire interest in properties. Like a mutual fund, it is also a pass through security. A *pass through security* passes through the income generated from the property to the shareholders. The income is not taxed at the corporate level but at the investor level, provided profits are passed through.

Unlike mutual funds that purchase shares of stock in companies that manufacture products, REITs purchase mortgages, rental properties, properties for resale, and so on. They are publicly traded companies that show up on the stock exchange listing, so owning shares is similar to owning shares of stocks.

REIT legislation does not require that a REIT own properties but that it earns income from real estate investments. These investments usually take one of two forms, either buying properties and investing in the equity (equity REITs) or investing in commercial mortgages that help to provide financing for someone to acquire buildings. In this manner the income comes from the interest on those mortgages (mortgage REITs). Of course, there's always one option that fits in the gray area in between; that's known as a hybrid REIT, which does a little of each.

REITs can be attractive investments. But, as with any other investment, you must do your homework. You need to look at the dividend yield, meaning how much do they offer when paying dividends and how that compares to the price of the stock. You also should look at the earnings growth (also known as "Funds from Operations"), which is the indicator used to determine how rapidly the company is growing, the types of investments held (which could include office buildings, shopping malls, retail locations, residential properties, hotels and resorts, and health care facilities), and the geographic locations, since some REITs invest on a national level and others specialize in specific regions of the country. You also want to look at how much they diversify their assets and the management to see if there is stability in the leadership.

NAREIT, the National Association of Real Estate Investment Trusts (with a Web site at *www.nareit.com*) offers a great deal of information on REITs. NAREIT can also provide you with information by calling 1-800-3NAREIT.

More Tech Than You Thought You Had

Before you buy the latest sector fund, look over the holdings of your other stock funds. Yes, the holdings will have changed slightly, but you'll get a good idea of the percentage of various industries you already own. For example, many funds were heavily invested in technology heading into the year 2000. Growth funds have been knee deep in companies making computer hardware, software, and semiconductors or dealing with the Internet or wireless communications in some capacity. Funds may be 60% into a sector, meaning you already have plenty of exposure to that particular industry.

Utilities	3-Year Returns Through 1999
AIM Global Utilities A	27.50*
AIM Global Utilities B	26.50*
Alliance Utility Income A	24.24
Alliance Utility Income B	23.34
Alliance Utility Income C	23.33
AIM Global Utilities A	24.47
Eaton Vance Utilities A	26.52
Eaton Vance Utilities B	26.25
Eaton Vance Utilities C	25.87
Federated World Utility A	27.77
Federated World Utility B	26.81
Fidelity Advisor Utilities Growth A	35.08
Fidelity Advisor Utilities Growth Institutional	35.31
Fidelity Advisor Utilities Growth T	34.73
Fidelity Select Utilities Growth	33.03
Fidelities Utilities	29.10
INVESCO Utilities	26.60*
MFS Utilities I	27.55
MFS Utilities A	26.82
Van Kempen Utility A	22.40*
Van Kempen Utility B	21.50*

*Indicates fund returns were rounded off.

Utilities show less dramatic returns than technical or communications industry mutual funds. However, they also show less volatility and will be more stable in a down market.

GROWTH FUNDS

Growth funds are mutual funds that invest in stocks that show steady growth. These are generally stocks in companies with high P/E ratios (price/earnings ratios). Since the stock market fluctuates, these funds will be volatile over the short run, but in the long term they will usually see growth and you should expect positive results.

There is less of a concern about the stock price than the idea that the stock will continue to go up. The buy low, sell high theory, does not apply, as a stock at $100 per share for a major company will be a growth-oriented security if that stock is expected to continue to see significant gains. The growth fund industry is built on sound reasoning that a company has potential to see higher share prices based on new products, new services, strong sales efforts, marketing and promotion, or other such factors. A hot industry and product demand is reason to believe a company will see growth, and hence the stock will fall into the growth category. Through the late '90s, growth funds have done well, outperforming value funds (explained later), which have frequently outperformed the growth funds in the past.

The more traditional growth fund, which is becoming harder to find with countless variation on a theme, does present some risk to your principal to see higher gains. Most of the investments are in mid- or large-cap companies.

Growth stocks usually represent companies that are big on research and development. Earnings in these companies are usually put right back into the business. Such companies can be found in any sector as long as there is potential for growth, and this provides a lot of stock selections from Yahoo! to FedEx to McDonald's. Popular growth fund holdings as of the start of the year 2000 included Microsoft, Cisco Systems, Lucent Technology, General Electric, Intel, and other big corporations.

LET'S GET AGGRESSIVE

Growth mutual funds today, like new cars, come with distinct options, beyond that of higher returns. The question, in a world of faster access, fast food, and shorter sound bytes, is how fast can you see your potential profits. The emergence of the aggressive growth mutual fund, also known as capital appreciation funds (which can turn out to be capital depreciation funds as well, but no one is going to name it as such), comes with the surge of new technology hat has factored into many of these funds. A turbo-charged sports car will get you to your destination twice as fast as

Most Popular Funds

The most popular funds today are stock funds (led by index stock funds within the category). Next in line are money market mutual funds, taxable bond funds, hybrids (which include asset allocation and balanced funds), and then municipal bond funds.

Five Things to Keep in Mind
When Investing in Sector Funds

1. Risk. Know the level of risk you are comfortable taking. Sector funds, because they depend solely on the success or failure of one industry, can be very risky.

2. Do your homework. Once you've determined how much money you are planning to invest, you'll need to study your chosen industry carefully. Past indicators are important, but since you can't invest in past returns, it's more important that you look to the future of the industry. Look at what is on the horizon in that particular industry. What are they writing about in the financial papers? Are there new products forthcoming? How much of a sure thing are these new innovations? Does the industry need a strong economy to flourish? Is the economy expected to remain strong? Take a look at world events and trends. For example, a decrease in international travel because of a rash of terrorism will affect the transportation industry.

3. Look for some big ticket items. Check the portfolio of the fund and see if they've got some of the bigger, more established companies. Investors with Yahoo!, AOL, and Microsoft in their tech funds in the late '90s not only did very well, but could rest comfortably if the smaller, lesser known companies in the fund went bottom up. This is especially true in a rapidly growing industry. Only the strong will survive, and you want your fund to have those in the portfolio.

4. Don't jump the gun. The next emerging industry may not emerge until 2003. Why invest now? Wait until you see something tangible. Even if you get in slightly after the industry begins its liftoff, you should have plenty of time to ride the wave.

5. Know when to get out. Is the industry falling out of favor? Has everyone bought it, seen it, done it? Has the attention shifted to a new hot industry? Real estate is a perfect example of an industry that has great highs and great lows, depending on when you look at it. Know when the industry you've chosen is headed for a major decline or is simply experiencing a bump in the road.

a minivan, but your hair may stand straight up from the ride. Likewise, an aggressive growth fund could show you returns of 100%+ in one year, but at what risk? These funds invest in highly volatile stocks in companies expected to grow very quickly. The opposite, however, is true, and they can drop quickly as well.

The top 10 aggressive growth funds in 1999, based on 1-year returns, averaged 238.2% returns (based on the top 10 NAV totals, only not weighing the net assets). The category of aggressive growth funds, however, was at a 46.4% average. While that is still a very high return, it is significantly lower than the top of the class, meaning there have to be funds out there pulling those astonishingly high numbers down. There are also incredible highs and lows from year to year with many of these funds. It is not uncommon for the chart-topping aggressive growth fund of one year to fall way off the mark the next. Over 5 years, the category average is a gain of around 24% to 25%, meaning that even with some incredible highs, these funds come crashing back down to earth.

The aggressive growth fund investor is willing to accept a high level of risk. He or she is usually not going to hold onto these funds for their long-term growth since only some have good long-term track records. These are funds you allocate out of.

GOING LONG (TERM)

Unlike the aggressive fund sports cars, long-term growth funds are designed to get you to a longer term goal in a slower and steadier fashion. Some variations on traditional index funds fall into this category, holding some of the biggest stocks in the S&P 500 or Wilshire 5000 that show the best steady growth. The key to these long-term mutual funds is consistency. While leaders in the field will show 1-year returns in the 75%+ area, more commonly long-term growth funds will grow by 20% to 25% in 1 year, then maintain a similar pace through 3 and 5 years, and still give you 17% returns after 10 or 20 years.

Long-term growth funds are less volatile than their short-term aggressive counterparts, and there is less risk. The expense ratios on

Sector Funds: Average Gains

Yes, some of this is skewed by the rise of the tech funds of recent years, but, as a whole, sector funds have fared well (but you must pick the right sector).

Through the end of 1999, all sectors together averaged the following returns:

1 year	44.0%
3 years	26.8%
5 years	24.7%
10 years	19.6%
20 years	15.4%

Past Performance

*Remember, past perfor-
mance does not guarantee
future results.* Long-term
past performance is a better
indicator than short-term
past performance as it
shows greater consistency
over time; however, this is
still not going to help you get
a definite gauge of the
future. Also keep in mind
that past performance may
be the result of a different
fund manager and a different
economic climate and
market. A particular sector
may have been the rage 5
years ago, so the fund
cashed in on that sector.
Likewise a market that has
been going poorly in recent
years—or several years—
may suddenly become the
hot emerging market, despite
past returns. A new infrastructure in a previously
undeveloped country may
turn their economy and business around, putting them
on the map for investors.

these funds are also generally less than that of aggressive funds.
Also, you will see lower capital gains taxes since fund managers are
not engaging in the same high rate of turnover. A fund like the massive Fidelity Magellan fund (which as of the start of 2000 led the category for 20-year returns at 23.5% and was closed to new investors)
stays in the middle of the pack when it comes to volatility, while
posting an expense ratio of under 0.50. *This also supports the
axiom that larger funds can charge a lower expense ratio.*

Any fund seeking long-term growth seeks out companies with
solid foundations and good management that are expected to grow
steadily over time and give you solid 5-year returns. This is often a
more secure fund to be invested in looking at a longer term
horizon and dealing with large companies with solid, long-term
track records.

GROWTH AND INCOME FUNDS

Another popular option is the growth and income mutual fund.
These funds are not as optimistically titled as "capital appreciation funds," but they are designed to pay you steady income
while investing in growth. These are not to be confused with
other income-producing funds such as bond funds (discussed
later). Growth and income funds seek out large-cap companies
poised to grow that also pay solid dividends. The risk to your
principal is low, since most of these are large, established companies (usually the case with companies paying dividends). It is not
anticipated that these funds will bring in very high returns, but
some did see 30% or better over the last 5 years of the 1990s,
with the 5-year average being around 20% (10-year average, around
14%). The idea behind a growth and income fund is to see a
steady stream of income while getting some decent returns from
growth stocks over a period of time. Many investors in these
mutual funds basically start with making the investment and then
just let it ride, meaning they hold these funds for a long time.
These funds do less speculating than growth funds, which makes
them less risky in regard to losing any of your capital. If you are

looking for both capital appreciation and steady income, these funds are good choices.

EMERGING GROWTH FUNDS

One other form of growth fund you may hear a lot about is emerging growth funds. These are mutual funds looking to find companies that they hope will take off thanks to new technology, corporate restructuring, new products, or other special factors that could increase the stock price. Often these funds follow the Russell 2000, not as index funds but as a comparative benchmark. Since small companies carry greater risks and because their earnings are less predictable, such a fund will show greater volatility and is riskier than a large-cap growth fund. Also, to constantly keep up with the latest potential winners, these stocks see a high turnover ratio, which will result in higher capital gains tax assessments.

If you are comfortable with smaller companies, many of which you (and most people) are not very familiar with, then this is a potential category for you to consider.

VALUE FUNDS

The late 1990s saw a shift whereby value stocks and value funds were outperformed by growth funds. Value and growth funds do go in cycles, so the tide will change periodically.

Value funds look for bargain stocks of undervalued companies. These are companies that are attractively priced in relation to their true value. Research is important when looking for such bargain stocks, and certainly an entire fund in this area requires a fund manager with an expert eye for finding the companies that should be valued higher. Value fund managers and keen investors doing their own research are more likely to look at a company's sales volume, book value, earnings, and cash flow. There are companies that are doing better than their stock price would indicate and vice versa. Often the value funds use the theory that once a large company has gone through the rough stretch, they will usually rebound and get back to where they once were. New

Web Indexing

Not an index of Web sites, but Web sites of the indices. Look at *www.spglobal.com* for S&P index information, *www.dowjones.com* for the Dow Jones, *www.wilshire.com* for the Wilshire indices, *www.russell.com* for the Russell 2000 and other Russell indices, and *www.ms.com,* which is from Morgan Stanley, to look at their international indices. For the social index investors, the place to turn is *www.domini.com* for their socially responsible index. Also, *www.barra.com* has the Barra indices. Other indices have sites too. Look around the Web!

products and technology, such as cellular phones for an older, established electronics company (like Motorola), can turn a company around. The Internet has sprung new businesses, but has also sparked a revival of certain companies that were unable to keep pace and can now do so through e-trading. If a company can utilize the latest in technology to serve their purposes, they may be on the rise once again. Pharmaceutical companies need only develop and own the patent to the latest wonder drug to be back in, or move into prominence. The bottom line, however, is that a strong management strategy needs to be in place and a vision and plan for the future. Fund managers look for this along with a good risk/return opportunity when selecting a value stock for the portfolio.

The other value stocks are found in newer companies that have all the makings of a bigger and more successful business but have not yet seen their stock valued as high as it should be.

The old, "buy low, sell high" approach fits value funds. However, the theory in recent years has been buy high (or at any price for that matter) and sell much higher. Many companies, such as the tech stocks, were selling for 30 or 40 times their earnings until the big drop in April of 2000 when the tech sector came crashing down.

Value stocks come from companies that have more room for growth. Essentially the difference between value and growth investing is analogous to picking the New York Yankees after a 96 win season to get even better and win 100 the next year, while value stock (and fund) picking is like picking the Orioles to come off a 78 win season and win 96 games because they have revamped their team and are poised to move up, despite the low, undervalued rating and predictions of a team that didn't fare well the year before.

A VALUE FUND IN ACTION

How does a value fund find its way when growth funds are in vogue? What might a fund manager do to run such a fund effectively? How would such a fund benefit your port-

Which Growth Fund Is for You?

Aggressive Growth Funds

For anyone with a comfortable lifestyle who can afford to take a higher risk but wants better odds than going to Vegas for the weekend.

For empty nesters who have safe, income-producing investments and want to have something extra put aside for travelling, ·for retirement, and for their children and grandchildren.

For people with long time frames to reach their goals who can start out more aggressively.

For people who have come into a lump sum of money and can afford to take the risk.

Growth Funds

For young couple or singles looking for stocks that will grow over a few years to build up their assets.

For people with some degree of financial obligations (such as young children, car payments, or a mortgage) who can't afford to take a very high risk while looking for capital appreciation.

For anyone looking for capital appreciation when growth stocks are in favor.

Long-term Growth Funds

For investors who have long-term goals but have too many current financial responsibilities and obligations to throw caution to the wind.

For people who prefer the slow and steady approach.

Growth and Income Funds

For those with older children approaching college who need to see growth and steady income to put toward tuition, while not taking great risks.

For anyone who wants to be invested in growth stock but wants to see some steady income at the same time.

For those who like the large-cap giant companies.

Emerging Growth Funds

Like the aggressive category, this is for someone who can take the greater risk at this point in his or her life.

For anyone who is looking for the hot, smaller companies that are poised for growth.

folio? After all, the big name companies in your growth or index funds are names you've heard of. But value stocks? Bargain stocks? Underachievers in the business world? Some are familiar names, but they are often the ones followed by the phrase "Are they still in business?" Even companies that you think are still doing well sometimes find themselves undervalued. A company like Mattel (the toy makers), for example, fell off pace with an industry that was moving ahead with newer technology. It doesn't mean they can't and won't catch up. The same holds true for many other companies that are not getting their just valuations.

Since value stocks are attractively priced, below where they should be, they generally have no place to go but up. Unless you want to be in the position of frequently reallocating assets, which can prove costly and time consuming as you look for where to move your money, you may be best served having some money in a value fund while the growth funds are your big ticket items, and vice versa if the trend is reversed. This way, you'll only need to make adjustments when the tide turns.

A typical value fund looks for the 25%, 30%, or 40% of the most undervalued stocks available to the fund, depending on the fund's universe, which is based on the type of fund. A small-cap value fund doesn't chart large-cap value stock but looks at the small-cap companies that may be undervalued. A large-cap value fund looks at the large-cap companies. If the stocks found have lower present earnings than normal or than anticipated, plus a good management team, growth potential, and a good strategy in place, then it is likely that this is a value fund candidate. A value fund manager, like other fund managers, will analyze the numbers and do a fundamental analysis of the company behind each stock. A technical analysis means numbers and data. A fundamental analysis means looking at the more practical how's and why's of why a company is where it is. They will also look at the risk factor involved and the volatility. The manager and his or her team will then choose the 50, 100, or even 300 stocks that seem the most undervalued and have the most potential for improvement, based on their analysis. They will rank them in order of desirability and buy shares accordingly.

Besides seeking out specific undervalued companies, value can also be found by looking at sectors and emerging companies. There are times when the hottest trends have all the assets funneling into certain sectors, while other sectors are underperforming. Rather than being a follower and going after the hot sector funds, you might look at an undervalued sector that shows promise for the future. In fact, many experts recommend the philosophy of going against the grain, pointing with conviction to past history, meaning buy value when growth is hot or buy undervalued sectors and be patient.

One other note about value stocks and the funds that hold them. Unlike growth where you are looking at a stock and a fund that is moving up and anticipating that it will continue to rise, you are looking at companies that may not simply take off or return to a higher valuation the moment you buy the fund. Value stock selection is often a waiting game, whereby a stock holds steady for weeks or months (hopefully not years) and then suddenly kicks into gear.

ASSET ALLOCATION FUNDS

Asset allocation funds try to help you maintain that delicate balance whereby you diversify just enough to minimize risk. Such a fund encompasses various investments including domestic stocks and bonds, cash investments, and international securities. They are commonly known as hybrid funds.

Asset allocation funds can be considered a one-stop shopping answer for investors looking for proper allocation but not comfortable in dividing up the pie themselves. One goal of such a fund is to seek a high total return from income plus capital appreciation. The other goal is to do so while maintaining a low level of risk. Asset allocation in general is designed to minimize risk, but it depends on how the assets are divided up. These funds lean toward the conservative side.

The two primary types of asset allocation mutual funds are strategic and tactical. Strategic asset allocation funds try to keep a steady, consistent allocation of x% in stocks, x% in bonds, and x%

Measures of Value Fund Investing

Questions value fund managers might ask (and so might you):

- How does the company stand within their industry?
- How fast is the industry growing? Is it an industry that is coming into favor?
- What is the public perception of this company? Have they done anything to antagonize or deceive the public at large? Do they still feature household names?
- Is the company developing new products? Do they hold patents on new inventions? Are their products competitive? Innovative?
- How effective is the management team? Do they have value fund experience?
- Is the company gaining market share?

in cash equivalent investments. This is marvelous if the fund's allocation matches your own personal allocation plan. For example, if you are looking at a relatively long-term goal and want to keep your assets primarily in stocks, a strategic asset allocation fund with a breakdown of 55% in stocks, 35% in bonds, and 10% in cash accounts would suit your needs. Of course, you should also look at the allocations within the allocations. Some asset allocation funds will diversify greatly across asset categories but lean more heavily to large-cap stocks, for example, within the stock portion of their holdings. Others will diversify widely within each asset class.

Asset allocation funds that maintain a set percentage of assets in each category are also known as balanced funds. These funds are relatively safe, low-risk, investments because of diversity and they have volatility. While balanced funds slumped in 1999 they had a 20-year overall average of just over 13% as a category for the last two decades of the 20th century. Often they are bought as a long-term conservative investment along with a stock fund, giving the investor some activity in the bond market without purchasing a bond fund. If you equally divide up your $20,000 investment, putting the same amount of money in a 100% growth stock fund and a balanced fund investing 60% in stocks and 30% in bonds (+10% in cash instruments), you'll have 15% of your portfolio in bonds, 80% in stocks, and 5% in cash instruments.

Tactical asset allocation funds try to stay one step ahead of the shift in market trends by moving the assets around accordingly. They are not trying to maintain a balance as much as they are trying to put the assets in the right place at the right time. If the fund manager sees the stock market dropping because of panicky investors, or for any other reason, he or she may shift large portions of the assets to bonds. Conversely, when the market is looking good, he or she will move the assets from bonds to stocks. While fund managers in general should be looking for what is in the best interest of the fund holders, an asset allocation fund's prime objective is to seek returns while maintaining low risk. The prospectus of the fund will usually indicate whether you are looking at a tactical or strategic type of fund. Although it may not be phrased as such, a fund prospectus will tell you if the fund is trying to maintain a certain percentage of assets in stocks, such as 70% (or thereabouts) or a range between 50% and 75%, giving the fund manager greater flexibility. Either way these funds are combinations of stocks and bonds.

The biggest problem with investing in an asset allocation fund is finding one. While asset allocation is considered by experts to be the most important aspect of putting together a successful portfolio, funds are rarely listed as "asset allocation funds." The marketing savvy behind this discrepancy eludes most of us. The terms *hybrid* or *balanced,* however, are usually the place to look for funds that span the asset board and invest in stocks, bonds, and elsewhere. You can find domestic and international hybrids which, as you might assume, invest accordingly.

While investors who purchase mutual fund shares are handing over the job of stock and bond selecting to a professional fund manager or management team, many investors are more comfortable doing their own asset allocation. There is also the argument that says it's to your advantage to have separate fund managers, one who is an expert in stocks and one who specializes in bonds. A counter argument is that having one fund that holds both stocks and bonds lowers fees and commissions.

FUND OF FUNDS

It's hard to believe, but you can actually buy a fund that invests in mutual funds. These mega funds, known as funds of funds, can help you diversify by owning various funds that own various stocks that represent various companies. Now there's a mouthful of fund talk! With any luck, in a few years, you'll be able to buy a fund of funds of funds that will own several funds of funds that own funds. Well, you get the idea.

There are actually over 100 funds of funds to choose from. You can find funds of funds that buy stocks, bonds, and money markets and others that specialize in a diverse range of stock funds. A stock fund of funds might include a blue chip fund, a mid-cap value fund, a global fund, and even a few sector funds. It's almost like buying a fully furnished apartment, or in this case a full portfolio.

Single Country or Continent Risk

If you're investing overseas, besides the usual mutual fund risks, you run the additional risk of investing too heavily in one country or in one continent. If you should choose to invest in a single country fund, you will be more directly influenced by factors pertaining to that country, such as currency risk, political risks, and the economics of that country. Single country, or even single continent or region, investing can obviously be more risky, so it's more important that you be very confident in the country or region in which you are investing.

Many fund families offer these as a way to invest in several of their own funds at once. Keep in mind that each fund within the larger fund will pass on its capital gains and all other taxable income to the larger fund, which will then pass them on to you. This can result in a large tax bite.

On the positive side, funds of funds provide maximum diversification, which can be across asset classes. Risk can be lowered with such a broad range of investments. You also have a professional fund manager handling all of your many funds, much like a financial advisor, only cheaper. Naturally it's important that you look at the track record of the fund manager and see that he or she has managed this type of portfolio before. The fund manager is picking and choosing the best funds that other fund managers are putting together and actively managing. You can also get into more funds for a lower cost than if you had to pay the minimum balance on each of five separate funds. Six funds at a minimum balance of $2,500 each would run you $15,000. You could buy into the fund of funds and have a piece of each of several funds for perhaps $3,000 or $4,000. And you only have to track the one fund!

A simple analogy can highlight some of the shortcomings of this type of mega fund. There are some people who enjoy having a combination personal computer, printer, fax machine, scanner, CD player, coffee maker, etc. There are others who would prefer to buy the individual components and put together the system they want. The all-in-one unit might cost less and save hours of shopping. The component method could be more costly and take awhile to find each part. However, the person buying components is buying each piece to fit his or her own personal needs. You might want certain features in a fax machine and other features in your PC. You also might want to change your printer after a couple of years but not the entire system. Also, if one piece breaks you can have it fixed without having to take out the whole unit. Likewise, a fund of funds does all the fund picking for you. However, you might not like each component.

If one fund is bringing down your portfolio you can sell off shares in that fund. If one or two funds are pulling down the returns of your all-in-one component fund of funds, you can't get rid of them. Likewise if the fund manager leaves and is replaced or veers off course from the fund's objective, all of your funds are

affected. Basically you are purchasing a fund portfolio; this is hard to do unless you find a mix of funds that is just right for you.

For the same reason that some people book full packages at hotels that include tours and meals while others book their hotel and eat in various restaurants, some investors go with funds of funds and others prefer to furnish their own portfolios. It's a matter of choice. Since there are over 11,000 to choose from, and you may want to buy several funds, the new funds of funds now serve the same purpose in relationship to funds that mutual funds serve in relationship to stocks, making selections for you. Whew!

For the investor who wants tighter control over his or her mutual fund portfolio and particularly in regard to tax managing their investments effectively, this may not be the route to go. For the investor who wants an instant portfolio complete with asset allocation, at a fraction of the overall cost, this may be the way to go.

Keep in mind that you will need to look closely at the holdings of a fund of funds and the allocation or breakdown regarding how much they own of an asset class. Unlike a mutual fund investing in so many stocks that a few losers will barely be noticeable, the 7, 8, or even 12 funds in a fund of funds will carry greater weight, so knowing what they are and how much the fund allocated to each is that much more important. In short, no one can name all 600 stocks in their mutual fund. If they can they have way too much time on their hands. However, you should know all the funds in a fund of funds, just as you'd know all the individual funds you select.

Also you should know that a big drawback of a fund of funds is that you have to pay expense ratios for all the various funds included, plus fees and expenses for this mega fund as well. This increase in fees and expenses can significantly cut into your returns, which is a cumulative return of all of the funds. Of course you paid less money than you would have to purchase all of these funds individually.

The best way to determine if a fund of funds is for you is to first determine your own needs and goals, then do your own asset allocation. Once you determine what types of funds you might want to buy, see if there is a fund of funds that can save you money with a similar grouping of funds. If the asset allocation is similar to what you wanted, the results should be about the same as if you

Who Are Funds of Funds Best Suited For?

1. Someone looking for a one stop, convenient, and simple investment.
2. Someone who wants to own mutual funds but doesn't have time to weed through and do research on the thousands available.
3. Someone looking for broad diversification in one investment.

put the portfolio together yourself. Despite the higher expense ratio fees, you may be able to afford to build such a portfolio by doing it this way. A fund of fund that specializes in index funds won't have an especially high expense ratio since such expenses are generally very low for index funds. This way you could have a large-cap, small-cap, and international fund for one minimum balance, and all would be under one roof.

SELECT FUNDS

Quite the opposite of the fund of funds is the fairly new breed of select funds. These are a more intimate grouping of stocks numbering around 20 to 25. The Janus 20 has been one of the most popular and successful select funds. Since there are fewer companies represented, fund managers invest more heavily in the companies selected to round out the portfolio. The right mix can be a strong combination for someone who really wants to be in the stock market but can't afford to buy each of the 20 or 25 stocks individually. The price is better buying them in this kind of fund. Along with following the success of the fund overall, the investor can also keep tabs on the stocks he or she owns since this is a small grouping. Of course, only the fund manager can buy or sell the individual shares. Needless to say, there can be greater fluctuation and volatility since the movement of one stock has a greater impact on the fund. The risk is also higher since there is less diversity.

An advantage to such a concentrated fund is that they can be easier for a fund manager to handle and carefully map out a strategy since there are fewer securities to deal with. There is also generally a low rate of turnover.

Select funds can specialize in a sector, or a cap-size, or be diverse. They may simply be 25 carefully chosen stocks that the analysts think are the best at a particular time or 25 selected favorites, one by each of 25 analysts. Perhaps they are the top performers in each of 20 areas or sectors.

INTERNATIONAL STOCK FUNDS

Two thirds of the world's economy is based outside the United States. This means there are a wealth of opportunities outside of the domestic markets in which to invest. There is literally a world of opportunities for overseas investing.

Plenty of internationally based companies are not foreign to you. Well known brand names in the United States such as The Benneton Group, Canon, Fiat, Honda, Heineken, Nikon, Mercedes Benz, and Sony are a few of the many companies that are found in international investing.

International stock funds fall primarily into five categories.

Diversified international funds invest in companies in other parts of the world.

Global funds can invest in U.S. companies as well as companies abroad.

Specialized international funds invest in companies in one specific country or in a region of the world.

Emerging market funds invest in companies in underdeveloped, up-and-coming markets around the world.

International index funds invest in stocks that try to emulate international indices.

Concentration

The term *stock concentration* describes how many stocks are in a fund or other grouping. The stock concentration of your portfolio is how much of your portfolio is made up of stocks. *Sector concentration* is how much of the fund or how much of your portfolio is in one sector.

INTERNATIONAL INDICES

Before looking at the various international funds listed earlier, it's worthwhile to have an idea of what these funds use as a benchmark by which to judge their success.

The Morgan Stanley Capital International Index—EAFE (Europe, Australia, Far East) is an international index that covers the stock markets in Europe, Australia, and the Far East. Not unlike the S&P indices and the Dow in the United States, this index is used as one of the premier benchmarks by which these significant markets are compared.

The International Swing

An international fund can provide greater diversity to your portfolio. While international funds have trailed the U.S. stock funds in recent years, the trend can swing the other way as it has at several points in the past.

The international market can be the place to turn when there is a downturn in the domestic markets. It can also be a place to turn when an industry that is doing very well in the United States, or other parts of the world, begins to have global implications. The technology and telecommunications sectors are possibly going to produce big profits in other parts of the world that have not yet been inundated by software companies, Internet sites, and wireless communications. The trick is to determine in which parts of the world these sectors will be profitable and when.

International index funds also try to mirror the benchmark Morgan Stanley Emerging Markets Free Index, which looks at countries that are primed for development and business growth. Morgan Stanley also has indices following the market in the Far East (excluding Japan), Europe, and Asia as well as the Morgan Stanley Japan Index funds, which include both large-cap and small-cap indices. There are other index funds for individual countries, such as the Tokyo Nikkei 225, which mirror the Tokyo stock exchange. Often an international index fund is a good way to start off in such a wide world of fund investments.

The international market bounced back in 1999, and the index showed a 27.3% return after showing only a 7% return over the previous 5-year period. Before investing internationally, however, it is important to get an idea of the market in the part of the world you are looking at. Politics and the value of the currency in that part of the world, plus the nation or region's economy will give you an idea where the market is headed in Japan or throughout Europe.

When looking at international mutual funds, you will find many investing in what are considered the more developed economies such as Western Europe, Japan, and Australia. These are stronger economic markets with high per capita income, a skilled work force, a solid infrastructure, and greater technological advancement. Many of the familiar international companies including auto makers, international banks, and electronics manufacturers are found in these parts of the world.

The opposite approach is to look at the emerging markets, which are countries that have less developed economies that may be ready to grow. Often, companies in developed markets step in and initiate economic growth by educating and assisting these countries in their manufacturing, industrial, and technological endeavors. Telephone companies and other communications industries are among the places where there is plenty of growth potential in these nations and plenty of potentially solid returns. Of course, there are greater risks as governments may be unsteady and the social climate can change at any time. Mexico, Hong Kong, Korea, and China are among a growing number of countries where markets have potential to emerge and grow. The international market is a place to look for value companies, and a good fund manager can

find undervalued companies in emerging markets as well as in the more developed markets.

Among the many cities that are home to their nations' financial markets (besides New York City) are: Amsterdam, Brussels, Frankfurt, London, Mexico City, Paris, Stockholm, Sydney, Toronto, Tokyo, and Zurich. You will find times when these markets and international funds react conversely to domestic markets. Therefore it can be a nice place to be when the United States market goes "bear." Certain sectors, like Japanese technology, however, will follow suit with the domestic funds. There are times when the world market follows trends in the American market.

INTERNATIONAL STRATEGIES

Strategies for international investing differ depending on your view of the investment world. One of the advantages of a global fund is that it also has holdings in stocks in the United States stocks, which means the fund manager can shift assets into domestic securities if world markets are struggling. A global fund obviously provides diversification because it holds securities from around the world. Global stock funds, however, are wide ranging in their success, as evidenced by one-year totals in 1999 for example, when the top global funds gained over 100%, while the category average was much lower at around 35%. This wide disparity of returns can be found with international funds that specialize in one country as well. While a single country may be flourishing, others won't be. It's rare that the majority of world markets are all flourishing at the same time.

Some investors will make a smaller investment in a global fund to get their feet wet and determine how the fund does before plunging in deeper. Other investors will select two established areas of the world that they have heard good reports on, such as Japan and Europe, and buy international funds focusing on these two areas. Many investors will steer clear of international markets all together as long as the domestic market is going well.

Another common question investors ask is whether international markets react in an opposite manner to the domestic market or do they follow suit? Do others act autonomously without regard to the

Hint

A global fund may be a safer way to start investing outside of American shores because it holds a mixture of both international and domestic stocks.

The Re-emergence of Emerging Market Funds

The very end of the 1990s and start of the new century was encouraging for a fund group that was listed on the endangered fund list—emerging market funds. Just as domestic funds seek out companies that are showing promise, these international funds seek out foreign markets that are expected to grow in the coming years. Since 1993, the emerging markets have not fared well, particularly while the large-cap U.S. companies were the place to be. Add to that the very unsteady financial markets in a number of countries and there was not much to cheer about.

Managers of such funds have a number of concerns, which include finding growing companies and the hot industries within foreign countries and keeping track of the overall global economic picture (which is no easy task). The international economy can present an analyst (and an investor) with a roller-coaster ride because so many factors (such as politics) come into play.

Some emerging market funds seek out companies first, while others look initially at a growing economy or developing industry in a particular country and then look to find the company that leads that industry.

One of the reasons for a more positive outlook regarding international and emerging markets is the growing telecommunications industry. While there was some concern as the world approached Y2K, the computer and technology sector is now creating a more compact global economy. The web of technology is reaching into more countries than ever before.

Encouraging signs, such as the T. Rowe Price Emerging Market Stock Fund, which gained over 87% in 1999, and the American Express Emerging Markets A fund, which gained nearly 79%, show that emerging market funds may finally be re-emerging. Of course the tide can turn back around very quickly.

U.S. market? After all, the U.S. market is only a small portion of the world's economy. However, it does play a major role in the global economy. The answer to this question is all of the above, which makes international investing a tad more risky. Depending on the leading industries, some markets overseas will pick up when the United States market is in a decline, looking elsewhere to do international business. Others, particularly emerging markets, will follow suit, with industries such as technology and industrials lagging behind the domestic lead. If a more developed nation is technologically at the point the United States was 3 or 4 years ago, then the next 3 years should see them doing well as they catch up. However, other factors can and will affect the markets in these countries. This is where they will react autonomously. A country, for example, that is now building up their infrastructure and enhancing their computer and communications capabilities will not succeed if tax laws are too prohibitive, if the government is in disarray, the political climate is shaky, or if other social or economic factors halt progress. There are few countries that are not affected by the U.S. market in some manner, for better or worse.

Some reasons investors often steer clear of overseas markets include:

- Unfamiliarity with many of the companies abroad which the fund is investing in
- Unstable governments and politics abroad
- Higher expense ratios on international and global mutual funds
- Potentially higher taxes in places like Europe, which can wipe out some of your returns
- The stability, or instability, of the market and the rate of currency in other countries

Some reasons investors seek out overseas markets and look to buy shares of global or international mutual funds include:

- Greater diversification with exposure to markets outside of the United States

Watch the Expense Ratio with International Funds

The long distance phone bills alone are reason to be concerned about high expense ratios when dealing with international mutual funds. You won't find many expense ratios under 1.20, and many will be in the 1.60 to 1.80 range. Also, international funds, both diversified and country specific, will generally be higher and more volatile than global funds that have investments in U.S. companies.

- The right markets, such as Japan in 1999, can be extremely profitable
- There is great potential in emerging markets with the growth of worldwide technology, improved infrastructures, and telecommunications
- It's a good place to be if there is a domestic bear market
- Great conversation at cocktail parties, talking about your more exotic funds

While Japan funds are the most popular single-country funds among American investors, and Europe (which generally focuses on Great Britain, France, Germany, and Italy) is the most common broader category, since the markets in most of these countries react similarly, there are many parts of the world that you can delve into as an investor. Some investors will strategize to have a high-risk emerging market fund countered by a less risky global fund or international index fund.

For most investors, buying an international or global fund is down the road, after you have set up your domestic portfolio with two to five funds you feel suit your needs and will help you meet your goals. Then, if all is going well with your funds, you might, and I emphasize the word *might* since this is not a prerequisite for having a successful portfolio, look to invest abroad.

Keep in mind that a portion of your current stock funds may be invested in foreign markets, usually only 5%. If you want more, go for it, but be very well versed in the fund or funds you are looking at and start small.

Types of Funds

Aggressive Growth Funds
For investors looking for very high capital growth, possibly in the short term, who are not afraid of taking a high risk.

International Funds For investors looking for steady, potentially high capital growth who are not bothered by higher expense ratios or a high degree of risk.

Growth Funds For investors looking for steady to high capital growth who are comfortable with a relatively high degree of risk.

Sector Funds For the investor looking for steady to high capital growth and who are comfortable taking a relatively high degree of risk.

Index Funds For investors looking for steady capital growth, low fees, broadest diversification, and less risk.

Growth and Income Funds
For investors looking for some growth but also steady income and a low degree of risk.

High Grade Bond Funds and Fixed Income Funds
For investors not looking for a great deal of capital appreciation, seeking steady moderate to high income and low risk.

Global Technology
and a Couple of Emerging Markets

China is one of the countries enjoying the new wave of technology with the telecommunications and Internet sectors growing fast. At the start of the new century, the top PC manufacturer in China, Legend, was poised for success, as PCs became more popular in the country. Hong Kong has also seen the emergence of the Internet and the new media. Companies like China Telcom, which is the leader in the mobile phone business in mainland China, are spurring a growing telecommunications market. The Heng Seng Index is a benchmark for the Hong Kong market.

Malaysia is another country benefiting from the need to be technologically up to speed. A reintroduction into the MSCI international index has made this a popular international emerging market for investors building global portfolios. In Taiwan, new products like DVD's, MP3, and large screen digital TVs are all hitting the market as of early 2000. The telecommunications industry is also anticipated to rise along with the semiconductor industry. All of this could bode well for business and for investing in this market.

What does all of this mean? It means emerging markets are worth keeping an eye on. However, be cautious, as these markets are risky. They will react to the inflation rates of the United States, international trading agreements and rulings, political changes or upheavals, and numerous other factors.

FUND LISTINGS

As you sift your way through 11,000 mutual funds, it may help if you write down a few in each category to help yourself compare and contrast the mutual funds that might be right for your portfolio.

Fund Category:

	Fund Name	Fund Family	NAV	% Sales Load	Expense Ratio	Assets Millions	1 Yr.	Returns: 3 Yrs.	5 Yrs.
1									
2									
3									
4									
5									

Fund Category:

	Fund Name	Fund Family	NAV	% Sales Load	Expense Ratio	Assets Millions	1 Yr.	Returns: 3 Yrs.	5 Yrs.
1									
2									
3									
4									
5									

Fund Category:

	Fund Name	Fund Family	NAV	% Sales Load	Expense Ratio	Assets Millions	1 Yr.	Returns: 3 Yrs.	5 Yrs.
1									
2									
3									
4									
5									

CHAPTER FOUR

FUND SIZE:
THE LARGE AND
SMALL OF IT

SMALL FUNDS

Contrary to the old adage that "bigger is better," "smaller" has often made the public sit up and take notice. Smaller cars replaced the larger gas guzzlers, small independently made films have taken awards usually reserved for big studio blockbusters, and many mom and pop businesses have thrived in a time when people have had money to spend. Even small video stores have been successful against the giant blockbuster chains by giving personal attention, reserving a film, or by giving you a select choice of quality titles as opposed to stocking up in mass quantity. The idea is often the same with mutual funds: quality investing versus quantity of assets.

Smaller funds can provide select quality investments their larger counterparts are often no longer able to do. The more assets that pour into a fund, the harder it becomes for the fund manager to find solid places to invest all the funds. Mutual fund managers or management teams handling billions in assets will find themselves looking to buy stocks they would not normally have been interested in purchasing for the portfolio. This becomes very difficult in a sector or emerging market fund where stock choices can be limited to begin with and especially difficult during a time period when more stocks are dropping than are gaining. There is a need to trade more, which raises the tax liability to the investor. You'll see small-cap funds buying mid-cap stocks in order to allocate some of their assets. A forced hand by a fund manager can often cause performance to fade. You'll also see larger funds being very heavily sector weighted to try to maintain a strong position.

Smaller funds, generally under $10 million in assets, and some-times much smaller than that, can see significant results from a good fund manager since he or she is able to carefully make stock (and bond) selections. As Greg Knopf of HighMark Funds, a small fund family of 14 core mutual funds (averaging around $1 billion in assets or less) explains, "A massive fund can buy the greatest stock and it will have very little effect. With a smaller fund, a good stock picker can make a very big impact."

A small fund can move assets more easily and take a position in a promising young company without driving their stock up sky-high. If they pick the right stocks, they can make a great impact on the portfolio of a small fund. The better small funds have fared well, bringing in returns over 80 points above average in their categories. The trick is finding such good small funds and small fund families.

HighMark is an example of a smaller fund family that is not as highly discovered or visible as the Vanguards or Fidelities of the fund world. Rather than trying to blitz the investing media, they distribute through 250 branches of Union Bank of California, through investment specialists, regional brokers, and fee-based investment advisors. This is an example of a fund family that can remain relatively small and benefit from a fund manager who is not trying to move enormous and cumbersome amounts of assets. They can also provide more personal attention to their investors. HighMark manages to stay around or below the average expense ratio of the overall fund world (which is around 1.20). Many smaller funds, because of the limited asset pool, are forced to have slightly higher expense ratios.

Smaller funds have the following advantages:

- Good stocks can make a greater impact on the overall fund.
- They can be more selective in stock choices and more specialized.
- They can move money more quickly when a bear market is approaching; they are more nimble.
- If they do not market to become a large fund, they can remain small and not be overburdened with assets.
- Returns of the better ones have been very good in recent years.

Smaller funds have the following disadvantages:

- Bad stocks can have greater impact on the overall fund.
- Frequently they have higher expense ratios, and they are very often load funds.
- They can be harder to follow if the fund does not yet have a ticker symbol.
- If they are doing poorly, such funds can be closed or merged into a larger fund that might have a different objective.
- Smaller funds do not have as much buying power in a good market.

Small Time Winners

Of the top 50 funds annually, usually half are less than 3 years old and have under $150 million in assets. In fact, as noted by Jonas Max Ferris, founder of Maxfunds.com, "according to a study (from the publication *Financial Research*) the smallest 25% of funds routinely outperform the largest 25% of funds, which is why it's important to consider having some smaller funds in your portfolio. But you have to research them and determine which ones are winners." You also have to know there is greater risk.

REALLY SMALL FUNDS

How small is a really small fund? According to Jonas Max Ferris of *www.maxfunds.com* in Ann Arbor, Michigan, there are hundreds of new funds started every year, and many begin in people's homes.

"Other than not having a criminal record, it's not that hard to start a fund," says Ferris, whose Maxfunds Web site is one of the few places you can find these little known (pre–ticker symbol) mutual funds. "A small fund can be a Janus Fund that in a short time, through marketing efforts of a major fund family, will grow to assets over $25 million in no time. A small fund can also be that started by a wealthy investor for $100,000. Some grow quickly and see tremendous returns while others are closed or merged away. It's all a matter of who is managing them and how good they are at picking the right stocks."

Small funds generally receive little fanfare or attention, particularly those that are from small fund families. Independent funds are quite unknown to the average investor. Such funds are marketed through banks and brokers and occasionally receive attention in a small financial publication if they're doing something particularly unique. Maxfunds.com is one place to look under the heading "undiscovered funds" where you can click to get a listing of these little known funds. Punching in a category and hitting "Go" will bring up groupings of such funds, including those that will grow out of the "undiscovered" category quickly because they are part of larger fund families, and those that may never get above $50 million in assets. It is also a great place to compare a small new fund with other more established larger funds in the same category.

Funds generally don't make any money until they have passed at least $10 million in assets. It takes that much to cover all the expenses necessary to build a successful fund. In fact, a fund won't receive a ticker symbol until it hits the $10 million mark, and then it receives only a supplemental symbol that doesn't appear in the newspapers or in the major financial media. At $25 million in assets, or over a thousand investors, a fund gets a full fledged NASDAQ symbol and makes the major leagues, so to speak, getting into the newspaper listings, receiving ratings, research, and media attention.

From Seniors to Football, Everyone's Got His or Her Own Fund

Associations and organizations are getting into the fund business, and so are former football players. The AARP, the American Association of Retired Persons, now offers various funds including balanced, capital growth, plus growth and income funds. Some of the former San Francisco 49ers also have started a mutual fund, including ex–all star Ronnie Lott. The mutual fund is primarily for former athletes who are looking to invest some of the money from those big salaries earned in their playing days.

Small Funds That Will Grow

New funds usually start out as small funds. Some 75% of them are the products of mid to large fund families, and such new funds won't stay small for very long. Fund families can help funds grow in assets by adding incentives to buy. Large fund families can absorb expense ratios in newer funds and keep them low. They can get the inside track on IPOs and add low or no transfer fees from other funds. In fact, new funds can also be heavily promoted to the holders of other funds in the family. The Internet and financial media can bolster a new fund with plenty of prime coverage led by fund marketing. Managers of new funds can then carefully handpick with a small number of assets exactly the ideal portfolio to get started. On the other hand, a brand-new fund is missing one important ingredient, past performance. This is why fund families will do what they can to entice you to buy shares. Since they need to compensate for no past performance data, they try to build up an initial positive performance so they'll have data for the next round of investors.

Small funds that are not emanating from large fund families but are independent or in a small fund family, have the dilemma of not getting coverage because they are too small and don't have the assets to market themselves to get larger. It's an uphill battle. Some funds catch on with targeted marketing and may even grow larger than the fund family may want them to. In some instances, they may close the fund to new investors at a certain point to maintain a small, easier to manage fund. If a fund remains open and grows too fast, or faster than management is prepared to handle, you will see a drop-off in returns. It is not uncommon to see an 80% return by a fund with $10 million in assets turn into a 10% return the following year because the fund has grown to $70 million in assets.

Another Small Fund Advantage

One of the advantages of a small fund is that, since the fund is trading in lower volume, purchases of stock can generally be filled in a shorter time than the stock purchases of a larger fund, which takes longer for the execution because of the higher volume of trading. A stock may be gaining momentum but the larger funds may not get it into the portfolio as quickly as a smaller fund, which can act more quickly, having fewer assets to move.

Many of the new funds that open every year will fail. Some, in larger families, are merged into larger funds or merged with other small funds to keep them going. Other funds will simply be closed down. There is risk, but not from the fund going bankrupt, since they will simply return your investment money. The money is kept in custodial accounts, and, unlike a low-grade bond, there is almost never a risk of default. There is a risk, however, that the fund's NAV can drop greatly if it is not managed well and the selection of securities is not a good one. A smaller number of assets can be greatly affected by the stocks selected and the manager selecting them. This can also make a small fund a great place to be if those running the show really know what they are doing. The Internet Fund started in someone's basement with $100,000 in assets. It racked up 300% to 400% returns and took off to over $1.5 billion very quickly; word spread fast! Needless to say, they're no longer in someone's basement.

It's to your advantage to do your homework with small funds, just as you would with larger ones. It may be harder if it is a new small fund since there is little in terms of past performance data to look at. Ask for a prospectus and any other literature available about the funds and the people who manage them. Once you purchase a small fund, keep tabs on it, just as you would any other fund. You may have to call the fund for updated information since, other than *www.maxfunds.com* and information about small funds at *www.businessweek.com/investor,* there are few places to go to find out how these funds are doing. You may find some very successful small funds, in which case, sssh, keep them a secret!

In investing, smaller generally means potentially higher returns, and potentially higher returns generally means there is a higher level of risk involved.

LARGE FUNDS

They are the funds you'll hear about in the financial magazines, see touted on commercials, and most often find as one (or more) of your 401k choices. These are the big guns, the funds that everybody has a piece of. The fund world has grown at such a rapid rate that there are no longer a select few large funds (although there are still only a few behemoths).

Holding over $10 billion generally classifies a fund as large, while there are mega funds holding $40 or $50 billion or more. There are advantages to being part of such a large fund. For one thing, the asset pool usually lowers the expense ratio. Large funds also have many more options and greater purchasing power. In a good (bullish) market for investing, the manager or management team can enjoy the wide range of stock choices. Such larger funds can (and are mandated to) spread the assets around, which will result in greater diversity and potentially less risk. The fund can lean heavily, and we mean heavily, into one sector. Risks can be much less in a large fund as well. Just as holding a winning stock in a smaller portfolio can have a greater impact, holding a losing stock in a large fund will have little to no effect on the fund overall.

Conversely, in a bear market (or even a highly volatile market) the fund manager of a large fund will also have to invest the many, many assets, and he or she (or the team) will have a harder time finding solid companies in which to put such assets. They may also have a harder time staying close to the fund's objective. Moving the many assets around in a large fund can also result in a high turnover rate—hence higher tax liabilities for you, the investor. Smaller funds with securities that hold up well through a bear market might do better. However, smaller funds hold fewer investments, and less diversity can mean more volatility and greater risk. In the end, and it's been written many times before, it's not the size but the performance that counts. Note that some of the larger funds grow to their enormous size largely from 401k plans, IRA's, and other retirement vehicles.

Large funds have the following advantages:

- Expense ratios are generally lower.
- They have tremendous leverage and buying power.
- Large funds offer great diversification and low risk.
- There's very little chance, if any, that the fund will shut down or merge.

When Funds Merge

This generally happens when a fund is underperforming or not attracting enough in assets to keep it as a separate entity. This can become a problem when you thought you were invested in a growth fund which just merged with a value fund and you already own a value fund.

While there are mergers, or proposed mergers, that will cause the SEC to stand up and intervene, many mergers simply go through as proxies distributed to shareholders who generally do not bother to read the fine print—or any of the print for that matter.

If you receive a proxy that informs you that your fund may be merging, read it carefully. If the fund's objective is no longer what you originally had in mind, redeem your shares.

Large funds have the following disadvantages:

- Fund managers can run into trouble handling so many assets when the market drops.
- Hot stocks have less impact on a large fund.
- Large funds can't always be as selective in stock picking.
- They can close to new investors.

The numbers may change, and some other players may climb into the company of these giants, but as of early 2000 these were the nation's 10 largest stock funds. While numbers 3 through 10 range from around $53 billion down to $24 billion, the top two are in their own category, with assets near $100 billion. Many of these funds are closed to new investors, but those that are not have the luxury of significant purchasing power and very low expense ratios.

Top 10 Biggest Funds	Category	Style of Investing (Types of Stocks Fund Invests In)
1. Vanguard 500 Index	Growth & income	Large cap, blended (index fund)
2. Fidelity Magellan	Growth	Large cap, growth
3. Investment Company of America	Growth & income	Large cap, mostly blue chip
4. Washington Mutual Investment	Growth & income	Mostly large cap, some mid
5. Fidelity Contrafund	Growth	Mixed
6. Fidelity Growth & Income	Growth & income	Large cap, blended
7. Janus Fund	Aggressive growth	Large cap, growth
8. American Century Ultra	Aggressive growth	Large cap, growth
9. Janus Worldwide	Global	World Stocks
10. Janus Twenty	Aggressive growth	Large cap, growth

As of April 2000, Vanguard edged its way past Magellan as the nation's largest fund, which ended Magellan's 11-year run on top. These two are the top performing mega funds, which explains why they just keep getting bigger and bigger. They will most likely remain the top two for some time, although Magellan has closed its doors to new investors, figuring that just over $100 billion in assets was quite enough, thank you. Remember, however, that while these are very successful funds, size is not everything.

At this point Janus Worldwide was the biggest U.S. international fund, while the Vanguard 500 leads all index funds and mirrors the S&P 500.

VOLATILITY

When selecting a mutual fund you will want to assess how rocky a road you will be travelling en route to reaching your goal. Greater risk means greater volatility. It also means you need more patience, as most funds will recover, some in a day and others in a year. Individual stocks are quite volatile. If you follow the day-to-day stock quotes, you'll see constant volatility. Even the most successful stocks, will take an up and down road while climbing to the top. Funds respond to the securities held within, whether they are stocks or bonds. The overall market will affect the funds. On a day like April 14, 2000, when five out of six stocks lost money, you can be sure most stock funds dropped with the tide. The notion that a rising tide raises all ships means that your fund may be as volatile as the overall market.

It is not only the market that causes a fund to be volatile. If your fund is experiencing volatility because of a change in managers or a change in direction, then you may want to investigate management more thoroughly and determine if the fund still meets your goals.

There are several other reasons a fund may be volatile, including interest rates (particularly pertaining to bonds) and foreign currency rates. A fund that is actively buying and selling more heavily and funds that invest more small-cap or micro-cap stocks or low-grade bonds will be more volatile. Look to see if similar funds, in the same category, are also experiencing similar volatility. You may simply find that the volatility of your fund is typical for all funds in that category. Usually you can expect greater volatility in the short term. From day to day you'll see stocks and funds bounce around, but over time there is a more steady path.

Clone Funds

Many of the top funds, in terms of number of investors and assets, at some point will close their doors to new investors. This does not make them closed-end funds, but simply open-end funds that do not want to grow any larger. The larger funds can become harder for the fund manager to manage. To make life easier on the fund manager and allow the investor a chance to invest in the fund, many mutual fund companies will set up a clone fund duplicating (with fewer assets to work with at first) the previous fund. For example, Fidelity Growth & Income is closed to new investors. Thus, Fidelity Growth & Income II was created. No, it's not a sequel but a clone fund that will closely follow the lead of the predecessor and be open to new investors.

BETA

While fund magazines may simply rank volatility from 1 through 10 or by giving grades to simplify matters, the official measure of volatility is called *beta*. Beta is a more official number system for rating volatility. It uses the number 1.0 as a base; anything above that will be a more volatile fund in relationship to the overall market. Any fund with a beta under 1.00 will be less volatile than the market.

One way to ease your mind regarding volatility is to hold onto your funds for a longer period of time. Even before the surge of the stock market in the late '90s, mutual funds demonstrated that they are solid, long-term investments. According to Lipper Analytical Services, Inc., for the 35-year span from the end of 1960 through the end of 1995 (and no, you don't have to hold your funds 35 years to see results), small company growth funds were up over 12%, growth and income funds were up over 11%, and growth funds up over 10%. Balanced funds checked in just under 10% and long-term fixed income funds (bonds) were just shy of 8%. You can be sure that 99% of these funds didn't start out at one net asset value (NAV) and move steadily upward, without volatility (bumps in the road) along the way.

Volatility alone is not going to affect your investment unless you act on it. If your stock or fund drops and you lose $500 in one day, it is still an unrealized loss (also known as a paper loss), which may very possibly correct itself by the following day. Even in the same day the stock market has taken investors on a fair share of roller-coaster rides of late, thanks to tremendous investor activity. This is due in large part to reactions to other financial indicators, words from the Federal Reserve, and good old fashioned panic, which is later reversed by level-headed veteran investors. A slight dip in the market will send many newer investors (who aren't used to watching the volatility of their investments) into a panic that will lead to their selling off stocks, bonds, or fund shares. The panic spreads and feeds upon itself. The more pessimistic the tone, the more selling that takes place. Seasoned investors, who are convinced that what goes down must go up, see downturns as a sign to pick up some great bargains. Likewise, good fund managers can get some deals when the market nosedives. A good fund manager may be able to pick up some good values during these moments of investor panic. You, on the other hand, should stay put. This is what volatility is all about; it

Make Your Own Fund with Investment Clubs

You already make your own salads at the salad bar and pump your own gas at filling stations, so why not make your own fund?

Perhaps you will soon see the make your own fund approach whereby shareholders can vote in certain stocks to be purchased or perhaps a specially designed fund just for you. I'm not sure where the pooled assets would come from, perhaps friends and family. In time, funds personalized in some manner will probably exist. In fact, there are a number of wealthy investors every year who start their own mutual funds and go out and market their new creations to the public. It doesn't take more than $40,000 in some cases and a filing with the SEC (and a good lawyer who knows what he or she is doing) to get a fund started. It does, however, take some skills to run it effectively and market it so that the operating costs are covered. Many of these wealthy investors also close such funds after seeing how difficult it is. The point, however, is that, one can start his or her own fund with enough backing and some good planning.

In essence, investment clubs, which for a time in the 1990s were popping up around the country, are designed to pool money for the purpose of investing in a similar manner to a mutual fund. The goal of an investment club is to bring together like-minded investors with the idea of compiling a portfolio that will benefit the whole group. While in theory this is a noble idea, it doesn't work most of the time and not because of bad investments. The problems that ensue with the majority of such clubs lie in the areas of control and club management, not to mention personality conflicts. Money, being the principal part of the equation, quite often brings out the worst in people, even in the best of friendships. There is a great deal of disagreement, not unlike that found on co-op boards where battles for power become reminiscent of great military struggles. Resentment and lost friendships are the results of more investment clubs than good returns.

Seven Things to Do When You See a Bear Approaching (Bear Market, That Is)

1. Stay calm!
2. Make sure you are diversified.
3. Look at how your funds fared during the last bear market.
4. Shift some (and we mean a small percentage) of your assets into cash accounts or your money market mutual fund. Move money from your higher risk/more volatile funds.
5. Don't be swayed by investor friends, neighbors, or relatives who panic.
6. Avoid reading too many financial papers (or looking at too many Web sites)—they'll depress you.
7. Remember that (according to history) a bear market shall pass.

is the ups and downs of the market and all related investments. It is not something to panic over. Doing nothing is almost always the wisest move, particularly with mutual funds which, because they are diversified, will take less of a hit than shares of an individual stock.

The stock market endured 25 bear markets in the 1900s, some longer lasting than others. It has always recovered and moved higher than prior to the fall. The biggest reason for listing the volatility of a fund is to inform you ahead of time that the roller-coaster ride has some major highs and some major drops. It's almost like that height line you see before getting on a ride, the one that tells children that if they are under a certain height they can't ride. The volatility ranking, or beta, is just like that line. If you're under it, don't take the ride.

How do funds generally rank in terms of volatility? There is no set formula, but from a general standpoint, here is a listing from more volatile to less volatile. The most volatile funds include:

Aggressive growth funds
High yield bond funds
Sector funds
International specialized (specific country funds)
Emerging market funds
Small-cap funds
Micro-cap funds

The least volatile funds include:

Balanced funds
Growth and income funds
Asset allocation funds
Government bond funds
Mortgage backed bond funds
Global funds
Large-cap funds

Growth funds can fall anywhere in the volatility range and are generally in the middle. Funds seeking higher capital appreciation have greater risk attached and also have more volatility. Funds looking at protecting your principal or producing income, which are less focused on capital appreciation, come with lower risk and are less volatile.

CHAPTER FIVE

THE NAME IS BOND,
BOND FUNDS

No, they're not as frequently talked about or hyped as stock funds, and there are fewer assets invested within them, but bonds and bond funds are an integral part of the financial picture. They are generally considered the lower risk portion of a portfolio. Bond funds focus on interest income and preserving capital more than on growth. The emphasis on interest over growth of capital means a bond fund manager will invest in securities that pay a fixed rate of return.

It's important, before passing over this section entirely, that you understand that bond funds paying 6%, 8%, or 12% returns are not designed to compete with growth funds paying two or three times higher. It is not an either/or proposition. Bond funds are usually funds that make up the more conservative portion of your portfolio. With the exception of international bonds and high yield corporate bonds, most of these funds are not bought for capital appreciation. The more conservative you want your portfolio, the more you will allocate to bond funds.

To better understand the nature of bond funds, it's a good idea to take a look at what bonds are all about. Unlike stocks, where you are buying shares in a company and its impending success or failure, bonds are essentially a manner in which you loan a company, municipality, or the United States government (or a foreign government) money that is to be paid back at a set date in the future. For lending them the money, the borrower (or issuer of the bond) agrees to pay you a rate of interest. Such interest is usually paid semiannually or annually and compounds. Obviously, the rate of interest will be a significant factor in your selection of a bond.

Bonds are considered fixed income investments because you know how much you will get back when they reach maturity, unless you sell, and then the price will need to be determined based on the market. They are sold in specific increments and can be bought on a short-term basis (up to 5 years), intermediate term (generally 6 to 10 years), or a long-term basis (which can be as many as 30 years). Longer term bonds will pay higher yields (they've averaged higher than 6%

over the last 50 years) than short-term bonds. They will also show greater volatility than short-term bonds.

It's important to remember that bonds react in an opposite manner to the changing interest rates set forth by the Federal Reserve Board. The reason for this is that a high-interest-paying bond needs to stand out among its bond peers, so to speak. A good ballplayer on a team of all stars will be underappreciated, while a good ballplayer on a mediocre team without any big stars will look like a hero. Likewise a bond paying 7% when interest rates drop to 4% will be a sought-after winner and be very much in demand. Conversely, a bond paying 7% surrounded by 9% all-star bonds won't be a big seller.

Bonds can be bought at different amounts, often selling at $2,000, $5,000, or $10,000. And that's where bond mutual funds come in. A bond mutual fund, for the same $2,000, $5,000, or $10,000 can hold hundreds of bonds—far more than you could afford without spending a great deal of money.

The buying and selling of bonds, which can be difficult, as they can sell at a discount or a premium to their face value, is not your headache, but that of the bond fund manager. The amount of buying and selling of the bonds in the fund will depend on the type of bonds the fund is investing in, the fund manager, the bond market, and the style of the fund.

While bond funds are lower risk investments, you can lose money if the NAV drops in value. Government bond funds (primarily those dealing in short-term securities) are the lowest risk bond funds in regard to safe investments. The bonds purchased are government bonds that will not default. Again, this does not mean that if you invest in a government fund you cannot lose money if the NAV goes down. This is unlike buying an individual bond and holding it to maturity, where your principal is protected unless the company defaults, which won't be the case with a U.S. government security.

Remember, while bonds will provide higher returns than many cash instruments or bank accounts, they won't measure up to the big returns you'll see from stock funds. Bond funds are generally for generating income and for managing taxes on your portfolio through tax exempt bond funds.

Bond Ratings

The grading systems established by Standard and Poor's, Moody's, and other financial services rate the solvency of the company behind the bond. In other words, it gives you an idea of the likelihood the company will default on the bond. The top grade (AAA, AA, A, Aaa, or Aa, depending on which rating system you are following), means that you are dealing with bonds backed by a solid company or municipality. BBB, Bbb, or Bb grade bonds are also high quality, but often the company is still growing. These bonds are considered safe investments. Bonds graded below B are low-grade bonds. The lowest grade bonds are known as junk bonds. Unlike most bonds, these low-grade bonds are also high-risk bonds. And what comes with high risk? You got it— potential high returns, or high yields as they're called in the world of bonds.

WHAT PUTS THE FUN IN BOND FUNDS?

Buying and holding a bond until maturity is quite simple and painless. You'll get interest income, and your principal will be safe with a high grade or government bond. However, to sell a bond and get a good price is more difficult. Bonds do not sell at their face value but at discounts or premiums depending on supply and demand. Therefore you can buy a bond at a discount, sell for face value (which is the amount of the bond, such as $10,000), and make money. Or you could buy at a premium, meaning you're buying the bond for more than the face value in hopes that it will go even higher in value. All of this will depend on which direction you see the bond market heading, based on the future of interest rates and how much you need the money from that bond. Most people still buy bonds with the intention of holding them.

To sell, you need a bond broker who can get a good price for you in the bond market. You also need a buyer for your bond since the company issuing the bond is not your buyer. If the bond market is not favorable, you may have a hard time selling. A bond fund, however, like a stock fund, makes selling much easier. Since you do not have to find a seller for the bonds, you will sell your shares back to the fund; it's very simple. Hence, a bond fund is more liquid than individual bonds. This means not having to worry about finding a seller for a bond or holding a bond to maturity. Those headaches belong to the fund manager. Furthermore, some bond funds offer check writing privileges (sometimes there's an additional fee).

Following the bond market and knowing which are the best bonds to buy and sell is also not easy on an individual basis since there is far less press and Internet space devoted to bonds than to stocks. Therefore, by letting a trained bond professional handle the selection process, you can avoid plenty of tedious research. It's easy to follow a bond fund; the NAV is the place to look. That will give you one overall total for the fund based on the bonds held within. Contrary to popular belief, bond funds do not buy and hold bonds to maturity; they buy and sell frequently, like stock funds. Bond funds are also a way to provide steady income if that is what you are seeking. This income may vary depending on the bond market.

There are also a very large percentage of no-load bond funds to encourage investors to get into the bond market. Expense ratios for bond funds are often on the low end (at least for funds primarily carrying domestic bonds).

ADDITIONAL BOND RISKS

INTEREST RATE RISK

When interest rates rise, bond prices will fall and bond fund share prices will drop as well. Higher yields may make up for some of the drop in share price, but your principal may not recover until the rates go back up again. Short-term bond funds, or short-to-intermediate-term bond funds have less interest rate risk since they are not holding securities for as long a period of time as long-term bond funds. If you do not have a long time to wait for the rates to recover and want to see better short-term results, go with funds holding short-term securities. Remember that bonds react conversely to interest rates.

CREDIT RISK

The basic bond risk to your principal is that the issuer, or company behind a bond, will default on the payments. Highly rated bonds have far less chance of this occurring. General bond funds are usually managed to protect your investment against this by balancing out higher risk, high-yield bonds with lower risk bonds. Government securities can completely minimize this risk. A bond fund can usually stand the hit if one company defaults because they hold numerous bonds. This is why a low-grade junk bond is a greater risk when held by an individual investor.

INFLATION RISK

Inflation is a common investment risk that hinges on whether your rate of return is beating inflation. This is more noticeable with bond funds than stock funds because the returns are lower. Remember that while income from fixed income securities is a plus, it's a minus if it is trailing the rate of inflation. A +3% return with an inflation rate of 4% is really a −1% return.

Minimizing Bond Fund Risk

To minimize your risks when you buy shares of a bond fund you can:

- Look for funds that invest in high-grade bonds to minimize credit risk, or the risk of the bond defaulting.
- Seek out bond funds that invest in shorter term securities. These can help you minimize interest rate risk since the less time until the bond comes due, or is sold by the fund manager, the less time the bonds will be affected by interest rate fluctuations.
- Avoid prepayment risk by not investing heavily in funds that deal in mortgage backed securities.
- Steer clear of tax risk (a risk of all investment groups) either by buying your bond fund shares in a tax exempt retirement plan or buying tax-free municipal bond funds.

PREPAYMENT AND CALL RISK

This is the risk that a bond will be called or the bond issuer will pay off the principal before the bond matures. Callable bonds may be called if the interest rates drop and the issuer wants to issue bonds at a lower rate. Mortgage backed securities, such as those in the home financing industry, can also have the risk that homeowners will prepay or refinance the mortgage on their homes when interest rates decline. If you believe interest rates are going to fall soon, you might not want to invest in funds that handle a lot of home mortgages. When this happens, the bond fund is forced to reinvest the assets at what will likely be a lower rate of return. Therefore the bond fund NAV drops. Since this risk may scare off investors, agencies like Ginnie Mae offer higher yields to balance out the risk to some degree.

Bond funds will discuss their risks in the prospectus and in their profile literature. Risks will relate to the percentage of the types of bonds held in the fund. Along with risks, the other drawback of bond funds of late has been that many categories have not fared well coming out of the 1990s. However, the short-term stumbles should not greatly concern long-term investors. Over 5 and 10 years, bond funds are generally seeing good returns.

TYPES OF BOND FUNDS

Stock funds are primarily categorized by a style of investing that features various stocks that are selected to fit the category. While cap size defines itself, a value stock or a stock that fits into an aggressive growth fund is determined by the fund analyst who is selecting it. Bond funds, however, are categorized by the types of bonds that are in the portfolio.

The five broad categories of bonds that are featured in bond funds include: corporate bonds, government bonds, mortgage backed bonds, municipal bonds, and international bonds. In addition, bond funds can be either taxable or tax exempt.

Bond fund managers look for the type of bonds that fit the fund category, the length of the bond maturity (short- or long-term), the rating of the bond (government bonds are not rated because they are all essentially top grade), and the tax status of the bonds.

CORPORATE BOND FUNDS

Corporate bond funds invest in the bonds issued (primarily) by U.S. corporations. This includes corporate bond funds investing in a range of bonds, high quality or investment grade bond funds designed to invest only in high-grade securities. This also includes high-yield bond funds, also known as junk bond funds, investing in low-grade bonds. Naturally the high-grade funds come with lower risks to your principal than the high-yield funds, which will be defined clearly as "high yield funds." General corporate funds allow managers to pick and choose from the largest range of corporate bonds, including high and low grade. They will generally lean toward the higher grade bonds but will seek out a smaller percentage of potentially high-yield bonds for greater capital appreciation. They can diversify enough so that the risks of these bonds are not great.

As of the start of the new century, corporate bond funds were not faring particularly well on the short-term basis. Five-year returns, however, from 1995 through 1999 were averaging around 7%, and 20-year returns were averaging over 9% closing out the century. Since inflation has been low in recent years, a 7%, 8%, or 9% return is more than adequate from this safer portion of your portfolio.

The risky, high-yield junk bond funds can boast 10% to 20% returns or nearly no gains at all. The rate of companies defaulting in the low-grade bond category has been rather low in recent years with the economic picture being fairly bright across the board. This adds some level of confidence to such investments.

High-yield bond funds are highly volatile, but the better ones were showing the best returns of all bond funds at the start of the new century. High-yield junk bond funds are like stock funds. The risk/reward is particularly similar to higher risk stock funds. However, bond funds deal with a different market, which is an advantage for allocation. If the stock market drops, your junk bond fund will not be directly affected. It will still be affected, if in no other way, by an inpouring of assets as stock market investors panic and shift their positions from stocks to bonds.

Mortgage Backed Bonds

Frequently, the portfolio of a bond fund, particularly a government bond fund, is made up of a percentage of mortgage backed securities. These are bonds backed by ownership in home mortgage loans. You're helping finance the growth of home buying in the United States when you, or your mutual fund, buy these mortgage backed bonds. The leading lender for American homes, the Government National Mortgage Association, also known as Ginnie Mae, is a government backed agency. Therefore the loans by Ginnie Mae are backed by the full faith of the U.S. government and are, like other government securities, safe investments against default. This still doesn't mean the NAV of your fund can't drop.

It's best to look over corporate bond funds carefully and focus on your longer term goals with funds that are buying shorter term bonds, which have proven the better bet of late. If interest rates or inflation changes, so might the bond market, so pay attention the next time Alan Greenspan or the Federal Reserve Board makes a significant announcement.

GOVERNMENT BOND FUNDS

If you're looking for a low-risk investment, it doesn't get much lower risk than this. Government bonds are backed by the full faith and credit of the United States government, which hasn't ever defaulted on a bond. The fund shares are issued by financial brokerage houses such as Fidelity, Dreyfus, Kemp, and other known fund families and not directly by the government. The government sells bonds but does not have bond funds to offer directly. Government bond funds buy primarily long-term debt securities: bonds and notes issued by the government and its many agencies.

Among the various investment vehicles of a government bond fund, you will find the following:

- Treasury notes, which are issued by the U.S. government and range from 1 to 10 years until maturity. They pay a fixed rate of interest semiannually.
- Treasury bonds, which are longer term U.S. government bonds ranging as long as 30 years. They also have a fixed rate of interest and payments every 6 months.
- Zero coupon bonds issued by the government, known as STRIPS, which are bought at a deep discount because they pay no interest while they are held. For example, a $10,000 zero coupon bond (or STRIP) might be purchased for $7,500. Upon maturity you, or in this case the fund, would receive the full $10,000. These are not good for people seeking ongoing income from interest. They do, however, produce a good rate of return. This example is 25%.
- Treasury inflation protected securities. Also known as TIPS, they are adjusted to deal with the rising or lowering of the rate of inflation. The interest is also adjusted as the principal changes.

Bonds Versus Bond Funds

- Bonds are costly to buy in quantity. Bond funds allow you to own many bonds.
- Selling a bond means finding a buyer. Shares of a bond fund can be redeemed by the fund company.
- Bond funds are more liquid than individual bonds.
- Bond funds provide professional management.
- There is greater diversification with a bond fund.
- Bond funds allow you to reinvest your income dividends easily and to add to your investment.
- A high-grade or government bond does not risk your principal; a bond fund can have a lower NAV than when you purchased the fund and you will lose some of your principal investment should you sell.

- Various mortgage backed securities issued by national lending associations such as Ginnie Mae and Fannie Mae. Ginnie Mae is backed by the U.S. government, while Fannie Mae is privately run.

Various government bond funds will invest in some or all of these vehicles plus other government issued securities.

There is some volatility in government bond funds, but it is minimal compared to other funds. These are generally thought of (from your standpoint) as longer term investments, so you should look at 5- to 10-year statistics where you can see returns of around 6% or 7% from many of these risk-free funds. Remember that a long-term goal on your part has nothing to do with long, short, or interim securities on the part of the bond fund. That refers to the length of time until maturity of the securities that they are purchasing. You, however, can hold a fund that buys and sells short-term bonds for 25 years and vice versa; one has nothing to do with the other. Bond funds investing in short-term securities are less volatile and have outperformed those investing primarily in long-term securities in recent years.

Also look to see whether they are investing in income-producing bonds or zero coupons, which are bought at a deep discount but do not pay interest. This is important if you are looking at a bond fund for steady income.

TAX EXEMPT MUNICIPAL BOND FUNDS

Bonds issued by municipalities are called *munis*. Munis have their own brand of tax exempt funds that can help you tax manage your investments. There are a wide range of municipal bonds including both the high-grade, lower yield variety and the lower grade, higher yield (higher risk) variety.

Tax exempt municipal bond funds can buy securities at a national, state, or local level. Naturally, national muni funds have a wider range of geographic areas in which to invest. The interest income is tax exempt at the federal level. State munis can provide greater tax benefits. They are exempt from both national and state taxes, provided you are a resident of the state issuing the bond. Large cities or a certain region can issue a triple tax exempt muni

Taxable Bond Fund Categories

Among the taxable bond fund categories you will encounter are corporate; corporate investment grade; corporate high yield; U.S. government general mortgage; U.S. government long, short, and intermediate; U.S. Treasury; global; international emerging growth; multi sector; bond index; long, short, or intermediate general bond funds. Yes, there are others, but this is just enough to get you started. And then there are the munis— high yield, national, single state, and so on.

While bond funds operate in the millions and not billions in assets as the stock funds often do, there are certainly a wide variety of categories to select from. Seek out those that fit into your portfolio and meet your needs.

that is also exempt from local or city taxes. In cities such as New York, where there are higher taxes at the state, local, and city level, this could be a significant benefit. Funds can focus on any of these types of municipal bonds. Keep in mind that a nonresident of the state in which the bond is issued does not get the tax break.

Municipal bond funds are not known for great returns. However, if you match up a tax exempt 5% return against a taxable 6.5% and you are in the 31% tax bracket, you will be better off with the tax exempt yield. For people who are in, or approaching higher tax brackets, this is a secure place (secure from taxes and secure for your principal with high-grade munis) to put the more conservative portion of your assets. It is also a place to generate income that isn't taxed at all levels. When you sell a tax exempt fund, however, you will still pay capital gains tax. The tax exemption is on the interest.

GLOBAL AND INTERNATIONAL EMERGING GROWTH BOND FUNDS

You may opt for a global or international stock fund, investing in companies abroad to diversify your portfolio. It is not, however, highly recommended, of late, to delve into overseas bonds. If you think it's hard to collect the money you lent to your friend down the block, try collecting money lent to an overseas government. The point is, too many factors, including unstable markets, politics, and inflation, make these types of funds quite risky. There is also a higher credit risk that there will be a default by either a company or a country. Some of the more established markets are safer in regard to credit risk, but the returns in recent years have not made them worth taking any risks at all. Emerging markets can be very fruitful, but they can also be a total disaster.

The best global or international bond funds, and they're all generally categorized under the same listings—Industrial Funds, have produced some 20%+ one-year returns, but the worst have produced great losses. The last three years of the 1990s saw returns under 4%

The Abbreviated Version of How Bond Funds Work

1. Bond funds collect the assets invested and purchase numerous bonds that fit the objectives of the particular fund.

2. The bond fund then buys bonds that fit the objective and the manner in which the fund is set up. Some funds are classified as buying long-term securities (primarily), and others buy intermediate or short term. The same holds true with categories. As mentioned earlier, there are corporate, government, municipal, mortgage backed, and international bond funds. Within each one are subcategories such as international emerging markets. While bond funds may have a narrow focus, such as short-term munis, there are also general bond funds that invest in all of these categories.

3. Bond funds do not have a set maturity like that of the individual bonds they own because the bonds are all have their own maturity dates. The fund has what is called a dollar weighted average, which is the average of the maturities of the bonds currently held in the fund. Short-term bond funds, for example, have an average maturity of less than 5 years from the securities held—hence the name *short-term* bond fund. This does not mean the fund needs to hold these securities until they reach maturity. The average maturity of a bond fund might be 3.2 years, meaning that is the average of the bonds held in the fund.

4. Bond fund managers actively trade the bonds in the portfolio in much the same manner as stock fund managers. Among the primary jobs of bond fund managers, however, is to follow the bond market, the interest rates, and the value of the bonds they hold. Fund managers handling many long-term bonds have the toughest job since the volatility is much greater. They may buy short-term securities to diversify within the fund.

5. The NAV for a bond fund is calculated in a similar manner to that of a stock fund, taking into account the current holdings of the fund. The NAV is what you track or follow, and it moves up or down accordingly with the success of management and the bond market as a whole. Interest rates affect the bond market, which is why, in this time of great volatility, many people are looking at high-grade, short-term bond funds, which hold high-grade bonds and are less volatile than their long-term counterparts.

6. You receive interest payments while holding the fund, which can be reinvested.

7. The fund charges fees and possibly loads in a similar manner to a stock fund. The fund also distributes capital gains that are passed on to you, the investor.

Don't Be Fooled by the Word *Conservative*

Bond funds are thought of as a conservative investment. Don't be fooled, there are risks. The word *conservative,* when dealing with bond funds, generally means (1) in contrast to stock funds and (2) you can get steady income and not take great risks to your principal with *certain* types of bond funds. Bond funds holding many long-term bonds or low-grade bond funds are far from risk-free investments. In other words, your principal is not protected. Therefore, you can preface the phrase "Bond funds are for the more conservative portion of your portfolio" with the word *some* in front of it.

for the category, which considering expense ratios, loads, and taxes, is next to nothing.

In short, there is no solid argument for buying overseas bond funds at present, other than if you should happen to hit the right emerging market fund at the right time you could do well. However, you could usually do better with an emerging market stock fund. International bond funds are too big a gamble.

THE BOND FUND PROSPECTUS

A bond fund prospectus is not different in structure than that of a stock fund. The fund goals will be clearly stated and may say something like: "To seek a total return through investments in fixed income securities." The prospectus will go on to detail how much of the fund invests in bonds, which will usually be around 70% or more, including investment grade corporate debt securities (bonds), debt obligations issued by the United States government (bonds or treasuries), and mortgage backed securities (also bonds).

A bond fund prospectus will also outline further investment details, such as how much of the fund can be invested in stocks or cash instruments, how much (if any) can be invested in the international market (foreign bonds), and how much can be invested in low-grade bonds (junk bonds). Then you will see the average duration of holdings, which is important to determine whether they are buying short-, intermediate-, or long-term bonds. There will also be a note about volatility, which is usually defined as low, moderate, or high, depending on the types of bonds (based on duration and grade) purchased.

The fund manager's plan of action will generally follow, explaining the method and why he or she makes specific bond choices. For example, the prospectus might explain that the fund manager looks at a variety of factors, including the current interest rate, rate of inflation, yields of similar securities, the grade of the bond, and other factors regarding the bond issuer and the overall bond market. He or she may also look to tax manage the fund with government securities.

There will be a discussion of risk, similar to that which we discussed earlier, and past performance data, generally measured against a benchmark such as the Lehman Brothers Aggregate Bond Index. Similar to a stock fund, a bond fund will have 1-, 3-, 5-, and 10-year returns listed, plus returns since the inception of the fund. A breakdown will generally give you an idea of what types of securities the fund is investing in and in what percentages. You can usually also find this in other fund literature.

For example, a bond fund may invest in the following sector proportions to show diversification:

Corporate bond	43%
Mortgage backed securities	28%
U.S. government backed securities	12%
International securities	7%
Domestic stocks	5%
Cash investments	5%

A breakdown of an intermediate-term bond fund might have an allocation similar to that listed and also give you a listing such as:

Years to Maturity	
Longer than 8 years	5%
6 to 8 years	15%
3 to 5 years	60%
Less than 3 years	15%
Short-term cash investments	5%

Any sales charges (loads), redemption fees, and annual operating expenses will follow (or also be included). The breakdown of when a back-end load (or commission paid when you sell fund shares) phases out completely will also be included if there is such a load.

State Risk

A bond issued by a particular state, such as California or New York, is (naturally) more susceptible to developments in that state. Therefore if inflation or unemployment affect the economy of a particular state, your bonds will also be affected. Funds that are geographically diverse, such as United States bonds, avoid state-sensitive risks. State bonds, however, can avoid state taxes.

BOND INDEX FUNDS

Just as you can find stock index funds that track the S&P 500 and numerous other indices, there are bond indices too. Among the most significant benchmarks in the bond arena are the Lehman Brothers Aggregate Bond Index, the Lehman Municipal Bond Index, and the Bond Buyers Guide.

A bond index fund will try to monitor the success of the index it is designed to follow. A bond index, however, may not own all 5,000 government and investment grade bonds in the Lehman Brothers Corporate/Government Bond Index, but will have a well researched statistical sampling and a similar average maturity. The goal of the fund will be to closely match the benchmark.

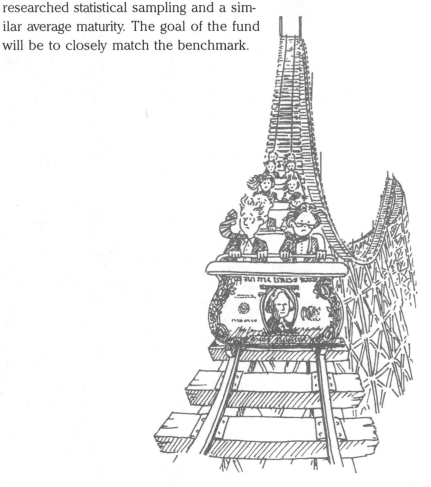

1999 Tanked!

"If you don't have something nice to say, don't say anything at all" is an old expression that might explain why there was comparatively little written about the majority of bond funds in 1999. It was simply not a good year as numerous government, municipal, and corporate bond funds saw negative returns. Despite the sour year, 5- and 10-year returns showed 6% and 7% returns, encouraging long-term investors—which is the route to take with a fund, particularly a bond fund—to stay put. These funds were also bought by many investors for the purpose of income interest and with less focus on capital gains.

BOND FUND COMPARISON

There are several types of bond funds to choose from. Here you can list and compare several funds in each category of interest.

Corporate Bond Funds

	Fund Name	Fund Family	NAV	% Sales Load	Expense Ratio	Assets Millions	1 Yr.	Returns: 3 Yrs.	5 Yrs.
1									
2									
3									
4									

Government Bond Funds

	Fund Name	Fund Family	NAV	% Sales Load	Expense Ratio	Assets Millions	1 Yr.	Returns: 3 Yrs.	5 Yrs.
1									
2									
3									
4									

Municipal Bond Funds

	Fund Name	Fund Family	NAV	% Sales Load	Expense Ratio	Assets Millions	1 Yr.	Returns: 3 Yrs.	5 Yrs.
1									
2									
3									
4									

Tax-Free Bond Funds

	Fund Name	Fund Family	NAV	% Sales Load	Expense Ratio	Assets Millions	1 Yr.	Returns: 3 Yrs.	5 Yrs.
1									
2									
3									
4									

CHAPTER SIX

MONEY MARKET FUNDS

Disclaimers

You will see a disclaimer with money market funds that says, to the effect, that while the funds seek to maintain the $1.00 per share net asset value, this price cannot be assured or guaranteed. Don't worry, this is primarily for the protection of the fund family or brokerage house. Better than 99.9999% of money market funds do not break the buck!

• • •

Discounts

Money market mutual fund managers buy securities at a discount that will reach maturity in less than 90 days. The discount is small since these are very short-term investments. Your interest, however, comes from the difference in the *face value,* or price realized at maturity, and that discount.

At the start of the 1980s money market mutual funds became very popular. They were paying a good rate, offering steady yields and they were very low-risk investments. At that time, when VCRs and answering machines were the latest in technology and the stock market was not yet going gangbusters, these were considered a solid investment. However, when interest rates dropped in the late 1980s, money market funds became less popular and investors looked for new places to put their assets.

Today, money market mutual funds are still in vogue, but generally not as a primary investment vehicle. Instead they are used as a safe place to put those additional investment dollars that are not in either a stock or bond fund (or individual stocks or bonds for that matter). They pay higher rates than bank accounts, while preserving your principal investment. No matter how shrewd an investor you become, or how much time you have until reaching your investment goal, you will still need to have some capital preserved. A money market fund will also be one place to move your money for safekeeping as you close in on your goals and start redeeming some of your other mutual fund shares.

Money market mutual funds invest in high-yielding, short-term instruments such as U.S. government securities, top-rated commercial paper, bank rates, U.S. Treasury bills, bankers acceptances, and certificates of deposit. The securities generally mature in an average of 90 days or less.

These funds are quite different from any other type of mutual fund in that they are considered *share based* investments, meaning they offer a rate of one dollar per share. This means simply that the number of shares you buy is the number of dollars you spend. Maintaining the one-dollar-per-share value is the prime objective of the fund manager. Interest is credited daily on these funds and reinvested.

Like other mutual funds, there is a fund manager running the show and a management fee, although usually this is kept relatively low, at a rate of around 0.75. Since they are dealing with safe investments, these funds have become a handy alternative to bank accounts, with higher yields in the 5.5% to 6% range as of early 2000.

Since money market mutual funds are run by financial institutions and mutual fund companies (and not banks like money

market deposit accounts), they are not insured by the FDIC, but are closely watched and regulated by the Securities and Exchange Commission. The SEC has guidelines regarding the types of investments, length of holdings, and so on. The companies that sell such funds stand firmly behind them. In fact, in over 20 years there has been only one reported case of such a fund "breaking the buck," which is the cardinal sin for these funds. One fund was forced to liquidate at 94 cents a share.

As safe as money market mutual funds are, nothing is 100% guaranteed. Therefore private insurance has emerged for money market funds, which may gain acceptance just as FDIC insurance has become common coverage for bank accounts. As it turns out, insurance companies are taking less of a risk with money market accounts than the FDIC takes with banks, because several banks have run into trouble in recent years. The savings and loan mess was not all that long ago.

Like the bond mutual funds, the money market fund managers keep a close eye on the interest rates. In contrast to stock fund managers, however, they are trying to keep a very low-risk portfolio of short-term securities rather than going for greater capital appreciation at greater risk. There are several other restrictions put on money market fund managers, such as not allowing them to invest heavily in one company or even one market. They must therefore diversify widely, which gives you more security.

Many money market accounts offer check writing privileges, although (like checking accounts) you'll usually need to maintain a minimum balance in the account of $100 to $500. You can also sell off shares of your money market fund without closing out or selling off the entire account.

Many investors will use their money market mutual fund as a safe haven in which to keep money that is earmarked for investing or re-investing in other mutual funds. Such funds also provide liquidity and pay interest when you need to shift assets out of riskier investments during a downturn in the market. They do provide a great alternative to volatility. When you have floating assets, which have just been redeemed or for any other reason, money market funds are now widely used by fund families and financial institutions as pit stops for assets earmarked elsewhere.

No FDIC, but SIPC

While the FDIC, which insures bank accounts and bank securities, does not insure money market mutual funds, the SIPC (Security Investor Protector Corporation) does. They insure many such money market funds against the company going bankrupt. They will cover up to $100,000 and in some instances more. The company from which you are buying the fund can tell you if they have such insurance.

Mid-Point

Money market mutual funds are a step between keeping money in the bank and taking a plunge into stock or bond mutual funds. To follow the progress of a money market fund, you will be able to see the 7-day current and the 7-day compounded yield. The current yield will give the basic or simple rate that the fund is paying, and the compound yield will include the recent compounding of interest. You can also look at 30-day totals and compare those to the current yields to determine whether the interest rates are rising or falling.

Assets are automatically moved into such a fund until you've selected where to roll them over or transfer them.

TAXES OR NO TAXES?

You can choose between taxable and tax-free money market mutual funds. It's worth your while to look more closely at the two choices. The tax exempt funds pay less interest, but sometimes, after taxes (depending on your tax rate) these work out in your favor. You need to compare the returns you will receive after paying taxes.

To confuse matters, there are taxable money market funds where you pay federal, state, and local taxes, and taxable U.S. government securities money market funds where you are often exempt from state and local taxes. In these funds you'll find Treasury investments including T-bills, T-notes, and T-bonds. Naturally the government securities make these very sound (safe) investments. The nature of the securities held in the portfolio will determine the local or state tax status. There are funds that invest only in U.S. Treasury securities. These are secure investments, and they are tax exempt at the state and local level.

Then there are the "tax exempt" money market funds which are tax exempt at the federal level. National money market funds, however, are taxable at the state and local level. These funds invest in municipalities from around the country. Single, double, and triple tax exempt money market funds invest in the municipalities of a single state or city. These funds are exempt from federal taxes, state taxes, and possibly local or city taxes as well.

Remember, the state and city tax exemption is for residents of that state or city only. Therefore, if you buy a money market fund that invests in New York while you are living in New Jersey, you won't be exempt from New York's higher taxes.

As you can see, there are a variety of tax breaks available with money market mutual funds. Naturally, the money market funds that are able to invest across the board, with no tax exemptions, can often pay the highest (pre-tax) yields. The tax breaks, however, may make funds with lower yields more attractive, depending on the state taxes you have to pay. It's a good idea to discuss your options with your tax specialist.

There are fees to be paid while owning a money market fund, including management fees. Such fees may be less if you have a higher amount invested in the fund. Money market funds have various levels, just as airplanes have seating classes. The more money you invest, the lower the fees. It is also not uncommon for a fund family to automatically sweep cash into a money market fund for you. This will be spelled out in the prospectus. Fund families encourage you to open a money market account when you sign up with the brokerage firm.

WHAT TO CONSIDER

The interest rates are the first thing to look at. Compare several, although they will be relatively similar at any given time. Make sure they are outpacing inflation, which they have been doing of late with inflation numbers being very low. This is perhaps the biggest problem with having too much of your portfolio concentration in money market funds. Should you be generating 5.5% returns and the inflation rate is at 3.0%, you are outpacing inflation by 2.5%. Taxes will also come into play, but you will still be ahead of the game. However, if inflation jumps to 4.9%, you will only be outpacing it by .6% returns, which might be totally negated by tax payments.

You also need to find out the minimum investment necessary. Minimum initial balances for money market mutuals vary widely from $500 to $100,000. Don't put a higher percentage of the assets you wish to allocate into money market funds just to meet a higher minimum investment. Simply select a fund with a lower initial minimum investment.

Also inquire about check writing and ask if there is a minimum balance for the privilege. If you have other higher asset investments, such as mutual funds with the fund family, some of these minimums or fees may be dispensed with. Fund families sometimes look at all the money you have invested in their various funds and count that toward your balance necessary to avoid fund fees in your money market account. On occasion you will also see all, or a portion, of the fund's fees waived as a way of promoting that money market fund over the competition. The more business you do with a fund family, the more you should discuss the fees and

Half a Dozen Positives about Money Market Mutual Funds

1. Money market funds are designed to provide a higher level of current income than traditional savings accounts offered by banks.
2. They offer greater stability than stocks and bonds by preserving your capital. In short, they're very low (essentially no) risk.
3. They are liquid investments.
4. They pay steady interest.
5. They are a perfect place in which to move assets between stock and bond investments and keep your cash reserve.
6. They are a good place to move money into when the market(s) are doing poorly.

Don't Forget the Fees!

Like other mutual funds, there are administrative and other fees associated with money market mutual funds. While they are no-loads, you need to clearly find out in advance what other fee costs will total. Do some comparison shopping. Since most money market mutual funds will do similarly, why receive just a 4.50% return instead of a 5.25% return because of fees cutting into your returns? Along with taxable versus tax-free, look at the fees. Often the fee structure will be based on what type of money market fund you open, and that type will be defined by how much you are putting in. Not unlike days of old when the small bank account got a fountain pen while the larger one got you a toaster, the "premium," "preferred," or "deluxe" account in which you deposit more money (and have more privileges) will have a lower fee structure.

the possibility of waiving some of them. For big fund families, money markets are the nickel and dime items. They want you to invest heavily in their stock and bond funds, so they are often willing to negotiate when it comes to these small ticket items.

Essentially, your money market mutual fund should be a fairly uncomplicated investment designed for safekeeping your money while maintaining liquidity. You won't find a lot written on money market mutual funds with their 5.65% or 5.75% returns. They are not flashy nor do they bring anyone sudden wealth or great capital gains for that matter. But they serve a purpose as a place to invest the cash portion of a portfolio for security. Davis, Excelsior, Fidelity, First Omaha, Invesco, John Hancock, Montgomery, Schwab, Scudder, Smith Barney, Strong, Vanguard, Wells Fargo, Zurich, and nearly all of the many mutual fund families and brokerage houses offer money market mutual funds.

Following a money market mutual fund is simple. Newspaper and other listings generally divide money market funds into two categories, taxable and nontaxable. Taxable funds include those that are general-purpose funds, meaning they buy a wide range of securities, and government only funds, which will be listed together and generally distinguishable by their names. Likewise, single-state tax exempt funds and national tax exempt funds will all fall under the tax exempt heading. The average maturity of the funds portfolio will also be listed. If a fund manager believes interest rates will fall, then he or she will hold onto securities longer and the average maturity will be longer. If a fund manager believes interest rates will not be dropping soon, then the average maturity of the fund's portfolio is shorter. Over 50 days would be on the longer end while 25 or 30 days would be considered short. Remember these are all short-term investments. You can then look at the 7-day yield and 7-day compound yield, which tells you what the fund is paying with and without compounding. Thirty-day yields, both simple and compounded, can also be found. Comparing the 7-day yields to the 30-day yields will give you an idea which direction the fund is heading.

MONEY MARKET FUNDS

Current rate of inflation _____

	Fund Name	7-Day Yield	30-Day Yield	Management Fees	Minimum Investment	Check Writing (Y/N)
1						
2						
3						
4						
5						

Tax-Free Money Market Funds

	Fund Name	7-Day Yield	30-Day Yield	Management Fees	Minimum Investment	Check Writing (Y/N)
1						
2						
3						
4						
5						

To determine taxable equivalent, subtract your tax bracket from 100 (a 30% tax bracket would give you 100 − 30 = 69). Then divide the tax-free yield of the tax-free fund by the reciprocal tax number or in this case the 69 that you have left after step 1. For instance, a 6% yield would be 6 divided by 69 or .086, which means an 8.6 equivalent needed in a taxable money market fund to equal your 6% tax-free fund in a 31% tax bracket.

CHAPTER SEVEN

MUTUAL FUND FAMILIES

There are plenty of mutual fund families, each offering a wide variety of funds designed to meet different personal goals and investment needs. Many fund families like American Century and Janus offer no-loads while others offer only loaded funds or both. You do not, by any means, need to invest in one fund family. You get no extra points for loyalty. However, one of the primary advantages of staying with one fund family is that you'll save some on fees and plenty of paperwork should you decide to switch funds.

The idea behind fund families, from the perspective of companies such as Dean Witter, Vanguard, Fidelity, or AIM, is to offer you a variety of funds so that if you are looking to buy several to diversify your portfolio, you'll do all of your shopping from one sponsor or one fund family. They want to, as All State Insurance has been famous for saying, "put you in good hands."

Most of the major fund families provide other services, including comprehensive Web sites with plenty of information about their companies and their products. While larger fund families may meet some of your needs, smaller companies can house highly successful funds as well. A smaller fund family may provide more personalized attention when you call custom service. However, a small fund family may need to charge higher fees; this is certainly not always the case. You'll also find that certain fund families are known for having specific types of funds. One fund family may have more sector funds and specialize in that area while another has more growth and income funds or retirement planning funds. By and large, most fund companies do try to diversify, allowing you to set up a well rounded portfolio.

Some of the major fund families include:

Advantus 1-800-665-6005	BlackRock 1-800-441-7762
AIM 1-800-347-4246	BT Investment 1-800-730-1313
Alger 1-800-992-3863	Calvert 1-800-368-2748
Alliance 1-800-227-4618	Chase Vista 1-800-348-4782
American Century 1-800-345-2021	Citifunds 1-800-721-1899
American Funds 1-800-421-4120	Citizens 1-800-223-7010
AXP 1-800-328-8300	Columbia 1-800-547-1707
Berger 1-800-333-1001	Concert Investment 1-800-544-5445

Davis 1-800-279-0279

Delaware Investments
1-800-523-4640

Dreyfus 1-800-373-9387

Eaton Vance 1-800-225-6265

Enterprise 1-800-432-4320

Evergreen 1-800-343-2898

Excelsior 1-800-446-1012

Federated 1-800-341-7400

Fidelity 1-800-544-8888

First American 1-800-637-2548

First Investors 1-800-423-4026

Firstar 1-800-677-3863

Founders 1-800-525-2440

Franklin 1-800-342-5236

Gabelli 1-800-422-3554

Galaxy 1-800-628-0414

Goldman Sachs 1-800-526-7384

Hancock 1-800-225-5291

Harbor 1-800-422-1050

Hartford 1-800-843-7824

INVESCO 1-800-525-8085

HighMark 1-800-433-6884

J.P. Morgan 1-800-521-5411

Janus 1-800-525-8983

Kemper 1-800-621-1048

Legg Mason 1-800-577-8589

Liberty 1-800-426-3750

Lord Abbett 1-800-874-3733

Mainstay 1-800-624-6782

Marshall 1-800-236-8560

Mason Street 1-800-627-6678

Merrill Lynch 1-800-637-3863

MFS 1-800-637-2929

Montgomery 1-800-572-3863

Morgan Stanley Dean Witter
1-800-869-6397

MSDW 1-800-6397

Nations 1-800-321-7854

Neuberger & Berman
1-800-877-9700

New England 1-800-225-7678

Northern 1-800-595-9100

One Group 1-800-480-4111

Oppenheimer 1-800-525-7048

Paine Webber 1-800-647-1568

PBHG 1-800-433-0051

Phoenix 1-800-243-4361

Pilgrim 1-800-334-3444

Pimco 1-800-426-0107

Pioneer 1-800-225-6292

Prudential 1-800-225-1852

Putnam 1-800-225-1581

RS 1-800-766-3863

Schwab 1-800-4345-4000

Scudder 1-800-225-2470

Seligman 1-800-221-2450

Smith Barney 1-800-451-2010

State Street Research
1-800-882-0052

Stein Roe 1-800-338-2550

Strong 1-800-368-1030

Sun America 1-800-858-8850

Templeton 1-800-342-5236

T. Rowe Price 1-800-638-5660

United Group 1-800-366-5465

USAA 1-800-382-8722

Value Line 1-800-223-0818

Vanguard 1-800-851-4999

Van Kempen 1-800-341-2911

Victory Group 1-800-539-3863

Warburg Pincus 1-800-927-2874

Wells Fargo 1-800-237-8472

WM 1-800-222-5852

Bouncing from Fund to Fund

While one of the pluses of a fund family is that you can move your money out of one fund and into another without much hassle, you should note that fund families do often charge exchange fees for overusing that privilege. Since funds are generally thought of as long-term investments, the fund family does not want to encourage excessive movement from one fund to another. Keep in mind that moving from one fund to another in the same fund family may indeed be easier from a paperwork standpoint, but you still pay taxes on the fund you have left as you are still, in effect, selling one fund to buy shares in another one. Therefore your paper gains by the sale of fund "A" are realized gains while your money is moving into fund "B," even if it takes only a few minutes.

WHAT TO LOOK FOR

When looking at a fund family in which to invest, you should look for information on the fund families and their offerings. The largest fund families, such as Fidelity, Vanguard, Merrill Lynch, Franklin Templeton, and others have a wide variety of selections. Since smaller fund families may specialize more in bond funds, international funds, or other types of funds, it's important to look at how several funds in the family are performing. Sometimes a fund family is built around a few core funds that reap rewards while their other funds do not fare as well. You will want them to cover the various bases of funds that you may be looking for as you build up your portfolio. In other words, if you think an index fund, growth fund, and a short-term bond fund are the best choices for your portfolio, you might want to find a fund family that has seen success in those three fund categories. Major fund families try to satisfy as many possible asset allocations as possible, that doesn't always mean they do it well.

Fund families can help you stay organized by consolidating your fund statements. They can also consolidate expenses within the company from their overall pool of assets, whereby a larger fund might pick up some of the expenses on a smaller new fund. This means lower expense ratios and lower fees for the shareholder. Remember, however, that you certainly do not have to buy all of your funds from one fund family.

Since there are many fund families that will meet your mutual fund needs, you should look into two key aspects behind each fund family.

INFORMATION

Thanks to Web sites, information is readily available at your fingertips. If you cannot easily navigate the site and find what you need, look elsewhere. The fund business is very competitive, so mutual fund families should be forthright in providing information and getting written material that you request sent to you promptly. Also, material should be comprehensive and not just promotional by nature. You should collect fund information from a few fund families and compare.

LEVEL OF SERVICE

This is the area that separates the pros from the amateurs. Too many stories, that don't make the financial pages, center around poor service from brokers at top financial families. Brokers from major fund houses have been known to call repeatedly promising you the world, until you sign up and invest in the fund, after which they suddenly become quite unreachable. This, of course, makes you curse the fact that you didn't buy a no-load since you aren't getting any service anyway. It also makes you realize that these brokers are not taking into consideration your goals and needs.

Other complaints include unanswered, or poorly answered questions and delays in processing or handling aspects of your transaction. One fund investor purchased a fund in August with an automatic investment program that was to begin taking $500 a month from his bank account. The broker, who made the initial transaction, neglected to have the money automatically deposited until February of the following year. The investor, therefore lost 6 months of accumulating funds in the account.

Another story recounts a major fund family suddenly being unable to locate $40,000, which was supposed to have been transferred into a money market account but mysteriously vanished. Eventually the investor found her money, which had been transferred accidentally to another fund family.

Use word of mouth and find out the horror stories and positive accounts of different investment houses. It's important that you feel confident in the fund family in which you're invested. No-loads also do not mean that you are not entitled to paperwork and information. You may not get financial advice, but you are an investor with all the same investment privileges.

OTHER BENEFITS

You might also inquire about other features that you, as a valued customer can receive. For instance, are commissions lowered on fund A if you have x amount of dollars invested in funds B and C already in the same family? The more you invest in one fund family, in terms of dollars and number of funds, the more benefits you should be entitled to. That is, of course, dependent on what the fund family offers. The level of investments at which a fund family reduces its commission charges is called a *breakpoint*. The fund family will let you know when you are about to reach such a level and must then reduce their fees (according to the SEC). Everything offered in a fund family should be clearly spelled out. If you don't see what you need to know in the fund family's literature then you should ask.

In one fund family you can deal with one set of rules and procedures since families in general have slightly different ways of doing the same things. Also, a benefit of being loyal to one fund family is not having to establish a rapport with five different brokers at five different fund families. This can be a benefit if you're dealing with a broker you trust. If you're buying online or no-loads through 800 numbers, this is essentially a moot point.

ON THE OTHER HAND

Many investors today, partially due to the ease of investing through 800 numbers and the accessibility of discount brokers through the Internet, are not loyal to any one fund family. In fact, such loyalty is thought of by some investors as not being diversified. Why not spread your assets around different fund families as well as funds?

When you look at the list of funds offered by most of the major players, you'll see a great deal of similarities. Major fund families generally have the usual smorgasbord of core funds. However, when you look more closely, you'll see diversity amongst the fund families. Some lean more heavily into tech sectors while others have a great deal of international funds, and still others

Fund Families
Versus Fund Supermarkets

While fund families offer their own funds, a fund supermarket offers funds by various fund families, serving as a clearinghouse for funds. Also known as *fund networks,* these supermarkets provide information from each of a wide number of major fund families and can offer you a wide selection of funds from one source. There are a growing number of these fund supermarkets. No, they don't have a special 10-funds or fewer checkout express, but you shouldn't be buying more than 10 anyway, although you can choose from literally thousands of funds in as many as 40 fund families. Fund supermarkets include:

Accutrade 1-800-882-4887 *www.accutrade.com*
Bull & Bear Securities 1-800-262-5800 *www.bullbear.com*
DLJdirect 1-800-825-5723 *www.dljdirect.com*
E*TRADE Mutual Fund Center 1-800-786-2575 *www.etrade.com*
Fidelity Funds Network 1-800-544-8666 *www.fidelity.com*
Quick & Reilly 1-800-262-2688 *www.quick-reilly.com*
Scudder Preferred Investment Plus 1-800-988-8316 *www.scudder.com*
Vanguard Brokerage Fund Access 1-800-992-8327 *www.vanguard.com*
Jack White Mutual Fund Network 1-800-233-3411 *www.jackwhiteco.com*

offer a wider array of value funds. The different fund families have winners in different areas. If a fund has several winners in one area, particularly if it is not the hot category across the board, you can assume this is their strength. If you find different fund families with different strengths, then why not buy five various types of funds by selecting the best one in each class or category, regardless of the fund family?

This theory has a lot of investors buying online from the new breed of mutual fund supermarkets, taking one winner from Janus, one from Fidelity, perhaps the Vanguard 500, plus a fund from a smaller fund family that is riskier but fills a particular niche in the portfolio. You'll be selecting what you want from where you want it. Why choose two mediocre funds as the fourth and fifth funds in your five-fund portfolio because the fund family has nothing better to offer in a particular category when you know highly rated funds in those categories can be found elsewhere? The savings on transfer fees won't be as significant as seeing better returns elsewhere.

This isn't to say a fund family can't meet all of your needs, but you can't always build the best portfolio in one fund family.

FUND FAMILIES CHECKLIST & WORKSHEET

❏ Does the fund family charge you a fee for transferring from one fund to another?

❏ What is the limit to transfers you can make in a year?

❏ Do you receive one statement for all of your funds?

❏ What is the fee structure?

❏ Can you trade through their Web site?

❏ Most importantly, does the fund family have the types of funds you want and how successful are their funds in each category? To compare, you can list a type of fund and the representative funds from each fund family. Remember, only compare like categories, otherwise you're comparing apples and oranges.

❏ Try to narrow down your field to at the most, four or five fund families. You might start by listing the types of funds you want. If you'd like to buy from one fund family, first look to see that the fund family has all three, four, or five categories that you are looking for. Then compare. If you were looking for a balanced fund, a large-cap growth fund, and an index fund for a more conservative slant on a stock portfolio you would first need to find a couple of fund families that have all three. Then compare.

For example:

Fund Family/Fund	Current NAV	Returns 1 yr.	3 yrs.	5 yrs.	% Sales Load	Net Assets (Millions)	Expense Ratio
INVESCO Balanced		14.4%	17.1%	20.7%	None	436	1.21
Scudder Balanced		10.5%	17.6%	18.5%	None	554	1.29
INVESCO Blue Chip Growth		33.3%	33.2%	30.6%	None	1,376	1.03
Scudder Large Cap Growth		29.3%	31.1%	29.3%	None	1,027	1.19
INVESCO S&P 500 Index (II)		16.0%	—	—	None	76	.60
Scudder S&P 500 Index		16.2%	—	—	None	309	.40

CHAPTER EIGHT

Closed-End
Mutual Funds

The common understanding of mutual funds is that of the open-end funds, meaning there is no limit on funds offering and selling shares. While some open funds will close their doors to new investors because they simply become too large, this is not the definition of a closed-end mutual fund.

Closed-end mutual funds are similar to their more popular open-end counterparts in that they pool the money of numerous investors and offer diversity, professional fund management, and dividends, and capital gains are reinvested. They also offer a variety of categories, which include domestic and international securities.

The primary difference, however, is that closed-end funds offer a limited amount of shares. The other major difference between open-end and closed-end funds is how they are traded. Closed-end funds require there be a buyer and a seller. Rather than buying and selling from the fund company, investors essentially trade with one another through brokers. The fund manager does not have to worry about the size of the fund fluctuating since they are not issuing additional shares or redeeming shares. They can stick to the business at hand, making investments that follow the fund's objectives. Also, closed-end funds trade on the New York Stock Exchange and on the NASDAQ. Like open-end funds, there is an NAV, or net asset value. However, the shares are not always sold at that value.

Closed-end fund (CEF) shares sell in a manner similar to that of the bond trading market. They go through a broker who finds a buyer and a seller. The supply and demand for the shares, and external factors affecting the economy as a whole, will dictate the price. Sometimes, if there is a greater demand and the economy is good, shares will sell for higher than their net asset value. When this happens, you have shares selling at a premium. On the other hand, outside factors, a slowing economy, investments in companies that are not yet performing up to expectations, and other factors can cause a lower demand for the shares, which will result in the shares selling for less than their NAV value. This is considered selling at a discount. Naturally you hope to buy at that discount. The buying or selling price of a CEF is, therefore, not necessarily the same as the NAV, whereas in open-end mutual funds the price will be the same.

When looking at the listings for closed-end funds, you will see something like this:

Name of fund	Stock market	NAV	Market Price	%
CEF A	NYSE	$15.00	$17.00	+13%
CEF B	NYSE	$16.00	$11.00	−31%

CEF A, the first closed-end fund, is listed on the New York Stock Exchange with a net asset value of $15. It is selling, however, at a premium price of $17, so the seller is making $2.00 per share upon selling the fund, or a gain of 13%. CEF B, however, the second closed-end fund (also on the New York Stock Exchange) has a net asset value of $16 per share but is selling at a discount, so the seller is getting only $11 per share. The buyer of B is buying at a discount, so that even if he or she ultimately sells the fund at the same unchanged NAV of $16 per share and a market price of $14 per share he or she will be coming out ahead. The NAV may not have moved, but the market price for the CEF will be higher than what the investor bought it at (up from $11 per share to $14 per share, or a gain of 21%). An open-end fund at the same NAV would net no profit since it hasn't moved, but a closed-end fund in this case brought the investor a gain of 21%. Therefore, while the NAV gives you an indication of how well the fund is doing, the true value of a CEF is the market price, which can be at a premium or a discount in relationship to the NAV.

Fees and commissions, very common and often debated in the open-end mutual fund world, are similar in the closed-end fund business as well. Commissions are paid to brokers to buy and sell shares, and fees are paid to operate the fund.

One of the advantages of a CEF is that, because the fund is dealing with a finite amount of assets, the manager can make decisions based solely on that amount. Open-end fund managers are often forced to buy and sell more often because the fund is growing at a rapid rate. Sometimes they have to buy stocks at higher prices to maintain a certain percentage of the assets invested in securities. They may also be limited from buying heavily into better companies at higher prices if the fund gets too small. Therefore their decisions often hinge on the size of the fund's assets. Managers of closed-end funds don't have these same worries.

Bumpy Rides

Many CEFs invest in overseas markets, and therefore the volatility can be cause for Dramamine. If you aren't ready to watch major highs and lows, stick with CEFs that invest domestically.

Another reason investors will sometimes look for a CEF is to get into sectors that are otherwise not as commonly traded in open-end funds. Perhaps you want to get into an emerging market that is not as widely traded in open-end funds, like Malaysia or Thailand. In fact there have been instances where a country has traded only via closed-end funds. CEFs offer good opportunities, often at discounts to the NAV, and less risk. Keep in mind that one advantage of a CEF is that if you buy at a discount (a price below the NAV) you can still come out ahead even if the NAV drops or remains unchanged, as illustrated in the earlier example. Therefore, risk is minimized against a downturn in the market.

On the other hand, if you buy at a premium and the fund starts selling at a discount, you can take a big loss even if the NAV doesn't drop much. For example, if you buy a CEF with an NAV of $15 and you pay a premium of $17 per share, hoping the NAV and subsequently the stock price go higher than the $17 you paid, you would be in trouble even if the NAV remains steady at an NAV of 15 if the fund is suddenly selling at a discount of $12. The drop in the NAV is only 6%, but you're looking at a loss in sales price from $17 to $12, or 29% per share. The bottom line is: don't buy a CEF at a premium.

Interestingly enough, a slight downturn in the market can prove profitable. Whereas the NAV may not drop very much the CEF may be available at a discount thanks to panicky investors. Therefore you can buy into a fund that may not be doing badly but is underpriced.

Another disadvantage of CEFs is that there are no no-loads since you are not buying directly from the fund but from a seller. There are deep discount brokers who charge less in commissions or flat fees, but you will pay commissions to brokers. However, and there are always two sides to the issue, there is also no need for marketing since the fund has no more shares to sell, so 12b-1 fees shouldn't be part of the equation. Also, CEFs generally trade less, and lower turnover of securities in the fund means less in capital gains taxes for you, the investor. So, in the end it may all balance out. Read the individual prospectus and do the math carefully when comparing open and closed-end funds.

TYPES OF CLOSED-END FUNDS

Viva variety! Yes, there are always choices these days, orange juice with pulp, original, country style, orange-pineapple, and so on. Nothing is simple, so why should choosing a closed-end mutual fund be any different? There are plenty of choices in the types of funds awaiting you should you venture into the CEF market.

Fund types include: growth funds, value funds, blue chip funds, market timing funds, and others that are similar in style to open-end funds. You will also find many sector funds to select from focusing on the media, technology, health care, gold, or other industries. There are also many CEFs that focus on regions of the world such as Eastern Europe or Latin America and others that focus on specific countries. Some investors find that placing international investments through closed-end funds is more comforting since the fixed asset pool prevents a flood of assets resulting in a fund manager looking for places to invest in a limited market. Also political and other news has less effect on a CEF. Investors in an open-end fund can cause the asset pool to drop if they bail out when negative news stories come out of a certain part of the world. It's harder to make a panic move in a CEF since selling takes a little longer. This can be to your advantage.

International CEFs include emerging market funds, which look to buy stocks in developing nations, and global funds, which have investments in both domestic and international markets.

So, you think you're ready to tackle closed-end funds? If you're familiar with stocks and bonds, you'll have a definite head start. In fact, if you look at the market price, which is the stock price, you need not even concern yourself very much with the NAV for trading purposes.

Bonds are not similar investments by any means to closed-end mutual funds. The one similarity lies in the idea of premiums and discounts while the other is in liquidity. Bonds are less liquid than stocks or open-end mutual funds, where you can sell and redeem your shares from the fund company at any time. Buying and selling CEFs, like buying and selling bonds, requires another party on the other end with whom to make the transaction, a step that means it is not quite as liquid an investment.

More Closed Mouthed About Closed-End Funds

Why do you hear less about closed-end mutual funds than open-end funds?

1. They are not as actively marketed or advertised as open-end funds.
2. There are no no-loads, which are very popular (and rightfully so) in the fund world these days.
3. The process of buying and selling with discounts and premiums makes them more difficult to understand for new investors.
4. Money cannot continue to pour into them as it can with open-end funds, so you have to find a seller (through your broker) to buy into a CEF. There are also IPOs (as there are with new stocks), but they can be difficult to learn about for the new investor.

There are brokers who specialize in closed-end mutual funds, many found at large firms. Naturally, you'll pay for advice, as the term *full service* always indicates from the gas pumps to the financial world. Discount brokers can offer substantial savings. Of course you won't get as much hand holding or advice as you (should) get from a full service broker. Most discount brokers make it easy to trade by phone or even through your computer and have Web sites designed to help you access information quickly. Deep discount brokers are the no-frills end of the spectrum. They work quickly, often by PC or phone, at a lower price. Commissions can range anywhere from $15 per transaction to $500 or more. More information on brokers can be found in Chapter 10.

WHY A DISCOUNT?

While it's advised to seek out closed-end funds that are selling at a discount to the premium price, it may help you find such discounts if you know some of the reasons CEF discounts occur. Most often it's a matter of supply and demand. If there are not a lot of buyers, as with anything else, sellers will have to sell for less money and the buyers have the discount in the market. You can get a CEF at a low price if the fund underperforms. This fund, however, will be harder to sell for much more than the price at which you bought it. A more promising reason for a discount is if you find a fund investing in a country or region that is not yet very popular, perhaps still underdeveloped. If the economic future looks promising for this area you should hurry before word gets out and there becomes a greater demand for such shares. These investments can be found in the emerging market and other international funds.

Besides undervalued companies and emerging markets in developing countries, some CEFs invest in companies facing leverage buyouts and other companies facing financial difficulties. Naturally, these are not heavily sought out and often sell at a discount. One other situation where CEFs can be purchased at a discount is when they don't receive much attention or much press, so the overall buyer demand is relatively low. For any and all of these reasons you may find discounts when looking to purchase shares of a closed-end fund.

THE BOTTOM LINE

All tallied, there are not many reasons to look into closed-end funds, as opposed to open-end funds, unless you are looking at a very promising emerging market or industry that you cannot buy elsewhere and can get into at a discount. Offering less liquidity and presenting you with a lot more to learn, closed-end funds are not as practical for most new investors when so many of their open-end counterparts are showing significant returns. Open-end funds have been well marketed and have become extremely easy to purchase without the need of a broker or a seller. Until closed-end funds are more user friendly to buy into and easier to understand thoroughly, they will lag far behind in popularity among fund owners.

Open- and Closed-End Funds: The Key Differences

Open-End Mutual Funds	Closed-End Mutual Funds
Around 11,000 to choose from	Just over 1,000 to choose from
Heavily advertised and promoted	Not advertised and rarely recommended
Sales value of the fund is the NAV less fees and expenses	Sales value of the fund is not as clear, depends on the buying/selling market, and could be higher or lower than the NAV
Can grow, creating greater diversity	Do not grow and therefore is limited in regard to diversity
Can become hard to manage in a down market if it's too large	Are easier to manage in a down market
Easy to find information about	Hard to find information about
Don't always handle obscure markets or unique industries	Delve into emerging markets and less explored industries
Very liquid	Not as liquid
Can sell for a profit only if the NAV is higher than when you purchased your shares	Can sell for a profit for a higher NAV or if you purchased the fund at a discount and the price is higher than your purchase price

The 411!

Since there is less talk and little written about the 500+ closed-end funds, you will want to seek them out online from the closed-end fund trade association at *www.closed-end.fund.com* for more details about this hush hush segment of the fund market. You can call them at 1-816-413-8900, or e-mail them from their Web site or write to them at: Closed End Fund Association, P.O. Box 28037, Kansas City, MO, 64188.

CLOSED-END MUTUAL FUNDS WORKSHEET

When comparing closed-end mutual funds, you may want to list a particular fund and then, not unlike a stock chart it over several weeks. However, in contrast to a stock, there will be a net asset value or NAV, and a stock price, which will be higher or lower than the NAV.

Name of Fund	Stock Exchange	Date	NAV	Stock Price	Date	NAV	Stock Price	Date	NAV	Stock Price

CHAPTER NINE

Loads or No-Loads, A Loaded Question, Plus Fees and Expenses

The A-B-Cs of Loads

Often the classifications of a mutual fund, listed after the name, differentiate the load. "A" is front end and "B" is back end. "A" loads have a smaller 12b-1 fee than "B" shares. Sometimes, front-load A-classified mutual funds offer you discounted prices for larger purchases. Class B shares are actually contingent deferred sales charges, which are sales charges that will eventually disappear if you hold the fund for a long time. The other side of that scenario is that if you sell the fund in the short term you pay a higher percentage.

There are also "C" shares that charge level loads, meaning smaller front and back loads, plus 12b-1 fees and service fees. "D" shares are funds with no front, back, or other loads, which are designated for employee retirement plans such as 401k's. These institutional shares can be sold in greater amounts to a number of employees, thus generating more investor assets. They are also long-term investments since they cannot be withdrawn without penalty until retirement.

T wo of the terms you will repeatedly hear when fund shopping are *load* and *no-load* mutual funds. Loads and no-loads are mutual fund terms for "with a salesperson" or "without a salesperson." A loaded fund means you are paying a commission to someone who has helped you determine which fund to purchase. A no-load fund means you have bought the fund on your own, usually through a toll-free (800 or 888) number. By calling a toll-free number, you can get the paperwork necessary to buy into a fund simply by sending a check along with your application. No-load funds have, therefore, become very popular as the wealth of information about mutual funds reaches a wider audience via the Internet, financial papers, the Financial News Network, and books such as this. Mutual fund information is easily accessible. Many potential investors are learning how to evaluate their own needs without brokers guiding them.

A typical commission on a load mutual fund is generally in the 4% to 6% range, meaning 4 to 6 cents on every dollar will be taken out for a commission. This is money saved on a no-load. Of course, if the load fund outperforms the no-load by more than the commission, you are still coming out ahead despite paying the load.

There are typically three types of load mutual funds. A sales charge applied upon the front end, or initial, purchase of the shares is called a *front-end load*. A sales charge that is applied upon withdrawing the money from the mutual fund or selling the shares is called a *back-end load,* also known as a *deferred sales charge*. A load that remains constant over time is called a *level load*. Front-end loads are most common. It's important that you look closely at the prospectus or discuss with the broker exactly which loads you will be charged.

While the front-end load, or up-front sales commission, is more easily explained as a set percentage of the investment when you first purchase your shares of the fund. The back-end sales charge, or contingent deferred sales charge, can decrease and sometimes disappear if you hold the fund long enough. This means you pay a fee when you redeem your shares. Holding onto funds that have a back-end sales charge has a benefit in that they are often phased out (usually) over 5 years if you hold onto the fund. This is a way of encouraging investors to hold onto the fund for a long-term goal.

If you are dealing with a fund that uses a front-end load, it will be subsequently added on to all new shares that you buy of the fund. However, most funds have dividend reinvestment plans, whereby your dividends are reinvested right back into the fund. These reinvestments are not charged with the load.

GRAY AREAS

As is the case with everything these days, there are options in between the load and no-load mutual funds. While no-loads have gained an edge on load funds, many companies have started offering loaded no-loads or *low loads,* which bill themselves as no-loads, then charge a small percentage and do not give the advice of a load fund. Loaded no-loads have catches to them whereby you will be paying a fee somewhere down the line for the privilege of not paying a fee. Whether the costs are for "special benefits," a personal finance report, or some other accompanying service, the bottom line is that these are not commission-free funds. There are firms that will sell you a no-load fund, then charge you 1.5% of your assets on an annual basis, which can come to far more than a 5% load on a single mutual fund investment. There are numerous ways that certain companies have found to slip fees and payments into their no-load mutual fund business. If, when reading the prospectus, hidden costs jump out at you and you are suddenly dealing with unexpected fees, then you should look elsewhere. You should be clearly choosing between a load and a no-load fund without any additional surprises.

You will also see what are called 100% no-load mutual funds that do not impose any sales charges to purchase or to redeem shares in the fund. There is also no 12b-1 distribution fee (explained on p. 149). A council called the 100% No Load Mutual Fund Council, formed in 1989, has thousands of members in the

Loads Versus Fees

Remember, loads or no-loads are commissions paid (or not) while management and other operating fees go to the fund company to be used for operating and marketing expenses. They are *mutually* exclusive of one another. Of course if they are both high, they will be cutting into your profit margin.

form of companies selling mutual funds to the public with no loads. If you are wondering about a no-load, you can check with the council. This is noted because of the confusion that has arisen because of the low loads, loaded no-loads, and other variations on a simple theme.

Naturally, with so many funds competing for your investment dollar, the different share classifications can sometimes get blurred as funds charge various loads. Read the prospectus very carefully to fully understand the share classification.

LOADS VERSUS NO-LOADS

Let's face it, no-loads are easy to explain. You find the fund you like, call the 800 number or punch it up on your PC, buy the fund and pay no sales commission. So why in the world, if there are no-loads would anyone buy a load fund? You receive sound advice from experts when you buy a load fund. They can save you valuable research time and effort. If this appeals to you then you might be a candidate for a load fund.

There are a plethora of articles telling you why no-load funds are better than loaded funds. It's very easy for journalists to write the obvious, so many people will do just that, penning articles on why no-loads are the only way to go. Whether you read a three-page feature in a financial magazine or a short online blurb, the essence of the story is the same, you'll save money if you don't pay a commission. Jeez, that was simple. But since loaded funds have not gone the way of 8-track tapes and vanished into never-never land, there must be some reason they still exist and people are still shelling out that commission. Are people just being foolish? Do they not know by now that they can get something for nothing? Try finding an article on the advantage of loaded funds, I dare you.

Am I a "No-Load" Type of Person?

No-load funds are for the person who is able to take the time to control his or her financial destiny by studying and learning about mutual funds (as well as the stock and bond markets, in which they are based). A no-load mutual fund buyer has assessed his or her level of risk tolerance and has determined where to draw the line, be it staying conservative, being aggressive, or playing the middle of the road. A no-loader is also ready to take the responsibility of his or her decisions. Remember, a confident investor, new or seasoned, can knock off commissions and earn more money from a good no-load investment. The key word here is good, as with any investment.

Loaded funds are not the enemy that the no-load advocates will tell you they are. Not that we are picking sides, mind you, just providing the more rounded picture so you can decide. Load funds are still offered in abundance and serve a purpose. The most obvious one is that a load fund seeing 50% returns is better than a no-load seeing 25% returns. If you need to spend a little more to make more, what's the big deal? No-load advocates will say, "But you can find a no-load in the same category that will also give you a 50% return." The problem is that many people do not have the time to learn about and sift through the 11,000 funds available. They may not have the knowledge of funds or the confidence to just dial an 800 number and buy a fund. This does not mean these are ignorant people; it means they may be either busy people or people who are more comfortable with the advice given in a load fund from an expert. Likewise, some people spend money on a therapist while others spend much less money reading self-help books.

There are literally thousands of funds, and your money needs to land in the right one. The logic is simply that it's better to give up 5% of a profit than 0% of a loss. Therefore, if you seek guidance in the world of investing, you will seek experience and go with loaded funds. Some of the most successful funds are load funds backed by sound research and good advice. No-load advocates point to the loaded funds that have not provided good results, adding that you didn't need to pay for advice to get only a 10% gain, then lose half of that on a 5% back-end load. True. Therefore, if you are going with a load fund, make sure the person doing the loading is worthy of the commission he or she is getting. Ask around; get recommendations instead of just going with the first broker who cold calls your house. Word of mouth, as in finding a doctor or dentist, or hairstylist for that matter, is important when dealing with your investments. So many people are investing these days, it's not hard to find those who are getting good sound advice.

More Money Talks

If you invest a larger sum of money, you qualify for a reduction in your front-end load. This is mandated by federal regulations stipulating that at a certain amount the fund must offer breakpoints to investors. For example, a load may be 5.00%, but if you invest over $50,000 in the fund it might drop to 4.50%, over $100,000 it might be 4.00%, over $200,000 it might be 3.50%. This can be on a lump sum investment or on the accumulation of investments made over time. Either way, the more you invest in the fund, the lower the front-end sales load.

Likewise, time is a factor on back-end loads. If you sell your shares of the fund after one year, the load may be 5.00%, after two years, 4.00%, after three years, 3.00%, and so on until the contingent deferred sales charge (back-end load) has been phased out completely.

LOAD FUNDS VERSUS NO-LOAD FUNDS WORKSHEET

Comparing loads and no-loads sounds like a no-brainer. Loads will cost you more money than no-loads. However, if you are looking at a fund that provides very good returns, you may still be doing better with a loaded fund. Look at Morningstar or Value Line for load adjusted returns or take the load percentage and deduct it from the overall percentage increase in returns.

   Once again, remember to compare funds that are in the same category.

		% Returns	Load Fund:	
No-Load Fund	Category	1 Yr./3 Yrs.	1 Yr./1-Yr. Load Adjusted	3 Yr./3-Yr. Load Adjusted

UNDERSTANDING FEES AND EXPENSES

Whether loads or no-loads, all mutual funds have operating costs. Loads, fees, and expenses are all money deducted from your overall returns. If we really wanted to depress you, we'd throw in taxes, and you would think you had nothing left of your profits. The truth is, that you can withstand any and all of these fees if the returns are better than other investments.

Operating costs are part of any company, and mutual funds are no exception. The term *expense ratio* defines the fund's annual expenses, which are expressed as a percentage of the fund's annual net assets. Just as Uncle Sam will take his cut out of your earnings, so will the expense ratio of a mutual fund. The money goes primarily to management of fund and operating costs. A fund is usually a large-scale business handling millions or billions of assets, and a significant amount of money is spent on running the show. To market that business, there are also what are known as 12b-1 marketing fees.

Fees and expenses are monitored closely by the Securities and Exchange Commission. With so many fund families competing for your business, it behooves fund management to try to keep expenses low to make the fund more attractive. Obviously, the lower the expense the better for you as the investor.

Each mutual fund operates like a smaller business within the structure of the larger fund family. A mutual fund is an entity unto itself in that the fund does not interact with other funds under the same umbrella company. They share printed materials and costs such as advertising the financial group, but from the perspective of the fund family, each fund is handled separately. The success of one fund does not hinge upon the success of another, nor do the fees and expenses. Often you will look down the listings of funds in one family and see some winners and losers along the way.

Similarly, expense ratios will vary. Generally, the cutoff point is around 1.20% as the number you won't want your fund to exceed; of course, that's a subjective number. Some investment professionals will advise you to stay around 1.10%. Different types of funds will have different expense ratios. In general, index funds will have lower expense ratios because they are considered unmanaged or not actively managed funds. On the other hand, international, sector

Loaded Confusion

No-loads, even those from companies in the 100% No Load Mutual Fund Council, can charge small redemption fees for shares held for a short period of time, usually less than a year. This is to curb short-term investors who want to buy and sell on a very frequent, sometimes daily, basis.

Back-End Fees and Redemption Fees

Back-end fees are contingent fees based on the length of time you own the fund.

Redemption fees, however, are set percentage fees of your assets, paid when you redeem your shares of the fund. They are paid directly to the fund and can be costly if you have a lot of money invested.

funds, and small-cap funds generally have higher expense ratios. The expenses will be deducted from the net asset value each day when the NAV is calculated. So what exactly are these fund fees? Where does this money go?

Typical fund fees include management, brokerage, and administrative fees, plus a 12b-1 fee.

MANAGEMENT FEES

This is the percentage that goes to managing the fund. The fund manager fee can be a flat percentage or it can be set up based on the growth of the fund and the returns. Under management fees are other service fees that are paid to the support team that works with the fund manager, including analysts and other financial advisors. There may also be a need for legal assistance and/or a tax specialist.

BROKERAGE FEES

These are turnover fees and costs resulting from the trading that takes place within the fund. There may or may not be a mention of such fees in the prospectus, but they will appear in the fund's statement of additional information. More trading will result in higher brokerage fees. These fees will also include commissions, if there are any, markups, or markdowns on securities traded such as bonds. Usually highly active funds with greater turnover, such capital appreciation and aggressive growth funds will have higher fees in this area; income funds, or other buy and hold funds such as bond funds, will not be as greatly affected by brokerage fees.

ADMINISTRATIVE FEES

These are the fees associated with running an office, including paying the office staff, renting office space, paying for equipment, phone bills, and so on. Sometimes these funds are absorbed under management fees, but that is not usually the case.

Administrative expenses incurred by a fund also include online support and information, check processing, auditing, record keeping, shareholders' reports, printed matter, rent, equipment, and so on.

Remember, a mutual fund is a company in business and they need to keep the business running. Like any business, they have to pay expenses from the money they bring in. Businesses in general work their costs into their prices, so helping to pay the rent and salaries of employees is common business practice. Sometimes these expenses are broken down into various categories, including shareholder service fees, which generally involve the information made available to the shareholder. This can be anything from placing orders, to written information, to questions answered on the 800 phone number. Miscellaneous expenses can also be factored into these expenses or listed separately.

12b-1 Fee

This is an extra fee that has generated a lot of attention. There is an ongoing debate regarding 12b-1 fees, as they are used to market or advertise the fund. This fee also covers distribution costs, which includes literature, sales incentives to brokers, and even, in some cases, the Internet costs of maintaining a Web site. Some investors feel that they should not be paying for the advertising of the mutual fund, and until recently it was often advised not to invest in funds that impose 12b-1 fees. The argument was that it is the mutual fund's responsibility to handle their own marketing. However, with the vast competition among funds, advertising and marketing is becoming more and more fashionable.

The opposing argument says that the upside of a 12b-1 fee is that advertising and marketing will help the fund to grow. The larger the fund grows, the more money will be available and the greater leverage the fund will have to buy more holdings. Also, in many cases the more widespread the fund becomes (in total number of investors and overall assets) through marketing and advertising, the lower the overall expense ratio. Therefore, the 12b-1 fee can work in your favor by building up the fund. However, it is worth noting that when a fund reaches a very high total of assets it may be harder for a manager to manage. A huge fund may also close to new investors, meaning for all practical purposes there is no need to promote or market the fund any longer. Therefore the 12b-1 fee should be dropped. However, it generally is not.

By the Numbers

- If you invest $20,000 in a 100% no-load fund (with no 12b-1 fee) that after one year gains 20%, you will have a total of $24,000 invested in the fund by year number two.
- If you invest $20,000 in a 5% front-end load fund (with a .5% 12b-1 fee) that gains the same 20%, you will have $22,680.

  A back-end load would take off a percentage at the other end of the transaction. Such "exit fees" are often a higher percentage if the fund is held for a shorter period of time, like under one or two years.
- Taking the same $20,000 but assuming the load fund gained 30% instead of 20%, with the same commissions and 12b-1 fee as in comparison 2, after one year you would have $24,570.

Therefore, all things being equal, no-loads will outperform load funds, particularly over several years.

Loaded No-Loads with 12b-1s

Actually no-loads and 12b-1 fees are mutually exclusive. Loads (or lack thereof) and fees are different animals, which explains the logic behind the following (whether you agree with it is something else).

Funds that do not charge a sales commission but charge a 12b-1 fee can legally call themselves no-load funds. The 12b-1 fee, usually between 0.25% and 0.50%, continues as long as you own the fund. B shares, or those with back-end loads, can also charge a 12b-1 fee. So look in the prospectus for the 12b-1 load even in your no-load funds. People are often surprised by this fee in a no-load fund and are any-thing but pleased about this little loaded loophole!

From an investor's perspective, the expense ratio is one of the key points of comparisons between two funds that may be relatively similar, such as two large-cap growth funds or two emerging growth funds. If the returns are similar then you'll want to go with the fund with the lower expense ratio.

It's harder to compare apples and oranges, or index funds and international funds, since the type of funds are completely different and your reasons for investing in one as opposed to the other will also be different; so will the average expense ratios.

Example of Annual Operating Expenses (as a percentage of average net assets)	
Management fees	.60%
Service and administration fees	.28%
12b-1 (distribution plan) fees	.10%
Total fund operating expenses	.98%

There should be a fee table in the prospectus (near the front) that outlines the various fees associated with the particular mutual fund. The actual fee breakdown will be listed and explained in the annual report, which will have a detailed itemized breakdown. Don't assume, by any means, that funds with similar objectives, similar names, or even those in the same fund family will have the same fees. See if the rate of return over recent years has been high enough to justify the higher amount of fees you will be paying. Fund fees and expense ratios do not necessarily correlate to the success or failure of the fund. A fund can prove very successful despite a high expense ratio. On the other hand, a fund can give you a double whammy by having a high expense ratio and an NAV that is dropping.

Expense ratios are more often affected by the size of the fund. The largest funds generally have lower ratios because the pool of investors and total number of assets is just that much larger. Often once the fund reaches a certain amount, the ratio will drop. For example, an expense ratio may be 1.00, but once the fund surpasses

$200 million in assets, it will drop to .75%. If the 12b-1 marketing fee is helping to reach this goal, and this fee is lower than the .25% difference in expense ratios, then this fee is working in your favor, say 12b-1 defenders. On the other side of the coin are funds that will start out not charging high expense ratios until they reach a certain amount of assets. This is a way to draw in new investors, make returns appear higher, and get the fund off to a good start. It will be specified at what point the expenses will kick in.

Average Fund Expense Ratios

Below are average expense ratios and the funds that fall in each category.

Average Expense Ratio	Fund
Under 1.00	S&P 500 index funds
1.30–1.40	Growth & income equity income
1.41–1.50	Growth—domestic, sector—utilities
1.51–1.60	Mid cap sector—financial services
1.60 +	Aggressive growth, international, micro cap, other sectors, including energy, natural resources, health, biotechnology, technology, real estate, and precious metals

Non–U.S. equity, emerging markets, and other global funds tend to average closer to 2% for expense ratios.

Keep in mind that while 1% of a $10,000 investment is only $100 and 1.50% of a $10,000 investment is only $150, that small difference can become much more significant over 10 or 20 years.

Expense ratios are factored into the NAV that you will see and evaluate. Remember, compare funds in the same category for the most accurate assessment.

Maximum Sales Charge and Maximum Sales Load

A maximum sales charge is another way of saying "front-end load." These are the common loads taken as a percentage off the offering price of the fund. A *maximum sales load,* however, is a sales load placed on the reinvested dividends. This is very rare, and if you see it, you should steer clear since the vast majority of funds do not charge anything to reinvest dividends.

CHAPTER TEN

BROKERS
AND PLANNERS

Once upon a time, playing the stock market meant you would first go out and find a stockbroker. Since the vast majority of people did not know such a broker, they didn't bother playing the market. The perception was long held that brokers were for the rich and that they dealt with big money transactions and certainly wouldn't want to be bothered with the little guy investing $2,000—not while a $50,000 investor was on the other phone line with an important question. In short, anyone who did not feel financially savvy would shy away from stockbrokers. Bonds were bought and sold through banks or by calling the U.S. Treasury. After all, the U.S. Treasury Department had to be fair and forthright to all those who wanted government securities. The proliferation of information that became available over the past 10 years, by way of financial literature, new publications, *USA Today,* and computer software, opened up the world of investing to many more people. Brokers saw it in their best interest to go after this much wider market. Sure, unscrupulous brokers would always go after the little guy trying to swindle him, but as the investing market grew more widespread, legitimate brokerage houses saw value to be gained by helping the average American invest. The average American investor now had more knowledge at his or her fingertips so that he or she simply would no longer be uninformed when dealing with a broker. Women, in particular, began playing a more active role in investment circles—once a territory marked by male dominance. The changing roles of women in the work force coupled with the information available opened up a whole market to investors. The 800 number and the PC, however, became major obstacles to brokers, who realized they were no longer a necessary part of the investing equation, particularly when it came to stocks and mutual funds.

But brokers fought back, and many discount brokers jumped onto the Internet, giving you plenty of information at your fingertips and low-cost commissions. So now you, the mutual fund investor, are faced with several options. You could go through a full-service broker, a discount broker, a deep-discount broker, or just dial an 800 number, depending on the type of fund you were looking for and your personal comfort level as an investor.

Choosing the way you will conduct your investing is an important decision. Each option has its share of pros and cons. Whichever way you choose to conduct your investment affairs has a lot to do with your investment smarts and how eager you are to get involved in the entire research process.

FULL SERVICE BROKERS

Full service brokers are expected to provide sound advice based on financial research. They should not be trying to sell you the hot funds on their list, but look to match your goals with the right fund.

Someone looking to invest who does not feel that he or she has the time to commit to studying the fund market might find a broker's expertise helpful as a means of saving time they may not have. Investors dealing with large sums of money, such as $100,000, may do some of their own research but also often wish to work with a broker with whom they can discuss various plans of action and get an expert opinion. Full service brokers also have the inside track should you be looking to get in on an IPO (of course, this is usually for major level investors). Some brokers will be your best friend until they've got your account set up, and then they'll be as difficult to get hold of as that waiter who served you but then went on his break. Others will maintain an active relationship whereby they will do more than get their initial commissions and work with you on financial planning. Naturally the second scenario is preferred.

For some transactions you will need a broker, such as buying and selling closed-end mutual funds. This, however, does not have to be a full service broker. Therefore, full service brokers are now in a position where they want your business, and if you are savvy and knowledgeable about the investment world, they have to prove to you that they deserve it by adding something to the equation.

DISCOUNT BROKERS

Commissions charged by brokerage houses were deregulated back in 1975, and this decision was truly the beginning of the ascent of the discount broker. Trades could be conducted for far less money

Just Say "No"

Don't be blindsided by a good used car salesperson. Many brokerage firms, including top name ones, will cold call you with the latest hot fund to buy. They'll even, for a fee, do an assessment of your needs and goals and then sell you the same fund anyway, making a nice commission on top of that. Once your money is automatically being guided into the fund via direct deposit, you'll probably have a hard time reaching your friendly cold caller who was so cheerful and ready to be your best friend with a dozen phone calls prior to your investing. Just say "No."

than investors were used to paying at full service brokerage firms like Merrill Lynch and Morgan Stanley. Discount brokers are now offering more services than ever before, and with all the new and faster technology, investors have all of the investment information they need right at their disposal.

If you are ready, willing, and able to investigate potential companies on your own, then a discount or deep-discount broker may fit the bill. Many individuals are finding that taking charge of their investments is an empowering experience. Once they become acquainted with all of the available information, such investors feel that they are in the best position to handle their investments and are happy to be in control.

Discount broker fees are considerably lower than full service broker fees, and often the simple guidance you may need can be found in the content on their Web sites. As long as the discount broker, or any broker, is easily accessible, this is a very simple way of doing business. Deep-discount brokers can save you even more on commissions but are risky as they can be very hard to reach when you need to make a transaction.

Internet, online trading is another way of utilizing broker services. E*TRADE and Ameritrade are two massive online sites devoted to doing the job of a discount broker via your PC. An up-to-the-minute portfolio is maintained, along with account information, news on the market, and financially significant stories. You can also access the market at any hour. Off-hour trading is now part of the lure of online trading. Sites like Quick & Reilly, E*TRADE, SureTrade, and Ameritrade are some of the popular dot com places to go to trade and to get quotes and information about funds and the various markets. Most have fairly low minimums and are very user friendly, allowing you to click on your portfolio and get an up-to-date assessment of your holdings, plus all available account information.

If you are surfing the Internet trading sites, there are several things you might look for. First, you may want to see if the site deals in funds (stock and bond) as well as money markets, stocks, bonds, and if you are so bold, futures or anything else you have in mind. Next you want to get the per trade costs and at how many shares or what amount of investment these costs change. See if the site is insured by the SIPC, which is like the FDIC except for fund companies. Finally, find out how long it is before your transactions are executed (online this should be very quickly) and make sure you will get written documentation to back up your transactions.

Discount brokers and online trading are for individuals who are comfortable taking matters into their own hands. It's all a matter of comfort level, type of investment you are looking to make, and research. Stocks are generally not no-loads unless you buy directly from a company, which is uncommon. Closed-end funds will also be brokered by full or discount brokers. Open-end mutual funds, however, offer the most ways in which to invest, including full service brokers, discount brokers, online investing, and no-load 800 numbers.

THE DO-IT-YOURSELF INVESTOR

The wealth of information available on the Internet and in books has made it easy to educate yourself about the world of investing. Beginning investors now have access to many of the same resources as full service brokers. Therefore, full service brokers are less popular with the new breed of hands-on investors who are reading the *Wall Street Journal, Barons,* obtaining Morningstar reports, and buying no-load funds. They are turning to their PCs and delving deeper into the financial market than ever before. Major financial companies, aware of this insatiable quest for financial information, are building bigger, more comprehensive Web sites with full fund reports, analysis, picks by experts, and, of course, the latest in fund news, market updates, and all the statistics you could ever need. And for anything you don't find there are search boxes and 800 numbers.

Beyond Web sites is the word of mouth method of obtaining investment tips. Casual conversation around the water cooler is no longer just "Monday Night Football," but also well researched tips on the funds to buy. For the do-it-yourself investor, it's easy to follow up on all leads and buy into a fund with a few clicks of a mouse or a quick call to an 800 number.

The proliferation of online discount brokers has made trading possible around-the-clock for a nominal fee. In some cases, you can

Checking Out Brokers

1. Be leery of cold callers. They are trying to sell based on their agenda and not based on your goals and needs.
2. Talk to a couple of brokers before making your decision.
3. Look for the right broker for your needs. For example, if you are nearing retirement, don't go to a broker who primarily deals with young investors looking for hot aggressive growth funds.
4. Don't stay with a broker you don't like. If you can't reach your broker, or if you feel your broker is guiding you into high commission funds that aren't right for your needs, you should get out. Also, if you feel your broker is *churning*, which means doing a lot of buying and selling to run up commissions, then you should also get out. This will only occur if you give your broker the right to make transactions on your behalf.

Apples and Oranges: Promotional Double Talk

Listen closely when you hear great words of wisdom from anyone trying to sell you a fund. They may be comparing apples and oranges. For example, someone could tell you that over any given 10-year period bond fund returns have never beaten stock fund returns. While they are correct, the reasons for buying stock funds and bond funds are different. Likewise, someone can tell you that since growth funds have outperformed value funds for the past 5 years, there's no reason to buy a value fund. Yes, growth funds have performed better of late, but history, beyond the past several years, shows that growth and value funds are cyclical and that more often than not, value funds have outperformed growth funds.

make a trade for $8 to $10. Trading online is ideal if you have done your homework and know exactly which fund or which stock you want to own. Of course it is also possible to overtrade. All the research in the world won't circumvent old habits, including those of overindulgence or simply panicking if the NAV or stock price has dropped one week.

The do-it-yourself investor, therefore, no longer needs the hand holding of the full service broker and finds "personal guidance" through some good self-talk and strong self-control. You need to be able to remind yourself of your long-term plans and not get caught up by every shiny new fund that rolls off the assembly line. One of the reasons full service brokers and, more significantly, financial planners are in business is to construct a practical approach and dilute one of the biggest drawbacks to sound investing, your emotions.

A good do-it-yourself investor does not let emotions dictate which funds he or she will buy. Yes, you may have a legitimate concern about the environment and not be comfortable investing in certain companies with business practices you find objectionable. There's nothing wrong with being socially responsible and investing in funds such as the PAX Fund (one of the leading socially responsible funds). However, there's plenty wrong with playing a hunch or going with a fund because your jeweler's nephew's sister saw in the stars that it would bring you great fortune. The toughest aspects of do-it-yourself investing are:

1. Allocating your assets.
2. Narrowing down your fund choices for your final decision.
3. Staying with the fund(s) through the volatile times.
4. Not letting your emotions get the better of you.

The best aspects of being a do-it-yourself broker are:

1. You can utilize the Web and find whatever information you need when you need it (once you become Web savvy).
2. You can save on broker commissions.
3. You have more to boast about at cocktail parties, or more to gripe about.

LIST OF DISCOUNT BROKERS

There are numerous discount brokers, but following are a few of the most popular. Prices vary.

Accutrade 1-800-228-3011, online trading at *www.accutrade.com*

American Express Financial Direct 1-800-658-4677, online trading at *www.americanexpress.com/direct*

Ameritrade 1-800-669-3900, online trading at *www.ameritrade.com*

Aufhauser & Company 1-800-368-3668, online trading at *www.aufhauser.com* (They also offer stock information and links to other sites at WealthWEB.)

Bull & Bear Securities 1-800-262-5800, online trading at *www.bullbear.com*

Ceres Securities 1-800-669-3900, online trading at *www.ceres.com* (No-frills trading.)

Charles Schwab & Co. 1-800-435-4000, online trading at *www.schwab.com* (High volume and low prices from one of the biggest of the brokerage houses.)

Datek Securities 1-888-GODATEK, online trading at *www.datek.com*

E*TRADE 1-800-786-2575, online trading at *www.etrade.com* (High volume, very popular site with low prices.)

Freedom Investments 1-800-381-1481, online trading at *www.tradeflash.com*

Jack White & Company 1-800-233-3411, online trading at *www.pawws.com/jwc*

Marquette De Bary Company 1-800-221-3305, online trading at *www.debary.com*

Max Ule 1-800-223-6642, online trading at *www.maxule.com*

National Discount Brokers 1-800-888-3999, online trading at *pawws.secapl.com/ndb* (Major discount brokerage house with research information available.)

Quick & Reilly 1-800-926-0600, online trading at *www.quickreilly.com*

Regal Discount Securities 1-800-786-9000, online trading at *www.regaldiscount.com*

Savoy Discount Brokerage 1-800-961-1500, online trading at *www.savoystocks.com*

Tradex Brokerage Service 1-800-522-3000, no online trading thus far

USAA Brokerage Services 1-800-531-8343, online trading at *www.usaa.com*

Vanguard Discount Brokerage 1-800-851-4999, online trading at *www.vanguard.com*

Wall Street Access 1-800-487-2339, online trading at *www.wsacess.com*

The Wall Street Discount Corporation 1-800-221-7870, online trading at *www.wsdc.com*

Waterhouse Securities 1-800-934-4410, online trading at *www.waterhouse.com*

Ziegler Thrift Trading 1-900-328-4854, *www.ziegler-thrift.com*

FULL SERVICE BROKERS GO INTERNET AND DISCOUNT BROKERS OFFER ADVICE

The ease and quickness by which one can trade online led to the assumption that only discount brokers (faster and cheaper) would be found on the Internet. That is no longer the case. The recent presence of full service brokers on the Net indicates that they also want to provide their more detailed services in the Web world as well. Thus Merrill Lynch, Morgan Stanley Dean Witter, Paine Webber, Prudential, and other full service brokerage firms have hit the Internet with well marketed sites to compete with the E*TRADEs, Schwabs, and Ameritrades of the discount world.

The problem is that much of what makes the Internet world so inviting is speed and quickness. If one is seeking and paying higher commissions for sound advice, this may be a paradox, since such investment advice is not usually quick and easy. Furthermore, the initial foray into the online world, for most of these full service brokers has been for the bigger players, with investment minimums at $20,000, $50,000, or $100,000.

Fees are generally either $29.95 per transaction or a percentage of your annual assets. While this percentage may be as low as 1%, if you have $50,000 in the account your $500 is the same as 50 transactions through a discount broker charging $10 per transaction. Some combine a percentage of your account with a per trade transaction fee. Ouch.

The justification of full service online brokers is that you have the same advantages of a full service broker including investment advice, research material available, plus access to other company information that may be more difficult to attain or cost you money to access online. For investors with large sums of money, the full service broker and the new online full service broker accounts may provide the necessary guidance and comfort for handling such assets. For the smaller investor, many of these firms are not in the ballpark and those that are may simply be asking too much in commissions to make them worth your while.

On the other side of the equation are discount brokers who are now providing advice. Schwab was the first of the discounters to buck the trend by offering portfolio consultation for $400. More than having just an Internet presence, Schwab's branch offices made it easier to add this "full service." Other discount brokers have since followed suit with more full service.

As competition between discount and full service brokers increases, you may see more concessions from both sides, potentially culminating in a combination discount/full service brokerage house offering various packages from no-frills buy-and-sell transactions, to some advice and reasonable broker rates, to full service, higher commission professional advisors all available under one roof (and online) with a rates menu *and perhaps even a salad bar.*

FINANCIAL PLANNERS AND YOU

If it's expert advice you're seeking, there are plenty of financial advisors out there ready to talk funds with you. They have their own theories and strategies that can help guide you toward your financial goal(s). Since essentially anyone can call himself or herself a financial planner, it's advisable to look for one of several credentials. Among the designations to look for are CFP, Certified Financial Planner, and CFA, Certified Financial Analyst, both of which are licensed. There are several other letter combinations you'll find, but the most important factor is that you trust and feel confident in your choice of financial planner.

In a world gone (investing) crazy, it's easy for a charlatan to masquerade as a well intentioned planner. You'll also find well intentioned professionals who put their own self-interest ahead of yours. Furthermore, you'll find planners who are not as well versed as they should be in the rapidly changing markets and even those who, unknowingly, are preaching a one-boilerplate plan of investing for all. There are first rate, well versed professionals out there with most of the correct answers to your financial questions. The trick is weeding through all of the others.

Obviously, word of mouth plays a big part, particularly in such a wide-open field. Find out who was able to put together an effective financial plan for someone you know and trust. Set up a meeting with the financial planner and assess what they can do

Know Your Broker Fees

It's important that you know all the fees associated with any services performed by your brokers. You will want to know about all potential fees, including those associated with opening, maintaining, and closing an account, getting checks, and buying and selling securities. To circumvent potential discrepancies, it's important that you obtain this information in writing in advance.

The National Association of Securities Dealers can answer your questions and alleviate your concerns about the practices of a particular broker by looking up his or her past record regarding any disciplinary actions taken or complaints registered against the broker. They can also confirm whether the broker is licensed to conduct business in your state of residence (NASD 800-289-9999).

for you. Many such planners will routinely be able to tell you how they go about evaluating your financial situation and then how they plan to help you handle your financial future. You should not feel too intimidated to ask questions. Find out what services he or she provides. Can they help you map sound strategies for reaching several goals, including tuition payments, new home purchasing, and retirement? Can he or she guide you in the areas of insurance? Budgeting? Money management? Tax planning? Estate planning? Beyond telling you which funds to buy and when, a good financial planner should get a solid, overall picture of your financial situation at the present time and where you see it heading in the future.

You can even ask to look at a sample financial plan set up for someone else (a fictitious model). It's also a good idea to find out if you are working with a one-man or one-woman operation or if he or she has others in the office who can help you if the planner is not available. Also find out if he or she can, and will be able to recommend other professionals such as an attorney or an accountant.

Some financial planners will give you basic information and construct an overall framework in which you can buy the funds that fit the criteria. Others will be specific about which funds to buy, how many shares, and so on. Still others are in the position of being able to make the moves for you. This last category opens up a new can of worms. You must now assess whether the financial planner is selling you what he or she will get a commission on or a fund he or she is connected with in some manner. Such a conflict of interest doesn't benefit you as the client. This can be hard to ascertain unless you ask for various options when they select funds. When you get financial information from a Web site run by Dreyfus or Fidelity, you know that somewhere on the page they will promote their own funds, but that's understandable since it's clearly their Web site. An impartial planner should be just that, impartial. He or she should not be trying to sway you to follow his or her own strategy and buy his or her favorite funds.

On the other hand, financial planners are people too. Good planners see the investment world through a perspective that comes from years of training and a great deal of research. They may be more conservative or more aggressive in their approach, but that's understandable as long as they and you find a comfortable fit. One planner may tell you that with 12 years until reaching your goal, you should allocate 80% of your assets into growth and income funds while another planner might tell you to put 50% in large-cap growth funds and 30% in small-cap funds. Neither is necessarily wrong. They both have different approaches to a very subjective game. As long as their focus is on your needs and goals and they can explain their planned course of action, they are doing their jobs. Keep in mind that they also need to assess your level of risk since it's your money and not theirs. It's easy for anyone to tell you where to put your $40,000 because if you lose it, all they have to do is apologize.

Another important part of financial planning that often goes overlooked is follow-up. A good planner not only devises a plan of action but checks to make sure it is implemented and monitors how the plan is working. If he or she sees something new on the horizon, be it a shift in the market, a new sector of funds on the rise, or anything from which you can benefit, they should contact you. It's important that a planner be along for the ride, not just around to get you started. Investing is ongoing, and asset allocation is part of the process. No, you should not need to call your planner for every major purchase, but he or she should be there for advice as needed. Find out how ongoing advice is compensated. Some planners charge by the hour while others charge commissions on the sales he or she makes.

Finally, be careful when letting a planner have too much control. It's ill advised for an investor to hand over their money, carte blanche, for a planner to handle. Even if a planner is bonded, you can still set yourself up for potential disaster even with the best intentioned planner. Let planners do what they do best, plan, but you call the shots.

There are many good financial planners to be found. Interview a few and go with one with whom you feel comfortable. You want to feel that you can fully disclose your financial situation to this person without being judged or

Regulatory Agencies and Organizations

If you have questions or concerns about a fund, a broker, or a brokerage house, there are several places where you can seek out information.

U.S. Securities and Exchange
   Commission (SEC)
450 5th Street, NW
Washington, D.C. 20549
1-202-942-7040 or 1-800-SEC-0330
for investor education and assistance
www.sec.gov

Created in 1934, the Securities and Exchange Commission (SEC) oversees the financial industry. It governs and regulates trading. All companies trading on the stock exchanges nationwide must be registered with the SEC. The SEC administers federal securities laws with the intent of providing protection for investors. The commission also makes sure that there is adequate and effective disclosure of information to the public and that publicly traded companies publish regular financial reports.

There is a Division of Enforcement within the SEC that is charged with enforcing federal securities laws.

If you need information on the registration or practices of a company, including a mutual fund company, you can contact the SEC for information. You can also file a report with them if you feel you have been treated unfairly. However, keep in mind that they are a highly overworked agency, because of the number of investment firms and new mutual funds popping up daily, so it may take some time for them to respond.

National Association of Securities Dealers
1735 K Street, NW
Washington, D.C. 20006-1500
1-202-728-8000 or 1-800-289-9999
www.nasd.com
NASD Regulation 1-202-728-8000

The National Association of Securities Dealers (NASD) was created in 1983 by the Maloney Act amendments to the Securities Exchange Act of

Regulatory Agencies and Organizations *(continued)*

1934. Through its many departments and offices, the NASD Regulation's jurisdiction extends to over 5,400 firms with more than 58,000 branch offices and over 505,000 securities industry professionals. The NASD Regulation, Inc. is the independent subsidiary of the National Association of Securities Dealers, Inc. charged with regulating the securities industry and the NASDAQ Stock Market. You can discuss the practices of a questionable securities dealer and find out if he or she is licensed.

While both the SEC and the NASD are places you can go if you have a problem with a brokerage firm, mutual fund company, fund family, or broker, you are often better off trying to settle disputes directly. Stay calm, explain your concerns, and see what can be done to correct the problem. Large fund families do not need negative publicity and are usually more than willing to try to help correct the situation, but be persistent; sometimes it can take some time. Mediation, whereby both sides try to work out a solution, is often the simplest answer.

However, if you feel you have a legitimate case against a broker, you can contact the Securities Arbitration Group at 1-800-222-4724. They are a non-governmental business designed to help investors who feel they have been wronged. They can respond quicker than the government agencies and have been effective.

Remember, however, that losing money in a fund does not give you the reason to find fault or point blame somewhere else. The Securities Arbitration Group will only take on a situation that they believe to be a valid claim. Also remember that fighting such a battle may win money, but at a cost. Your time needs to be factored in as well. A lengthy arbitration for a small sum of money is not necessarily worthwhile; only you can make that determination. Most often fund families will try to settle minor disputes in a fair manner and will acknowledge and rectify general administrative errors on their part.

feeling intimidated. Anytime you feel you are committing to investments only because you do not know how to say no, you are not with the right financial planner.

DO YOU NEED A FINANCIAL PLANNER?

No, you do not *need* one, but you might feel more comfortable with someone helping you.

Let's face it, we are all individuals, and we go through life marching to different drummers. For this reason there are 11,000 funds to choose from, designed to try and match all of those beats. Likewise, there are different categories we fall into as personality types and subsequently as investors.

Beyond the do-it-yourselfer mentioned earlier, there are those people who are willing to take the initiative, do the research, study up, but ultimately want validation from someone more knowledgeable. These people seek out a planner not so much to do everything for them but to work with them on their financial goals and strategies as a consultant. They are seeking a second opinion from an educated source.

There are also people who simply do not want to be bothered taking control of their finances for one of two reasons: lack of motivation or lack of time. Either way they will turn to a professional and say "whatever you say." If it's the right professional and you as the investor have taken the initial time or been motivated enough to set the relationship off on the right path, having thought out your goals and provided proper information, then this method can be effective as well.

BROKER CONCERNS

While the majority of brokers are reputable, hard workers with the best of intentions, there are rotten apples in every "core" group. Brokers can be suspect for a number of reasons, and you need to keep tabs on their activities and do just enough fund homework to make sure you are receiving the professional service you are saying for.

What can brokers do wrong? There are a few common concerns, including misrepresentation, suitability, and omissions of material facts. These are all reasons to question the actions of your brokers. They are also strong arguments for having paperwork to verify all claims and recommendations made by your broker.

Misrepresentation is a situation whereby your broker has not accurately informed you about the company or the security you are purchasing. If you ask for material to back up whatever it is the broker is telling you and you do some follow-up research, you can avoid such problems. A broker who misrepresents a stock or fund because he or she stands to profit from the transaction is engaging in a conflict of interest.

Issues of suitability involve a broker selling you the fund he or she wants to sell you, despite the fact it is not right for your needs. A fabulous high-risk fund is not right for someone who needs income and principal security. A broker should know your goals, needs, and financial situation before trying to sell you on his or her favorite (high-load) product. There are stories about brokers selling high-commission, inappropriate securities to uninformed, unsuspecting customers. Suitability issues can also be avoided if you are a knowledgeable investor and have researched the broker.

Omission of information about a fund is similar to misrepresentation, only the broker hasn't told you something wrong, but neglected to provide you with key information at all.

Commission grabs is where a broker is churning your account or making more transactions to make more in commissions. This is avoided simply by not allowing your broker to make transactions without your approval. Unauthorized transactions is yet another serious problem whereby the broker is making transactions on his or her own with your money and without your consent.

Keep in mind that most of these areas of misconduct are very hard to prove unless they are quite obvious and you have some type of proof. It's often your word against the word of the broker. A broker can also claim that he or she simply made a recommendation, but that you were free to investigate information or request

You're Entitled!

Funds are required by the SEC to provide you with certain information. You should receive:

- An annual report
- Periodic statements
- Tax information in a timely fashion at the beginning of the calendar year
- All fee structure information

You should have access to all appropriate information regarding the fund, including a distribution schedule, the fund objectives, the management team, and all fees on a fee schedule. If a fund is negligent in furnishing you with such information within a reasonable time frame, you can contact the SEC. Most information should be in the prospectus or annual (or semiannual) report.

any documentation. You should, in fact, ask for documentation to support a broker's claims.

Your first course of action, if you feel you've been treated unfairly, is to talk to the consumer service representatives at the fund company and possibly speak to a manager. Try to talk with and work with the fund family to get an agreeable solution, or at least a solid understanding of why you were sold a particular fund. Be persistent until you are satisfied that the fund has not intentionally tried to mislead you.

If you have talked with the broker, his or her supervisor and anyone else who may be helpful, and you still feel that you have been wronged, you can request arbitration. This can take time and be potentially costly if you need to have a financial advisor or accountant with you.

The bottom line is that a mutual fund is a business and the customer still comes first, even if your $500 investment is not as significant as another investor's $50,000 investment. Investors are key to the success of a fund. and you should be treated properly and professionally.

One final note: Cold callers, from big, small, or midsized agencies, are not doing anything wrong by trying to sell you their fund(s). However, you should simply decline graciously, no matter how good their sales pitches are. Investing is about buying funds that suit *your* needs; this person doesn't know what your goals and needs are. "Thank you, but no. Bye."

BROKER CHECK LIST

When checking out a broker there are several things you need to remember. Here's what you want to know...

❑ What is the sales experience of the broker? _____
_____
_____

❑ What is the history of the firm or brokerage house? _____
_____
_____

❑ How much will you be paying in commissions? _____

❑ What fees will you be paying to open or maintain an account? _____

❑ Are there any additional fees? _____

❑ Does the broker or brokerage house specialize in a particular area of mutual funds?_____
_____
_____

❑ Can you conduct business online?_____

❑ Has this broker dealt with people in similar financial situations to yours? _____

❑ What kind of turnaround time can you expect from this broker for transactions and receiving statements and any other pertinent information? _____
_____

❑ Can this broker refer you to tax professionals, legal advice, and other professional services? _____

❑ Can you get references or do you know people who can tell you more about this broker? _____
_____
_____

Note: It's important to find out from other people how accessible the broker is and how prompt he or she is at getting back to you and making your transactions. If you're looking at a full service broker, other people can assess the advice given by this broker.

CHAPTER ELEVEN

FUND MANAGERS: WHO ARE THEY AND WHAT YOU SHOULD KNOW ABOUT THEM

The fund manager, also known as a professional money manager or portfolio manager, is hired by the investment company that is the actual mutual fund. Don't forget, within a fund family each fund is essentially a separate company. Often a team of money managers and analysts work with the fund manager to research and determine which stocks, bonds, and securities to purchase (and sell) for the best success of the fund.

Before going into greater details about the high-profile fund managers and fund management teams, it's important to take a look at the overall business structure of a mutual fund. The sponsor is the initiator who creates the fund, such as the brokerage house or fund family. The fund is then registered with the SEC. There is a lot of information that must be disclosed to the SEC including the investment objectives, types of investments, fees, and risks involved. Each fund, even within a major fund family, must be registered.

A mutual fund, like many businesses, has a board of directors. The board of directors oversees the fund's management as well as the daily business activities of the fund. The board is concerned first and foremost with making sure the company meets the shareholders' interests. After all, like any other consumer-based business, without investors there is no mutual fund. While a large portion of the board of directors can come from the fund family, brokerage firm, or whoever is sponsoring the fund, there must be a percentage of outside parties also sitting on the board.

The fund manager or portfolio manager is in the position of managing the fund in accordance with guidelines and objectives set out by that fund. Fund managers can take different approaches. Some, more experienced, will choose to run the show more autonomously while others place greater dependency on their management team to work closely with them. Analysts are common throughout the mutual fund world, doing detailed research on companies and their potential for growth.

The background of the fund manager is detailed in the prospectus, and it's a good idea to look over the past history of the manager. You can assess how the manager has done in his or her tenure with the fund you are considering as well as previous funds he or she has managed. You can also get an idea of the style by which the fund manager does business. Does he or she have a buy and hold philosophy or a wheeling and dealing philosophy with considerable turnover? Depending on the type of fund you are looking at, this can make a difference. It's also important to see how long the management team has been with the fund. Frequent turnover in leadership is generally not a good sign. Even if the fund has performed well over the last 3 or 5 years, you don't want to have new management every year.

Another factor you might consider when looking at the track record of a fund manager or management team is how well they've done when there has been a downturn in the market. If they have been able to manage the fund through bear markets without major losses, then it shows they can handle the tough times as well as the market's prosperity. In fact, many potential investors look carefully at this area, determining how the fund fared in the bear markets. Even a fund manager who has a buy and hold philosophy may need to make adjustments during these more difficult times.

In essence, the more successful funds have good people running them—not only the fund manager but the teams of professionals working on the fund. A fund can serve as a training ground for young professionals who work their way up to eventually managing a fund of their own. They also serve to create a new breed of popular fund managers who are generating the attention once reserved for ballplayers. Short of collecting trading cards, some seasoned investors are bantering names about of the hottest fund managers. Plenty of financial magazines are interviewing and writing up features on the most successful fund managers. Everyone wants to know what makes a winner. This, however, will subside if the market should take a prolonged downturn, no matter how well he or she keeps the fund afloat. The reality is, even when baseball slugger Mark McGwire hits an incredible 65 home runs, there was far less interest than when he shattered the old baseball record with 70. Likewise, even if a fund manager brings in a strong 35% return, if he was bringing home 90% returns with a hot tech fund during the surging market, he will be easily forgotten. You're only as good as your last season or latest fund returns.

RESUME AND CREDITS, PLEASE

If you're the investor, or customer, then you want to find out not only about the business, but also about the fund manager. If the fund has

The All-Stars

All-star team fund managers are the ones who have shown strong results consistently and have held their fund above the benchmark through bull and bear markets. These are not the 1-year wonders who took a gamble on a few riskier, more volatile stocks that went through the roof and made them look good, but the managers who have stayed focused and shown that they could do well without their funds becoming high risk or highly volatile.

had the same manager for the past 5 or more years, you can look up 5-year returns and compare the fund's returns to the returns of other similar funds in the same category. You can look at *www.managerranking.com* and get the background and performance stats of the fund manager. Perhaps, in some ways, it is getting like collecting baseball cards, complete with stats and everything.

Important questions:

1. How long has the fund manager been with the particular fund?
2. What are the returns of the fund under the manager's reign?
3. How well has the fund manager fared in bear markets?
4. How are the fund's assets allocated?
5. Does the fund manager have a track record handling the same style of fund? The same asset size?
6. Does he or she generally guide the fund alone or work as part of a team? (Most funds have several analysts and others involved, but at what level?)

Beyond the numbers, you can get a feel for the ability of a mutual fund manager to stay within the style of the fund by what stocks he or she has purchased. You'll also be able to see what kinds of risks are being taken. Perhaps the manager is buying into lesser known companies or more volatile stocks. A fund manager could be leaning more heavily into one sector of the market that he or she believes in. This is not necessarily a bad thing, but it may mean less diversification. Obviously a manager making transactions within a sector fund will be dealing with stocks in one industry. He or she may, however, be leaning toward industry favorites or may have a penchant for going with the new companies on the block. Be sure that the fund manager stays close to your own philosophies. A more conservative investor will select a more conservative fund, run in a conservative manner. It's hard to be as well versed in the details of fund management as a professional, but you know what best meets your own goals and needs. A fund manager with an all-star record at managing global funds is

Why a New Fund?

Mutual funds come into existence for a number of reasons.

Fund managers may see investors showing a sudden interest in another part of the world such as Japan and design a fund that focuses on that country's most sought after stocks. A growing sector may also prompt the emergence of new funds. Another starting point for new funds is the direction of various indices. For example, if the Russell 2000, charting the small-cap companies, is consistently moving upward, then there will be more interest in small-cap companies and more small-cap funds will appear. It's a combination of where the best returns are coming from, the direction the market is heading, and what the public wants. It is also a matter of filling in the voids. A fund family wants to have your portfolio needs covered, so they will try to create funds that fill in any gaps, such as your more conservative or income-producing needs. They will also open new funds occasionally in the off chance the market shifts directions. Janus, for example, after tremendous success with their growth funds in the late 1990s, finally added a value fund in 1999 just in case anyone wanted to diversify in that direction, expecting the tide to swing back to value investing.

Funds need to fit broad categories and follow their objectives. They can fit a theme or create a new one. The bottom line is that a sponsor will generally assemble a new fund when they feel that such assets will provide a profitable return. The problem arises, however, when such sponsors jump on the latest bandwagon and play "catch up," or try to "follow the money." They run the risk of joining the latest hot sector after it has peaked and the risk of creating one too many funds in a market that doesn't need more. Many new emerging market funds, for example, will not survive, as there are limited places in which they can confidently invest their assets. The funds will begin to duplicate one another, and since the sector is a risky one that doesn't attract a vast percentage of investors, many will not generate enough assets to succeed and be profitable for the sponsors.

of little use to you if he or she remains in the international fund market and you're searching for a domestic growth fund.

MANAGEMENT STYLES

Whether it's a large-cap or small-cap fund, stock portfolio managers are generally following an investment style, or a combination thereof. Managers who are looking to do growth investing for their funds have their analysts reviewing the companies that they feel are solidly managed and that, despite their current earnings, can and will continue to grow. Price/earnings ratios, earnings growth, and quarterly income are important factors for analysts and managers who are measuring potential growth. Sales, product development, and where the company is positioned in their sector are all significant factors, as is the particular industry's position in the overall economy. Growth fund managers and their analysts have to be careful to distinguish a stock's volatility (and this is a more volatile type of fund) from a sales downturn.

They must also look carefully at overvalued companies and determine when the bubble might burst or if the overall potential for continued growth will win out.

Value fund managers have had a tougher job of late finding the right stocks, but at least they have had to deal less with volatility than their growth fund counterparts. Value fund managers look at price earnings ratios, price to book value, and other measures to determine whether the company is undervalued. Analysts are looking for companies whose stock prices are selling at a relative bargain and show evidence that they will reach its fair market value. When the value stock goes up to its assessed valuation (reaching full value), the manager will then generally sell it.

There are other managers who will look to do what is called *momentum investing* whereby they try to catch the latest wave and ride the stock and/or the sector as high as possible until it slows down. These managers are essentially going with the hot tickets as far as they can. This is a quicker buy and sell strategy that works for some fund managers. Naturally, many fund managers will incorporate some, or several, of these styles into their portfolio.

ALL THE
ANWER

Some managers will have several analysts looking at different styles of stocks; others will break their teams down into sectors. There is a great deal of number punching to get all the statistics in order before lists of the best and worst are made up within a fund's universe of appropriate choices. A fund manager, for example, may want to study and track the top 200 mid-cap companies rated for potential growth and then determine the best 20 to buy. Fund managers may also have their eyes and ears out for international stocks that meet the fund requirements to fulfill 5% or perhaps 10% of the international investments the fund may hold.

Beyond looking at what to buy, the fund manager must continuously be on top of the securities currently held by the fund. He or she has to keep all the plates spinning and make the key decisions on which ones to drop first, if any. Some managers take the buy and hold philosophy while others are buying and selling at a hair-raising rate. The approach that fits the style of the fund keeps the investors happy and brings home the best returns.

Fund managers usually have a portfolio mix that consists of the following:

> *The "Must Haves"* These stocks are in the portfolio because the type of fund practically demands it if you are going to succeed. These are name stocks that the investors know and expect.
>
> *The "Safe Havens"* Not the biggest earners in the group, these stocks are less volatile even in a volatile category. These are the ones you can count on to keep you afloat when all else is sinking.
>
> *"Everyone's Hot Prospects"* These are the hot up-and-comers that all the printouts, all the analysts, all the king's horses and all the king's men say are the most likely candidates for rookie of the year honors.
>
> *"Personal Favorites"* These are the stocks that you became a fund manager to own. When they go up, you tell Kipplinger and Barrons they were your hand-picked winners. When they go up down, you shake your head in disgust.

Style Drift

Style drift is the term to define a fund manager who has drifted the fund away from its original objective. If a small-cap fund suddenly owns shares of IBM, Disney, and other large-cap giants, that would be more than just a drift, that would be a derailment.

Often a fund may veer off course quite unintentionally as fund managers find themselves with companies growing larger than their small-cap designation. Managers might find that some of their value stocks have done well and are no longer undervalued. To remain a value mutual fund, they would need to sell off these stocks that have regained their values.

Market cap is the biggest area to watch to see if a fund is veering off course. While sectors are more clearly defined and a manager buying finance company shares in a tech sector fund would be clearly `off course, market-cap sizes are not fixed. The precise definition of a small-, mid-, or large-cap fund depends on which financial listing you look at.

Old Fund + New Manager = Good Sign (Maybe)

Perhaps you've discovered a fund with only mediocre returns. Perhaps that same fund is being taken over by a fund manager with a consistently strong track record—particularly in handling that style or category of fund. By all means consider that this fund may be in for a change for the better. Since people are behind the funds (with help from their trusty computers) there is no reason not to think that the fund stands a good chance of turning around. After all, the fund manager has bought and sold the securities before to do so. You may not rush right out to buy the fund, especially since turnover (of securities) may be high for some time until the new manager has made the adjustments that he or she deems necessary. You can chart this fund for a little while and see if it starts turning around. Get the prospectus before the fund manager takes over. Then get the next updated information on the fund.

There are, however, times when a fund manager leaves a successful fund in which you are already invested and you worry whether the new fund manager will reap the same or similar rewards.

Generally speaking, fund manager transitions are smooth. Nobody on the board of directors wants to bring in someone who is going to rock the boat or tamper too much with a good thing. Often the new fund manager worked for the fund in another capacity and is well aware of the objectives and operating procedures of the fund. In fact, he or she is sometimes trained by the fund manager.

Nearly 90% of the time a new fund manager will do a similar job to the old one, sometimes better. The exceptions are often in a smaller fund when someone from the outside is brought in and tries to make his or her mark by making significant changes. This can be a big gamble, one which fund companies generally do not take unless they're bringing in a proven all star in the same category of fund.

The bottom line is, if the fund manager changes, keep a closer watch on what's going on with the fund for a few months. See if the turnover ratio has changed significantly or the types of stocks (or bonds) are noticeably different than in the past. Most of the time this won't be the case, so don't panic.

CHAPTER TWELVE

FUN READING:
THE PROSPECTUS
AND THE ANNUAL
REPORT

Thanks to the intense competition among fund families, the prospectus for a mutual fund is just a phone call or a download away! But what is it?

THE PROSPECTUS

The prospectus is essentially the Bible of the mutual fund. However, it is generally written in a combination of hieroglyphs and legalese. The combination is boring and often confusing. Some funds are trying to improve upon the dryness of the prospectus, hoping that if you can read something palatable, you would be more inclined to buy shares of the fund. Most funds, however, employ few people who are able to explain the fund information at a broad enough level for the purposes of new investors. Therefore, you're often better off reading the fund profiles by Morningstar or Value Line. Funds themselves also provide a profile of their own prospectus, which is essentially the shortened version. While you still need to do a once-over of the whole prospectus, this short version may be the one you spend more time with. The SEC requires a lot of vital information be included in a prospectus and that you receive a prospectus for each and every fund you are planning to buy, even if there are several within one fund family.

A few of the important details you should look for include discussion of the fund's objective, investment risks, breakdown of holdings, and a financial history of the fund.

FUND OBJECTIVE

The fund should have a clear statement of what the objective is. Is it a growth and income fund? A value fund? Does it buy large-cap stocks? Small caps? The objective of the fund should be clear. If it is not, either seek out a fund that is more clearly defined, or ask someone in the fund's Customer Service or Investor Relations Department. Get hold of the annual report and look at the fund profile and make sure they show you a similar objective. The objective, whether it's providing growth, finding value investments, or providing income, will help categorize the fund.

Fund objectives may be stated as follows:

To provide capital growth and income through investing in bonds
To provide long-term capital growth by investing in stocks
To preserve capital by investing in short-term bonds
To seek out growth by investing in the stocks of undervalued
    companies

INVESTMENT RISKS

The mutual fund prospectus should discuss the level of risks the fund will take in conjunction with their objective. Stock funds should discuss the types of stocks they are buying. Look at the volatility of the securities they are buying and of the fund overall. It should be outlined in the prospectus what level of risk you are taking on as an investor.

INVESTMENT BREAKDOWN

The fund will clearly lay out the percentage of holdings they are committed to holding in each fund group. They should say, for example, that the management is required to hold at least 70% of domestic common stocks or a maximum of 10% in international investments. The breakdown and parameters of the fund give you an idea of where your money will be invested. Other types of investments, such as cash instruments, should also be included. There are legal guidelines that funds must adhere to as well. The Investment Company Act of 1940 explains that what is considered a diversified fund (a fund that is not investing strictly in one industry or sector) with respect to 75% of its assets, is not allowed to have more than 5% invested in any one company.

COSTS AND FEES

A fee table should outline all the fees associated with that fund. Read them carefully and make sure you are left with no surprises. This is one of the most significant areas to look over. The fund will try in ever so delicate language to inform you how they can only do their job by charging you these fees. However, if you're looking

Additional Information

When you are looking to buy shares of a fund, you can request further information than that which is on the prospectus. Additional information may include more details on fund policies, plans, and objectives as well as bios and background information on the chief officers of the fund. Basically, if you are looking for more information about a fund, ask for it. Fund families are aiming to please, and there's a good chance they have the information you are seeking.

at one fund with a high expense ratio of 1.80% and one at 0.95%, their argument sounds less valid. It's less important where each portion of the expense ratio goes. Many people balk at the 12b-1 fees, but the reality is a 1.00% expense ratio is not bad whether it does or does not include the 12b-1. Redemption fees, on the other hand, are separate from the expense ratio and often signal investors to steer clear unless they are infatuated with the track record of a fund and must have it. We overlook a lot when we fall in love, and sometimes we get burned.

As for loads, it's the same old story. The prospectus is required to define the loads and the structure: back end or front end? When do back-end loads phase out? No-loads are highly touted and in vogue these days, low-loads also exist, but have not gained much respect. You decide. Just look over each prospectus to know what you're deciding between.

FINANCIAL HISTORY

A prospectus will also give you the history of that mutual fund. The financial information should provide the per share results for the life of the fund, or for funds that have been around for a long time, at least the past 10-year history. You can gauge the total return of the fund on an annual basis. You can also look at the year-end net asset values, the fund's expense ratio, and any other information that will help you gauge how the fund has performed over time. Dividend and interest payments are also listed.

In the end, the prospectus should answer all of your questions and concerns about a particular fund. There may be a lot of extraneous verbiage for the sake of "legally covering themselves" and some marketing hype, but the information you need should all be included in the prospectus. Obtaining a prospectus, by the way, should be as easy as calling the fund's 800 number or, in many cases, clicking to download one from a Web site.

Keep in mind that once you've made it through the prospectus, or read all of the key points carefully, you should look at Morningstar or Value Lines's data on the fund. You can also use the fund profile and literature about the fund family to double-check that which you may not understand. Often the literature about the fund family explains general rules for investing in all funds, such as transfers and certain fees, in a more succinct manner, as these are written by the marketing department in a manner that is clearer and less legalistic.

DERIVATIVES: WHAT ARE THEY?

The term *derivative* appears on the prospectus and in other fund literature, but rarely is it ever defined. It's one of those things that most investors have heard of but have never bothered to learn about because it does not directly affect most investors. Nonetheless, there are a great deal of derivatives being traded. Brokers, funds, banks, and other financial institutions deal in derivatives in some form. Individual investors can also play various forms of derivatives. For our purposes, however, we only want you to understand the basics and have a general idea of how derivatives affect mutual funds.

A derivative is defined as a financial arrangement between two parties where the value is derived from the performance of a security based on a benchmark. Huh? When someone talks about a derivative, it is almost as though they are talking about a wager between two people, one saying, for instance, that a stock or bond is going to beat the index while the other is saying that it is not going to beat the index. A derivative is therefore not a real, tangible thing, such as a bond or ownership in a company, but a speculation on the outcome of the performance. Although these are not bets but investments, they are almost like making a side wager on a fund.

For example, if you were to believe that our fictitious "Richie Fund" is going to beat the S&P 500, you could take a position whereby you stand to profit if the fund has a higher return after *x* amount of time (you could make it one year or one month) while the other party is taking the opposite position and stands to make money if the "Richie Fund" comes up short of the S&P 500 index. They are "shorting" the fund and betting that it will drop. Yes, there are investors who bet on losing money.

Unlike a stock, where all shareholders of the company can make money, with a derivative there is a winner and a loser. For everyone who makes money, there is someone losing money. *This is, by the way, the force that drives the commodities, or "futures" market, which is named for speculating on future performance.*

A lot of funds do a great deal of trading in derivatives. They are either hedging or using derivatives to provide insurance against risk. In other words, one side writes up the derivative, *which is basically coming up with the "side bet,"* and the other side, buys it, *or accepts the bet.* The buyer can take a position whereby they are going against the grain. In other words, if you are in the business of marketing a fund to make money, believing the market is going up, you can essentially take a position that says the market is going to drop. This covers you so that if you are right and the market goes up, your fund will gain assets, but you will lose money on the derivatives (saying the market would drop). The opposite scenario is also a possibility whereby you make money on the derivatives after losing money in the stocks that dropped. Basically you're covering yourself.

There are thousands of strategies and derivatives on the theme of derivatives, but what we've explained is the very basic principal that funds, banks, and other investment companies utilize all the time. It provides them with a way of cutting their losses. Another example would be if a bank made a substantial number of loans in the form of variable mortgages (whereby the rate of interest is the variable). The bank is liable if interest rates go down. They would be collecting interest at a very low rate. They need to hedge that risk, so what they will do is buy derivatives taking a position that interest rates will go down. Therefore, if interest rates go down they'll make money by having bet against themselves. They will make money on the derivatives and lose money on the loans. This could work in the opposite manner as well. Either way they're covered.

This manner of using derivatives to protect a fund or financial institution from a downswing in the market is not generally something that will greatly affect the individual. However, a fund can also buy derivatives to double up exposure to a particular security, sector, or index. In other words, the fund can buy the S&P 500 stocks in hopes that the stocks in the index will go up and then double up their exposure to that index by purchasing derivatives that also say the index will go up. Therefore, if the index does go up 10%, you will gain 20% in returns because you have the fund holdings in the S&P 500 (which went up 10%) and derivatives that took the position saying that the S&P Index would go up 10%. The downside to this double exposure is that if the S&P were to drop

10%, you'd lose because the index dropped (and the securities within) and because you lost the side bet which also said the index would go up. Therefore you'd have a 20%, or double, loss.

Funds can use derivatives in your favor or out of it. They can provide amplified exposure to a stock or index or protect themselves against risk. Funds that are using derivatives to amplify their position are obviously riskier since every dollar you invest is really two dollars.

Many funds have permission to use derivatives. The fund prospectus will provide you with such information. Sometimes you can tell by how a fund reacts to the market. If you know the S&P is up 5% in 2 months and your index fund following the S&P is up 10%, that probably means they are using derivatives to amplify your exposure to the S&P. (By the way, derivatives do not apply only to the S&P, but to all indices throughout the investment world. We're simply using the S&P as an example.)

International funds sometimes use derivatives to hedge currency risks. A Japan fund might, for example, take a position that the yen will decrease in value, which will protect you against currency risk. Therefore, you'll only lose money if the stocks in the fund go down.

The derivatives of a fund are not a top priority of the average investor, but they are something you should know about in case you are looking at a fund that is dealing in them in such large amounts that it is affecting your return. Otherwise, they are something to be aware of but not necessarily concerned about.

THE ANNUAL REPORT

Some companies combine their annual report with the prospectus. Most do not. Companies send you an audited annual report and a semiannual report. Some will send quarterly reports. If nothing else, an annual report is generally slightly more readable than a prospectus. Companies are trying hard to make the annual report more appealing to the eye and more user friendly. Often the fund manager gets to explain his or her philosophy, which can give you an idea where the fund may be heading in the future.

Often people think that if they do not already own a fund they can't see the annual report. This is not true. Unless a fund is doing poorly, fund companies generally make their annual reports available.

Key Prospectus Points

When reading through the prospectus, you should pay particular attention to:

1. The objective of the fund. Does it match your goals and objectives?
2. The fees and costs. Are there too many fees and costs associated with the fund?
3. The ground rules and manner of doing business:
   What is the minimum investment?
   Is there a minimum amount for subsequent automatic investments?
   How many transfers can you make in a year? At what cost?
   Can you buy more shares online? By phone?
   Look for all the rules and ways in which this fund does business.
4. Fund performance. How has the fund done in the past year? Three years? In the last bear market?
5. Top holdings. This will give you an idea of what you are investing in.

These are the most important areas to read carefully when looking over the prospectus. It's a good idea to have a pen and paper nearby should you have questions to ask the broker or fund representative.

It's also a good idea to follow up reading the prospectus by looking at one or two of the reviews or ratings by the companies that evaluate mutual funds like Morningstar, Value Line, or one of the Internet sites dedicated to mutual funds.

If the most successful funds had their way, they'd have them in Barnes & Noble.

The annual or semiannual report looks more closely at the fund's performance—after all they have to maintain current investors' interest. The "what have you done for us lately?" question is answered and explained as the manner in which the fund has conducted business. The holdings of the fund are listed in the annual report. This, however, is the list of holdings at the time the annual report is printed. It's very hard, if not impossible, to get a current listing of what your fund is holding. Funds will claim it's a combination of paperwork and confidentiality. It seems odd that you can own a fund and not know at any given time what the fund's holdings are. Nonetheless, funds buy and sell often, and it would be too difficult for them to keep all shareholders apprised of every move they make. It would also be very costly and that cost would come back to you, eating away at your return. Fund managers also don't want other fund managers knowing their secrets, at least not until they've had a little time to determine if they made a good or bad move.

By collecting information from the prospectus, the prospectus profile, profiles from leading financial services like Morningstar, or other publications and annual or semiannual reports, you should have all the knowledge you need to decide which funds are for you.

LEGALLY SPEAKING

All literature, particularly the prospectus, annual reports, and sales material, distributed by a mutual fund has to meet federal (and sometimes state) guidelines. The SEC must have the fund registered and be apprised with regular reports detailing its operations. All fees, investment objectives, and risks must be spelled out in the prospectus. In essence, mutual funds are closely scrutinized to avoid the type of fraud or deception that the penny stock industry has faced. Funds, for the most part, have had fairly clean, upstanding records, despite some occasional complaints about poor customer service. Fund families are very aware that a scandal or even any type of significant inquiry into their business practices by the SEC could ruin their reputations, as mutual funds are highly competitive.

A Fund by Any Other Name

Perhaps Shakespeare said it best, but he wasn't a financial advisor. In the world of funds, the name should give you an indication of the fund. But, it doesn't always. While it's a good assumption that the Scudder Fund called *Japan* invests in Japanese companies, what do the funds *Capital O*, *VoyagerII*, and *Nifty Fifty* tell you about the type of investments or category of the fund? Even with apparently more clear-cut names, funds aren't always what they seem. While you can't judge a book by its cover, you can judge a fund by its prospectus. Delve deeper than the name. *Didn't Shakespeare say that?*

THE PROSPECTUS AND THE ANNUAL (OR SEMIANNUAL) REPORT

Before reading either the prospectus or a report from the mutual fund company, you might want to have a checklist of areas to look for. This will help you gauge whether or not you are getting all the information you need from the document before you.

The Fund's Objective: _____

_____

_____

Are risks clearly explained? Y / N

What is the asset size of the fund? _____ million / billion

What is the minimum investment? _____

What is the breakdown of holdings? (i.e., 70% cap stocks, 20% bonds, 10% cash instruments. This may be broken down by caps, by domestic and international holdings, etc. It may also use ranges, such as 60% to 80% domestic stocks.)

_____

_____

What is the expense ratio? _____

Is this a no-load fund? Y / N   If not, what is the load? _____ What is the load adjusted return? _____

Is there a back-end load? Y / N   If so, does it explain when this is phased out? Y / N

Is the history of the fund clearly defined including previous year returns, 3 years, 5 years, and life of the fund? Y / N

What is the tax-adjusted return? _____

Is there information on the fund manager? Y / N

What is the beta or volatility rating of the fund? _____

Are the top 10 or 25 holdings listed? Y / N

If any of the above information is not available from the fund company, look at Morningstar, Value Line, or other ratings services for further information.

CHAPTER THIRTEEN

KEEPING TRACK
OF YOUR MUTUAL
FUNDS

Whether you are doing pre-investment research or following the fund you already own, it's important that you have a basic understanding of how to track a mutual fund. The first significant number is that by which the share price is calculated for mutual funds. This is called the net asset value, or NAV. Each day the NAV is calculated so you can see exactly how your fund is doing in comparison to when you purchased the shares. This is the per share price of the fund with fund expenses deducted.

Essentially the NAV is the market value of the securities less the expenses divided by the number of outstanding shares of the fund. In other words, if our fictitious "Richie's Mutual Fund" has assets of $10 million and expenses of 1.50%, then you would subtract $150,000 and have $9,850,000. If there were 1 million shares outstanding, then you would divide $9,850,000 by 1 million and have an NAV of 9.85. If the total at the end of the previous day's trading was 9.45, then you would have an unrealized paper gain of .35 on each share you own.

NAV is essentially like following the per share price of an individual stock. It is that which you go by to judge the overall return of the fund. In the case of a mutual fund, it is a way of measuring all the stocks in the portfolio.

It's important to know that distributions affect the NAV. When a mutual fund makes a distribution, the NAV will drop by the same amount. If your mutual fund has an NAV of $18 per share and a distribution of $3 is sent out, you will see the NAV drop to $15. You are not losing anything, however, since the $15 per share price and the $3 you receive per share is equal to the same $18 per share. If you had 1,000 shares at $18 per share, you now have 1,200 shares at $15.

You do, of course, need to pay taxes on the $3 per share dividend. This is why it's recommended that you do not buy shares of a mutual fund right before the distribution or you'll pay tax on that distribution; so why not get the distribution dates and buy the fund shortly afterward.

LOOKING AT RETURNS

When you are studying which mutual funds to buy, you are looking at 1-, 3-, 5-, and 10-year returns. Once you own a fund, you want much more current data such as year to date (YTD), month to date (MTD), weekly gain or loss, and daily gain or loss. And yes, the current NAV is also available! Online financial sites and Web servers such as Excite, Yahoo!, AOL, and others make it very easy to look up your stocks or funds under their financial areas. Generally, it's not necessary to follow a mutual fund on the same daily basis as you might follow a stock. Although both should be thought of as long-term investments, many stock investors like to buy and sell more frequently. This is not the general idea behind mutual funds.

Don't forget, you actually have potential for making money from a mutual fund in three ways. The movement of the NAV listed from day to day primarily represents your unrealized capital gains or losses, just as a stock price represents an unrealized gain or loss if you sell the shares. Once you sell your shares, your unrealized gains or losses become realized. You can also see dividend distributions from stocks (cash dividends), from bonds (interest payments), or capital gains distributions from your fund(s). Remember that the NAV will drop by the same amount as the amount paid out. You'll know from the distribution dates of your fund when this will happen, so you'll be aware that the NAV will drop and you won't panic.

The most important return to look at for the best measure of how your investment is doing is the total return. Total return includes:

1. Unrealized capital gains reflected in the change of the fund's NAV
2. Distributed investment income from the interest or dividend payments
3. Distributions from realized capital gains from securities the fund has sold

If you take the fund's NAV at the beginning of the month (you can use a year, 2 months, whatever time frame you want to look

Plenty of Paper

Perhaps it's not the most ecologically sound method, but it is important that a mutual fund provides you with all the information you'll need on paper, including:

- Fund profiles
- A prospectus for each fund in which you are interested in investing
- Your application for purchasing the fund
- Transaction statements/confirmations
- Statements of account activity (should you request one)
- Semiannual reports, including financial statements and securities held
- Annual reports, including financial statements and securities held

at) and subtract the NAV at the end of that month, then add the capital gains distributions and dividends distributed (dividends from stocks or bond interest), then divide the number by the NAV at the start of the month, you'll see how much you gained (or lost) on your total return. This is assuming that all distributions are reinvested in the fund.

For example, let's suppose you wanted to know your total return from the date you bought the fund, August 31, 1999, through August 31, 2000. Let's say the NAV on the first date was $26.00 and as of August 31, 2000, it was $30.00. Subtract the $30.00 – $26.00 and you have $4.00. Now suppose the income distribution was $0.80 per share and the capital gains distribution was $3.00 per share. You add on $0.80 and $3.00 to your $4.00 total and you have $7.80. Not too hard so far. The last thing is to take the $7.80 and divide it by the original NAV of $26.00.

$7.80 divided by $26.00 = .30 or a 30% total return.

Pretty good!

Now comes the not so good part. Keep in mind that while the fund expenses are factored into the NAV, sales loads or redemption fees are not. If you really want to burst your bubble, throw in taxes. All of these will take away from your total return. While taxes are only avoided in tax-free bond funds or deferred in a standard IRA or in retirement plans, it's important to adjust your return to factor in the load since the funds don't usually have the load adjusted return in their promotional materials.

When looking to buy funds, Morningstar and Value Line are two places to get detailed fund reports that will give you quarterly total returns for several years, as well as load-adjusted returns for 1-, 3-, 5-, and 10-years. You can also look at your statements and determine the same calculations using the actual numbers. If your 30% total unrealized return was a $6,000 profit and you had a 5% back-end load of $300, you would have a $5,700 realized profit after the transaction. Your tax would be 20% if you held the fund for more than a year and it was considered a long-term capital gains tax. Therefore, you would pay 20% of $5,700 or $1,140.

Morningstar and Value Line each offer a wealth of investing information about mutual funds, including detailed reports that you can order. Find out more about ordering Value Line information from *www.valueline.com* and about Morningstar at *www.morningstar.com* or *www.morningstar.net*.

When looking at mutual funds, if you see an NAV and a separate offer price, the offer price is the NAV plus the load per share. No-loads will show the same NAV and offer price since you're not paying any additional commission. However, watch for back-end loads and redemption fees. Keep in mind that a no-load saves you the most money in terms of transactions and loads take a percentage of your investment dollar. Anything that cuts into your returns on the back-end is cutting into your investment return dollar, which can be the worst scenario. Any time a fee is based on a percentage of your overall assets, that can ultimately be the highest payout.

FOLLOWING (AND FINDING) FUNDS ONLINE

Almost every fund family is well equipped online to help you follow your funds. Once you know your fund symbol—"XWYZ," for example—you can look it up at the fund's Web site. This is one of the reasons funds have grown in popularity. While stocks have been easy to follow ever since the advent of the ticker, funds were never quite as prominently displayed. Although they are thought of as a longer term investment (stocks should generally be a long-term investment too, but some people love wheeling and dealing), it's a good idea to check how they are doing periodically. You can also read up on news regarding the fund and see if there have been any significant changes made, such as in the fund's management.

There are numerous financial Web sites—too many to count. For your purposes, you want to get to know:

- The Web site of the fund family in which your fund sits.
- One or two good places to look up funds, follow the latest in fund news, and track your own funds.

The reason for narrowing your search to a couple of user friendly, comprehensive sites is to save yourself the trouble of looking for fund sites and searching through each site to find what you need.

What makes up a good financial site for mutual fund information? For one, an emphasis on mutual funds. Some of the sites we have mentioned don't emphasize just funds but do have major areas of fund concentration. Others, with funds being as popular as they are, have a great deal of well researched information on funds, that is *easy to access*. It's important to have information at your fingertips, and a good site should get you to your fund information in one or two clicks of the mouse. A good financial site also:

1. Is not pushing one product on you.
2. Is not overloaded with advertisements (including banner ads).
3. Provides clear explanations of the material on hand.
4. Is displayed in such a way (on screen) that makes it easy to navigate. Boxes within boxes within boxes can be difficult to deal with.
5. Is updated frequently, like throughout the day. Anything that doesn't feature the current (usually within 10 to 20 minutes) news and quotes does not cut it in the financial world.
6. Is not extremely opinionated. A point of view is one thing, but if the site insinuates that it's "the only point of view," it's not a good Web site.

It's a good idea to look at a few sites before you settle on your financial information favorites.

Morningstar and Value Line both provide the premier printable materials available for purchase. The Morningstar Web site is also extremely comprehensive, with a wide range of easily accessible (easy to navigate) unbiased information on stocks and funds. The Value Line Web site, also with plenty of information, does lean more heavily toward Value Line's own funds.

Research Actively / Follow Passively

When you are researching which fund or funds you want to purchase to make up your portfolio, you should examine and follow each fund of interest. You will need to evaluate which funds meet your needs (in terms of your goals and how you want to allocate your assets) and track the success of each fund. Unlike stocks where you might miss a sudden surge and curse yourself for not buying it yesterday, this is a long-term investment, so a few days spent waiting and watching generally won't make a great difference. Read the prospectus, look at the fees, and find the right fit just as you try on several pairs of shoes before buying a pair. Narrow down your field. If you are looking for dress shoes, or in this case a large-cap growth fund, look only at those in that category.

Once you have decided on a fund or on a few funds, you should start following passively, meaning you aren't about to go wheeling and dealing if the fund has a bad week or month or several months—or even a year! If you're buying funds for the long term (or any investments for that matter) you'll need to "sit on your hands" while looking at your PC so you aren't tempted to click sell if your returns are down. The market is volatile and on the short term, from day to day, you will see ups and downs constantly. The longer the time span, the less volatility you'll notice.

For example, our own fictitious "Richie Fund" might read as follows:

5/24/99	NAV:	32.00
5/26/99	NAV:	30.00
5/28/99	NAV:	33.00
5/30/99	NAV:	28.00
6/24/99	NAV:	34.00
5/24/00	NAV:	51.00
5/24/01	NAV:	56.00

You'll notice the initial volatility over the first 6 days that produced a return of −13%. At the end of one month the fund was up just 6%. After one year, however, the fund was up nearly 60%. The second year from 5/24/00 to 5/24/01, the fund didn't do as well, gaining just under 10%. The 2-year total was a return of 75%. The point is, if you based your decision on a week or even a month, you wouldn't have done very well. So don't let short-term volatility scare you. In fact, you may not even look at the fund's NAV more than once a week, or once every other week after the first few days when your investment still has that new fund smell.

Follow your funds without making drastic moves. You should continue to add to your investment. That is most easily done by dollar cost averaging, regular investing, through an automatic investment plan.

THE TOP FIVE

Along with *www.morningstar.com,* the other four best Web sites for mutual funds, whether you're researching new ones or following those that you already own, include:

www.bloomberg.com Very comprehensive Web site from the financial folks at Bloomberg News includes market news, plenty of charts and graphs detailing anything you need to know plus a Market Monitor section where you can sign up to track 10 funds, stocks, or indices with up-to-the-minute updates of their performance.

www.brill.com The Mutual Fund Interactive site is a Mecca for mutual fund information. This award-winning Web site has a fundlink section whereby you can find nearly any fund out there, a question and answer section, feature articles, fund manager profiles, a Funds 101 section for new fund investors, and a place to look up any fund and receive all information including performance, fees, expenses, portfolio manager information, top 10 holdings, and more.

www.cbsmarketwatch.com This CBS financial site has plenty of info on funds including profiles, a place where you can download a prospectus (only on a few funds), plus articles, lists of top funds, links to fund families, and a fund university.

www.mfea.com The Mutual Fund Investor's Center has a host of current feature articles on fund investing, plus all the tools and listings you'll ever need—even funds for $50 or less! You can look up funds based on key investment criteria and do the calculations on your investment goals for retirement or college planning. There are also model portfolios and plenty of other information.

There are plenty of other places to find funds, get info on your funds, and read general, up-to-date information about funds.

www.cnnfn.com CNN Financial News Network offers a site with an extensive amount of information about U.S. and global markets, including the latest financial and market news, "Consumer Strategies," "Deals and Debuts," and much more.

www.cyberinvest.com Cyber invest has links and information to cool investment sites with information on everything from tax planning to Internet fraud. Look for fund-related features. Some links are better than others.

www.investorama.com Invest-o-rama's site is a major directory to personal finance and investing sites linking to over 14,000 such sites. Pages are a bit overcrowded, but there is a wealth of information including fund listings.

www.maxfunds.com This new site is a place to find new and small uncharted mutual funds and compare them with the bigger players. There is a comparison of fund families plus stats, analysis, articles, and various member services. You can also download a prospectus from a number of funds.

www.quicken.com Well planned site with plenty of news and information. Click on investing and then go to mutual funds. There are constant updates plus stats, articles, and calculating tools. The site is very comprehensive, but what else would you expect from the people at Quicken?

www.quote.com From Lycos, Quote.com provides mutual fund info, including the top 25 listings and portfolios plus analysis, commentary, and, of course, quotes. Very current and user friendly.

READING THE NEWSPAPER

Yes, there are still millions of people worldwide, even those with PCs, who read the newspaper—actual newspapers where the print can rub off on your hands. The Internet has sealed off some people from the rest of the world, but newspapers continue to thrive with vast readerships. The financial pages are brimming with information and stories about the markets, the Dow, the S&P, and all sorts of investment wisdom, some worthwhile and some not worth the print. Along with the financial news of the day are stock, bond, and mutual fund listings. There are often stories about top-performing

Tangible Publications You Can Hold

Morningstar has detailed comprehensive reports on 1,700 mutual funds from top fund families. Funds are evaluated and rated, with style boxes and analyst reviews. There are updated reports twice a month. A 1-year subscription (U.S.) is $495 with a 3-month trial (with six updates) available for $55.

Morningstar
1-800-735-0700

Value Line introduced their mutual fund survey in 1993. They provide comprehensive reports on 1,500 mutual funds, including rankings and data. Two-week updates and a 12-page newsletter are also part of the package. A 1-year subscription (U.S.) is $345, and a 6-week trial costs $50.

Value Line
1-800-535-8760

funds and how they got to be the leaders in their categories. While you may not run out and buy shares in one of these hot performers, you might get ideas of what to look for in other funds. For example, a fund may have certain holdings that interest you, such as General Electric, Yahoo!, and Cisco, or you might read about how the fund manager keeps the expense ratio low, indicating that perhaps you can find a fund in the same category with a similar ratio. There is a lot to be picked up by reading about specific funds, especially when it's unbiased reporting in newspapers or magazines. Fund literature will obviously accentuate the positives.

The newspaper listings are fairly simple to read. The fund families are generally listed alphabetically with their funds listed below. Sometimes they are abbreviated, so learn the abbreviation when you first purchase the fund. The NAV is listed plus the offer price, which takes into account the load if there is one. The listings are as of the close of the previous day's market, unless you happen to have a newspaper that prints late enough in the day to include that day's closing market—but that's unusual. The "+" or "–" in the last column will show you how much the NAV has changed since the close of the previous day's market.

The different loads, A,B,C, and so on, will differentiate different share classes. Remember which ones you own. Also, if a fund has closed and started a clone or follow-up fund, you may be looking at "Spartan Fund II" rather than "Spartan I." In the case of mutual funds, often the sequel is as good as the original and follows the same objective.

Other symbols you may find include: "r," which stands for a fee charged when you redeem your shares, or "p," which means the fund has a 12b-1 fee. Many newspapers aren't this detailed. If you already own your shares, you should already know what fees need to be paid. If you are charting other funds for possible future consideration, you'll read the fund profiles and or prospectus, and learn about such fees before buying shares. Newspapers of choice for domestic and international fund buyers and followers include *USA Today,* the *Wall Street Journal,* and the *Financial Times.*

FOLLOWING YOUR FUNDS

List funds on top of page and update going down from the top with updated number of shares and NAV Mutual Funds Owned Worksheet. (*Note:* Update shares owned and amount invested to include reinvested dividends.)

Name of Fund _____	Name of Fund _____	Name of Fund _____
Fund Family _____	Fund Family _____	Fund Family _____
Fund Objective _____	Fund Objective _____	Fund Objective _____

Initial Purchase Date	Number of Shares	Net Asset Value	Initial Purchase Date	Number of Shares	Net Asset Value	Initial Purchase Date	Number of Shares	Net Asset Value
/ /	_____	_____	/ /	_____	_____	/ /	_____	_____

Date	No. of Shares	NAV	Date	No. of Shares	NAV	Date	No. of Shares	NAV
/ /	_____	_____	/ /	_____	_____	/ /	_____	_____
/ /	_____	_____	/ /	_____	_____	/ /	_____	_____
/ /	_____	_____	/ /	_____	_____	/ /	_____	_____
/ /	_____	_____	/ /	_____	_____	/ /	_____	_____
/ /	_____	_____	/ /	_____	_____	/ /	_____	_____
/ /	_____	_____	/ /	_____	_____	/ /	_____	_____
/ /	_____	_____	/ /	_____	_____	/ /	_____	_____
/ /	_____	_____	/ /	_____	_____	/ /	_____	_____
/ /	_____	_____	/ /	_____	_____	/ /	_____	_____
/ /	_____	_____	/ /	_____	_____	/ /	_____	_____
/ /	_____	_____	/ /	_____	_____	/ /	_____	_____

CHAPTER FOURTEEN

MUTUAL FUNDS AND TAXES

D on't you wish this chapter wasn't here? Imagine how many more billions of dollars would be invested in mutual funds if they were all tax-free! Unfortunately, you will be paying taxes on most mutual funds, and this section is designed to explain how funds are taxed and how you can best prepare for April 15th and select appropriate funds to minimize the tax bite.

TAKING THE FUN OUT OF FUNDS

One thing can be said for mutual fund marketing that truly defies the imagination. Fund families, brokerage houses, and clever advertising and marketing companies have, somehow, managed to promote the fun of funds (high returns) without factoring in the inevitable. Even the majority of fund magazines did not, for a long time, include the tax-adjusted returns. Perhaps the inflated economy and a vast majority of films with Hollywood happy endings created a positive mood whereby investors were turning a blind side to any negatives. The "don't bring me down," "don't burst my bubble," "don't rain on my parade" state of optimistic thinking has amazingly created a mindset where until the 1099s appeared in the mail, most fund investors did not even consider the tax bite of their funds, and fund advertising weren't about to bring up the point. What's interesting is that much more attention was paid to the difference in expense ratios between funds when the difference in returns after taxes was, and is, potentially much more significant. Expense ratios average around 1.20% to 1.25%, while taxes will take an average bite of 2.5% out of your returns. Once again, you can thank marketing for that little incongruity.

However, as of early 2000, the inevitable tax situation became a growing concern among investors, and the SEC stepped in and made disclosure of tax-adjusted rates of return a more common practice. Funds now have to provide this information.

TWO TYPES OF TAX BITES

The phrase "twice bitten" applies to mutual funds. Commonly, investors are under the misconception that they will only pay taxes on the shares of the fund that they sell. This is not the case, thus waking many investors up to an unwelcome tax surprise.

Mutual funds are set up so that you pay taxes in two ways. You will pay a tax should you sell your shares of the fund (any amount of shares), and you will also pay tax on the earnings in the fund, while you own it, through the sale of securities within the fund. This second tax (for mutual fund shareholders who have not sold the fund), is very important to understand, and it is why some people tend to shy away from mutual funds. A lot of turnover (transactions made within the fund) can run this amount up. Many funds have, of late, been showing high returns so that if you sell the fund, the bite taken out by taxes still leaves you with a better return than most other investments. However, a fund with high turnover, yielding 10% after taxes, fees, and, in some cases, commissions, could end up bringing in less than a 6% money market account. Therefore, very actively managed funds, such as growth funds, have to show higher returns to offset the tax bite and other costs. The tax you incur within the fund is the capital gains tax from the sale of stocks (or other securities) within the fund. Even though you have yet to realize a capital gain by selling the fund, you are realizing the tax on the gains made within the fund. Some fund managers are good at offsetting such gains with enough losses, which will minimize the taxes passed on to you.

Besides diversity and low expense ratios, the popularity of no-load index funds also includes less turnover, which leads to lower capital gains within the fund and lower taxes passed on to you. Such funds generally only make adjustments that are made by the index being mirrored, and those are not usually very many.

A CLOSER LOOK

A mutual fund will pass the earnings on to its shareholders, which keeps the fund from paying taxes on the profits made from its investments. Therefore, you will pay taxes on both capital gains distribution and income distributions. Whenever a fund sells a security for a profit there is a capital gain. As the fund sells shares for profits and losses, there will be an ongoing tally of capital gains

Tax Info on the Horizon?

As of early 2000, the Securities and Exchange Commission had proposed to Congress that mutual funds be required to report their after-tax returns. Congress agreed. It's amazing; it's taken this long and that the public hasn't demanded such returns. Nonetheless, Morningstar and some of the fund evaluation and rating services have been providing tax-adjusted returns for awhile.

Look carefully at tax-adjusted (and load-adjusted) returns for a better gauge of what a fund is really going to do for you.

Timing Is Everything (No, Not Market Timing!)

Example: You buy a no-load fund in January for $10,000 at an NAV of 12 and in 10 months it goes up 25% to 15. You now have $13,000. If you sell in November, you'll pay 28% of your short-term capital gain of $3,000 or $840 and end up with a gain of $2,160 (not taking into account the expense ratio for the purpose of simplicity).

Let's say you hold the same fund until January and sell it at an NAV of 15 or 25%. Now your $3,000 is taxed at a long-term capital gains tax rate of 20% or $600. You therefore end up with $2,400. This illustrates how holding onto a fund can help from a tax standpoint.

and capital losses. If the total capital gains are greater than the losses, the mutual fund will have what are called *net realized capital gains,* and you, as a shareholder, will pay taxes on these gains even though you still own the fund and have not yet made any money from selling your shares. This can also present a problem for fund owners as they have made no profits yet but need to dip into some pool of money to pay these taxes. Since interest and dividends are generally reinvested, this money is not available, unless you have an income-producing fund or are not reinvesting your dividends. Incidentally, if the fund shows net losses, this is not passed through to the shareholders but can be used by the fund to offset future capital gains. Therefore, a bad year from a buying and selling standpoint can work in your favor in the future.

The other tax for a mutual fund holder is on all income distribution, including interest and dividends paid out by the stocks or bonds in the fund. Whether you choose to reinvest these income distributions is up to you, but either way you will have to pay federal and state taxes (unless you're in a state with no state taxes). Tax-exempt bond funds can shield you from local, federal, or state taxes or even from all of the above. However, when you sell your shares you will still be taxed. You should also note, in regard to local and state bonds, that they are taxable to residents of other states.

There are several different ways to report the capital gains made from selling shares of a mutual fund. If you sell some shares, but not all, you need to determine which shares were sold. Your accountant will best advise you in each situation which method works best for you. Methods include *average cost*, which uses the average of all the shares you own and the *first in first out* method that says that the first shares you bought were the ones you sold. You can also *specifically identify shares* you wish to sell each time you sell shares of the fund, but this will mean contacting the fund and making sure you are selling specific shares. The fund company must verify which shares you are selling. This is cumbersome, more time consuming, and adds more paperwork. If you keep excellent records of your buying and selling activity and know which shares were bought at which price, with documentation, this more detailed method can be the most tax-efficient. There are reasons for and against each way of calculating the shares sold, based on your specific investment and tax situation.

There are actually two methods of using the average cost method: single and double category methods. Single category averaging is often used and is calculated as follows. As a regular investor your monthly $200 input to your mutual fund for 2 years (24 months) is $4,800. During that period, $300 of dividends were reinvested, making your "total basis" of money invested $5,100. You own 200 shares, making your total basis average $5,100 divided by 200 or $25.50. Let's suppose the fund is at an NAV of 33.33 and you redeem (or sell off) $1,000 from the fund, which results in selling off 30 shares. You multiply $25.50 x 30 and get $765. You therefore report a gain of $35. ($1,000 – $765 or $35.) Keep in mind that you are required to start by using first shares purchased in the averaging method, so you'll start with the oldest, long-term shares.

Once you elect to do an averaging method, you can't change your mind on that particular fund. You can, however, use different methods to calculate other mutual funds, even in the same fund family. You should include a note explaining that "a single category averaging method was used in determining gains or losses for Such & Such Mutual Fund." Remember that it's important to keep records not only of the purchasing and redeeming of the fund, but of your own calculations (or those of your tax advisor or anyone else helping you) to show the IRS (should you have to) how you came about the totals you reported.

Should you use a double category method, you should also include a note that that method has been used. One category is a short-term average for shares bought within a year, and the other is for the long-term shares held for more than a year. You need to simply divide the total cost of the long-term shares held by the total number of long-term shares and do the same for short-term shares. Generally, if you are only selling some shares, but not all, the fund company will charge the shares against your long term, oldest shares first, provided you have long-term shares. Remember

Hard to Avoid Capital Gains Taxes

Outside of a tax-deferred retirement plan, such as a traditional IRA, 401k, or 403b, it's hard not to have capital gains taxes. After all you are investing your capital with hopes of seeing some gains. Money market mutual will have you paying income taxes but not capital gains taxes. You're more likely to see higher capital gains taxes with a growth stock fund or growth and income fund and lower capital gains taxes with most (but not all) bond funds. That is also because you are likely to see lower returns with bond funds than growth stock funds. Even with bonds, however, if you are receiving steady income from interest payments, you are paying tax on that interest.

January Can Mean December

Some mutual funds will treat dividends you receive in January as though they were paid the previous year. It's not a trick or a miscalculation, it's allowed, and therefore you have to treat them accordingly as December dividends in the previous calendar year. Watch for this carefully.

• • •

Wait, It's Too Easy

If it's not complicated enough, there is other information a mutual fund can provide you with that should put you on the phone with your tax preparer. If the fund paid any exempt interest dividends, you'll need to know how much could be subject to alternative minimum tax, how much comes from various states, which could affect your state taxes, and how much is exempt from state income taxes.

that shares need to be held for more than one year to be long-term shares.

It is best to evaluate your own personal tax situation when selling shares of a mutual fund. Often, for simplicity's sake, people will use the first in first out method, but your tax advisor should be able to tell you if there are reasons you should use another method. Always weigh the tax and time benefits. If there are substantial savings, you will want to lean toward the most tax-efficient method. However, if 4 hours of additional paperwork and correspondence with the fund company will get you an additional $100 off your taxes, you need to determine if there is a better way in which you could be spending those hours more productively, at least $100 more productively in quality time.

COST BASIS

If you'd like to figure out for yourself how much you will need to report to the IRS, you will need to begin determining your gain or loss by first figuring out what is known as your *cost basis*. Your cost basis is the amount of money that you have invested in shares of the mutual fund. This includes any sales or redemption fees you paid when you bought your shares of the fund, as well as reinvested dividends.

To figure out your cost basis, you need to know the number of shares bought (and the dollar amount), on the date you bought the shares. You also need to know any fees or sales charges that you paid. Then you can select in which manner you want to calculate what you will pay. The first in first out method is commonly used, and, if you do not specify one of the other methods, the IRS will assume this is the method that you have selected.

HOW MUCH DO YOU ACTUALLY PAY?

If you sell your shares you will pay either short-term or long-term capital gains tax rates. Short-term gains (or losses) are securities held under 1 year. They are taxed at your own personal income tax rate. Long-term gains, held for more than 1 year, are taxed at

First in First out Versus Specific Shares Method

When determining how much you will be paying in taxes, two of the methods you can use are the first in first out and the specific shares methods. Although the specific shares method requires better recordkeeping on your part and is more time consuming, it can save you in taxes. Here's an example of how:

Let's suppose you bought 1,000 shares of a growth (stock) mutual fund at $15 per share in January 2000. Later, in April of 2000, you bought 1,000 shares at $20 per share. Then, lo and behold, in May of 2001, you see the fund's NAV is up to $40 per share, but it seems to be slowing down and you'd like to put some of your profits into a lower risk fund that will better preserve your newfound income. You sell off 1,000 of your 2,000 shares (we're assuming you didn't have shares being reinvested).

If you sell off your shares using the first in first out method, you will have purchased the 1,000 shares at $15 each, or paid $15,000. At $40,000, your capital gain will be $25,000 ($40,000 – $15,000) and a 20% long-term gain tax payment will be $5,000.

However, if you sell the second 1,000 shares you bought at $20 per share, or $20,000, at the current $40,000 that the shares are now worth, your tax bite for your long-term gain of $20,000 ($40,000 – $20,000) will be (at 20%) $4,000. Therefore, you could save $1,000 in taxes.

That Darn Tax Form

Okay, you need to report your dividends on your 1040. You have your 1099-Div, so now what do you do? If your total dividends are $400 or less (from all sources), take the total amount of ordinary dividends (box 1 on form 1099-Div) and enter the total on line 9 of your 1040. If the total will be more than $400 from all of your sources, then go to line 5 on schedule B, where you have several lines on which to list each source, or in this case each fund, and put the dollar amount next to the fund name on the right. Take your total from line 6 of schedule B and put it on line 9 of your 1040. Okay, let's review.

20%.) Long-term capital gains are 10% if you're in the lowest tax bracket. Therefore, how long you hold a fund, coupled with your personal income tax rate, are factors in your investing philosophy.

You might choose to hold a fund longer if you are in a higher personal income tax category. For example, if you pay 28% tax, you could hold onto the mutual fund into a second year to cut the tax amount down to 20%. Of course, if the fund is dropping and you sell it, this won't apply since you'll take a capital loss.

If you move from one fund to another, even within the same fund family, guess what! You will have to sell off one to buy the other, and, yes, that is taxable capital gains income too. Often people believe if they make a transfer from one fund to another within a fund family they won't have to pay taxes.

The fund will tell you the amount of long- and short-term gains it distributes. You will receive an IRS 1099-DIV form early in the year that will give you the information on what you need to report on your tax return. Even if you have the money reinvested, which is common, you will need to pay the tax on the earnings even though you haven't actually seen them. The long- or short-term holdings, in this case, are based on how long the fund has held the security and not on how long you've owned the fund. Should there be nontaxable bonds in the fund, you will also be told how much income was generated from these bonds. Form 1099-DIV reports the ordinary dividends you receive, including the taxable interest paid to you, the shareholder, and all short-term capital gains received by the fund that have been passed on to you. Total capital gains distributions will be listed so you can determine your long-term capital gains. Both nontaxable distributions (if there are any) and foreign taxes paid (if there are any) are also included.

If, however, you pay tax on $5,000 accrued in interest and dividends within the fund and you later sell the fund, you won't be taxed on that $5,000 again when you sell the fund. When funds make their distributions, they will take the money off of the NAV price. In other words, a fund selling at an NAV of $25 a share will, when they make their distributions, let you know that the taxable portion is on $5 per share. The NAV price then drops to $20. You're not really losing any money in regard to the NAV because you have the distribution of $5 per share plus you won more shares at the $20 per share rate. You then have to pay taxes on that $5 per share that you received.

You should get a schedule of when the fund makes distributions before buying into the fund. This way you won't buy in right before they make distributions and get hit with a tax bill right after buying the fund. On the other hand, you may want to buy into a fund right after the fund has made its distributions and the price is lower, plus you won't have to deal with taxes until the next distribution on the schedule.

If you sell the fund or transfer your investment to a different fund in the same family, it will show up on your 1099-B form, which will also arrive at some point in January with the previous year's transactions.

CHOOSING FUNDS: WHAT TO WATCH FOR TO BE TAX-EFFICIENT

While taxes are inevitable on stock funds and even most bond funds, you can keep an eye on certain factors that may influence your buying decisions. For example, what kind of approach does the fund manager take? For that matter, what type of fund are you talking about? A more aggressive growth fund will likely be doing more buying and selling (more turnover) than a fund designed for long-term growth and income. An index fund, by contrast, will have little turnover in regard to the stocks in the fund.

Turnover is defined as how much buying and selling goes on within the fund. If a fund, for example, has 200 stocks at the start of the year and all 200 are replaced by other stocks by the end of the year, that is a 100% turnover. While this is common among more aggressive funds, you may want to minimize the tax bite by finding stocks with turnover ratios in the 50% to 75% range. A turnover ratio from 75% to 80% is considered average among stock funds.

You may also have the benefit and the tax bite of dividends. Many large companies still pay stock dividends, although they are generally only a small percentage. If your stock fund has a lot of these companies, you may have a larger total in dividends and be paying more in taxes. If you are realizing long-term gains, however,

Tax-Efficient Funds

In the 1990s the number of tax-efficient funds rose from a handful to nearly 100. These are largely funds with buy and hold philosophies (low turnover). Funds can be tax-efficient by selling stocks that drop in price to balance out their gains. Look for these funds if you are in a high tax bracket or heading into one and are trying to minimize your taxes.

Taxable or Tax-Free, Figure out the Difference

Sometimes tax-free funds with lower returns can be better in the long run than their taxable counterparts. Here's a way to determine the difference between the taxable and tax-free funds:

Step 1: Subtract your federal income tax rate from 1.00

> For example, if your rate was 36%, you would put 1.00 − .36 = .64

Step 2: Divide the yield from the tax-free municipal bond fund that you are considering buying by your answer to step 1. If the yield is 5%, divide that by .64. You'll end up with 7.81%. Therefore a taxable bond fund will have to produce a yield of at least 7.81% to be as good as the 5% tax-free fund for your tax purposes. Actually, the yield can be slightly less than 7.81% to be equal because you may be paying state taxes in your "tax-free" fund. It can become more complicated, but you can add in state tax as well to do this equation. Many online financial services such as Quicken.com have online calculators that will help you do this type of equation.

If you are feeling lazy, here are a few of the comparable numbers based on federal tax payments:

To match a 4% tax-exempt yield, you'd need:

5.6% at a 28% personal income tax rate
5.8% at a 31% rate
6.3% at a 36% rate
6.6% at a 39.6% rate

At a 5% tax-exempt yield, you'd need:

6.9% at a 28% tax rate
7.3% at a 31% rate
7.8% at a 36% rate
8.3% at a 39.6% rate

At a 6% tax-exempt yield, you'd need:

8.3% at a 28% tax rate
8.7% at a 31% rate
9.4% at a 36% rate
9.9% at a 39.6% rate

Therefore, you can see that there is a significant difference as you fall into a higher tax bracket.

this won't affect your tax bracket; you'll simply pay 20% of what-ever additional income you make. Thus 20% of found money is still 80% in your pocket, and dividends are like found money since it's simply coming your way with no strings attached for being a shareholder.

Tax-managed mutual funds try to balance out capital gains and losses within the fund. A good fund manager can lighten your tax load if they do their job well. You need to stay focused on the long-term investment and these funds can pay off. Balanced funds are also an option with stocks and bonds.

If you are looking at a bond fund, look at the returns between tax-free municipals and other types of bonds. A higher yield in a taxable fund may not be a higher return after all. Municipal funds can save you on paying federal, state, or local taxes, depending on the fund. This can be advantageous when you compare the after-tax results of a taxable fund.

Also, if your funds are in a tax-deferred retirement account, like a 401k, you can avoid paying taxes on the mutual fund all together. This is one of the reasons mutual funds in retirement plans are so popular. If you are in such a plan, do not buy municipal tax exempt funds since there is no need for the tax break; you're already getting a tax break in the retirement plan.

TAX PLANNING: A BASIC REVIEW

1. Look for at any new changes in tax laws. It seems that every few years the IRS decides to change the rules slightly. The 20% rate for long-term capital gains (depending on your tax bracket) was established in the late 1990s. Keep abreast of the latest tax law reforms each year, especially any per-taining to capital gains and investments.

2. Keep in mind that you can minimize your tax bite by offset-ting your capital gains with capital losses. Not that you want to have a fund performing poorly, but you can take some solace in the situation by taking a capital loss. You're entitled to take a capital loss of up to $3,000 against your ordinary income, which might serve to lower the taxes due on your

Realize This!

Realized gains means seeing the actual money from an investment. The opposite are *unrealized* or *paper gains,* which means the numbers are still on paper or invested. For example, if you've invested $5,000 in a fund and it has gained 40%, you now have $7,000 invested in the fund. However, as long as you do not sell your shares, the $2,000 is a paper gain. You made it, but it's still in the fund, as opposed to in your pocket. If, however, you sell the shares and collect the $2,000, that is a realized gain, which you can be taxed on.

Within the fund there are also realized and unrealized gains. A stock within the fund can go from a share price of 25 to a share price of 35, gaining 40%, but if the fund manager holds onto the stock, it's still an unrealized gain. If the fund manager sells the shares for the $10 per share 40% profit, you will be taxed on that realized gain.

capital gains. You can carry excess capital losses into the future. *So, go out and buy a loser! Okay, maybe not.*

3. Remember, don't buy into a fund just before their annual distribution or you'll pay tax on that distribution, which is no way to get started and happily invested in a new fund.

4. Keep in mind that if it's a bond fund that you are seeking, unless you're looking at those high-risk, high-yield funds, consider weighing the returns carefully between taxable and nontaxable funds.

5. Select the method of paying taxes that best suits your financial situation. Averaging or first in first out is fine for most investors, but if you have purchased shares at significantly different prices and have a good sum of money in the fund, you might want to be more selective about which shares you sell. Keep in mind when selecting which shares to sell that you will only be taxed at 20% on long-term capital gains.

6. Consider tax-managed funds and balanced or asset allocation funds as better for tax efficiency, but only if the returns are good.

7. Look at turnover rate and tax-adjusted returns.

8. Buy funds with higher turnover and more potential taxes in your retirement fund and funds will not be as tax-burdensome outside the tax-deferred plan.

CHAPTER FIFTEEN

MUTUAL FUNDS AND RETIREMENT PLANS

THE LONG, LONG TERM

People are living longer today than ever before. They are not simply retiring from a job but moving onto new ventures and even new businesses. Retirement plans are tax-deferred places in which to let money compound in the long term. One of the many reasons for the popularity of mutual funds is the ever-growing popularity of retirement plans. While there has been an emphasis on saving up for retirement for many years, the new breed of investors are taking advantage of IRAs, Roth IRAs, Simplified Employee Pension Plans, and both 401k and 403b plans. IRAs can be purchased from banks or brokers while 401k's are corporate employee plans and 403B plans are for employees in the areas of education, charitable, or sometimes health organizations. There are also 457 plans for government workers. All of these have different specifications but are similar in that they are retirement plans.

Traditional IRAs can defer taxes until you start withdrawing the money at 59½ years of age, at which time you can set up a manner of withdrawal that best suits your tax bracket at that time. Roth IRAs do not allow you to deduct your annual contributions but allow you to withdraw money without paying tax. This can be a substantial amount at the point of retirement. Either way, IRAs are excellent ways to save money for retirement purposes. One of the reasons for the incredible surge of mutual funds assets has been the growth of retirement plans. There has been much greater interest in these plans in recent years, and people are far more knowledgeable about how they work. You can buy mutual funds in your retirement plan, often for a lower minimum purchase. Fund families offering a fund at a $5,000 minimum for investors outside of such a plan will have a $2,500 minimum within such a plan. They can do this because:

> They are receiving a greater number of investors through a company, thus boosting the asset pool.
> They are signing up long-term investors.

There's no reason in the world not to sign up if you do not need all of your income for your daily living expenses. In tax-deferred

401k plans, the company will generally match a certain percentage of the amount you put in, be it 10% or even (but rarely) 50%! You also save in taxes in two ways. First, the plan is tax deferred, meaning all the money that grows in the IRA or 401k within the plan is tax deferred. Second, the amount contributed comes off of your paycheck, and that portion of your salary is not taxed as it goes directly into the plan.

There are limited choices of mutual funds within such plans, but there is generally at least one major index fund like the Vanguard 500 or a favorite like the Fidelity Magellan Fund (which has finally closed to new investors as of the start of 2000). Nonetheless, look over the fund choices carefully and remember that you can spread your money out in the 401k, or in an IRA. You do not have to hold just one mutual fund. Funds will often have some restrictions, but many will also waive some of their fees. This can amount to significant savings over many years.

Companies with investment plans generally have a fund administrator who handles much of the paperwork and communication with the fund(s). You pay no fee to this administrator, as they are paid by the company. They may be able to make some suggestions, but remember they are usually not financial advisors.

APATHY

One of the problems with retirement plans is that people tend to forget that they can make changes in the funds in these plans. It is not uncommon for someone to select a fund or several funds from the list of choices in a 401k plan and let it ride forever. These are retirement accounts that cannot be closed without penalties until you are 59½ (with some exceptions), which does not mean you cannot make some adjustments *within the plan*. While a good long-term fund may perform well for 20 or 30 years, you can make a change when you feel it is not the best fund for your needs. Not that you want to go shifting investments often, but there are times when you may decide you've found a better investment, or you want to go more conservative or more aggressive with your fund choices.

It is also not uncommon for 401k investors to go with the flow and select the fund that everyone else is choosing. People get apathetic and don't read the literature about the funds. No one knows why this is, considering that a retirement account is generally a significant aspect of one's financial future. However, if you ask 60% to 75% of employees what they hold in their 401k plan, they'll say a mutual fund. When you ask them which one, they'll have to think about it and often say, "I'm not sure." Why not be proactive in this plan? It's your money.

Within an IRA or 401k, it is important to read about the funds, determine which are best for your needs, and even diversify. Furthermore, you should not be intimidated by the fund administrator at the office or anyone else. After all, you know your own goals, needs, and level of risk tolerance better than anyone else, and it's too bad if someone else needs to do some extra paperwork. You'd be surprised how many people do not make adjustments in their company plans because they simply do not want to bother the plan administrator.

You also need to ask about and find out about any services that are available though the plan, as well as all of the guidelines. There are limits as to how much you can put into an IRA ($2,000 for an individual and $4,000 for two separate accounts for a couple filing a joint tax return). You should also learn the differences between Roth and traditional IRAs, the principal one being that your annual contributions to a traditional IRA are tax deductible (but you pay taxes when you withdraw the money at 59½ and after), and the Roth IRA offers no tax deductions upon contributing but when you take the money out of the plan (also at 59½ and after) you will not have to pay taxes. There are other factors involved in setting up an IRA, including eligibility.

Benefits of a 401k

- They grow tax deferred.
- They allow you to select your investments from several fund choices and adjust your investments when you need to reposition your assets.
- They provide additional income, as the company will match a certain amount of your contribution. Therefore, if you invest $2,000 per year and the company is putting in 25%, your $2,000 investment is now $2,500 without even a day of returns. Keep in mind that companies will limit how much you can contribute. In other words, the IRS and the overall structure of any 401k plan puts a maximum contribution of $10,500 (as of the year 2000), however, a company might add their own annual limitations and say that you can contribute only up to 7% of your salary. If your salary is $60,000, you could contribute only $4,200 annually, or 7%. It's common for companies to set their own guidelines. They will still match a portion, so your $4,200, with them adding 25%, would bring your contribution up to $5,250.

To give you an idea of how much you save from taxes in a tax-deferred plan, if you put away $30 a week for 20 years at an 8% return, you'd save over $21,500. How much, if anything, is paid in local and state taxes can be different from state to state, and, yes, you do pay Social Security on your contributions.

A couple of other notes on 401k plans: you will usually have to be employed for a certain amount of time before you are eligible for the company's plan. This can be 3 or 6 months, again depending on company stipulations. Once you become vested and are eligible for the plan, you can begin contributing.

Also, if you lose your job or switch jobs, the money can be transferred to an IRA to keep it tax deferred, or transferred to another company plan. You can leave it in the existing plan for 13 months but can no longer contribute to it. If you are moving from one company to another or moving the money from the 401k into an IRA at the end of your employment, you need to have the money rolled over in a direct transfer from one account to another. If you end up with a check in your hands, you will likely have to pay major taxes. Even with the best of intentions to put the money into another retirement plan, you don't want to close a retirement plan to open a new one, but simply have the money transferred directly without any gap in between.

As for the fund or funds you are already invested in, when you transfer your retirement account you may be able to leave the money in the same funds if they are in the new plan as well. If not, you may have to select similar funds. It's a hassle, but often there are similar choices.

RETIREMENT STRATEGIES

Be conservative; look for investments that preserve your capital while generating income. This is the common course of action and the usual professional advice. It's not necessarily the only route to follow.

An argument gaining a great deal of support says that there is no reason to take strictly a conservative road during your retirement years. There is a much greater likelihood today of living another 20 or 30 years past your retirement. Therefore, you will want to see a greater growth rate in your investments—one that you can't get from very conservative funds or bonds. A portion of your portfolio in stock funds will generate higher returns that can always be sold, or become realized returns should you need income at any point. Remember that mutual funds are very liquid investments.

The key to investing at any age is to have enough money for living expenses and invest money beyond that which you need on a daily and weekly basis. Unless you tie up money in nonliquid assets, you can get your money out of such investments should you need it. Naturally, you want to preserve your capital as best you can. However, by diversifying and maintaining a portfolio that includes stock funds, you are stretching your investment dollar further and giving yourself capital appreciation as well as some income.

For many retirees, investments also provide a marvelous place to focus attention. While it may be more than a hobby—after all, money is involved—many retirees have more time than ever to do their investment research and homework and enjoy following their stocks and funds. For so many people over the age of 65, retired or working, investing is an interest that can be shared with friends and family and a great subject for conversation. For some it's a whole new avenue of added income. In fact, one gentleman who had never earned more than $40,000 during his many years of employment, retired and put a good portion of his accumulated savings, including money from his pension plan, into one of the hot Internet stocks. Within a couple of years he made nearly $1 million. He sold the stock and found another interest—traveling with his friends and family.

The bottom line is, investing is not just a way of reaching a goal, it's also a way of keeping active with the finances you've worked for so many years to accumulate. In the 1990s, for example, the safer bond funds produced 7% to 8% returns (at an average), while growth funds investing in growth stocks topped 14%. Those numbers are for any age investor. Many retirees have lower living expenses, which are covered by interest from savings in money market funds and other accounts. Allocating 60% to stock funds and 40% to bond funds and money market funds may provide all the income you need. And don't forget there are major companies that pay dividends, so stocks can provide income as well. So unless you feel more comfortable with income from bond funds for your day to day needs, swing a little more of that allocation into stocks; it's the new way of thinking in an age of living longer.

Variable Annuities

Variable annuities are retirement vehicles generally sold through insurance companies that provide fixed income for life while allowing you to invest in mutual funds. They offer the same deferred benefits as retirement plans plus insurance options. Unlike more common insurance policies that pay solely a beneficiary, annuities are designed to pay you ongoing income after you retire for the rest of your life and then pay your beneficiary. A joint annuity between a husband and wife will pay the remaining spouse income after the death of the annuity holder. The life insurance portion of the annuity essentially means that your beneficiaries will receive the amount accumulated in the annuity should you die during the accumulation phase. Such death benefits may be payable in one lump sum or in annual payments. There is generally a guarantee by the insurance company that if the investments have lost money the beneficiary will be paid the full amount that was invested.

You can purchase a variable annuity, not only directly from an insurance company, but also through many types of financial institutions, including banks and brokerage firms. A variable annuity is not a mutual fund unto itself, but works in a similar manner to other retirement accounts in that it allows you to select from a variety of investment options that include stock and bond mutual funds. These investments are called *subaccounts*. Similar to other retirement plans,

Why Funds?

Funds are preferable in retirement plans because they offer you maximum diversity and buying power, plus they are good long-term investments. It is also easier and more manageable for a plan manager to cover more bases with a fund than having you select 25 stock choices.

you will be taxed when you withdraw the money from your annuity. The amount taxed is based on a life expectancy table and on the amount invested and withdrawn in a set withdrawal schedule.

One aspect that differs from other retirement plans is that you pay a variety of fees, including administrative fees, to the insurance company plus subaccount fees for the person handling your investments. These are separate from the expense ratio or management fees that are already factored in the mutual funds. There is also an insurance charge to cover the mortality and expense risk and contract fees. These additional fees are a concern to investors looking at variable annuities. Mutual funds, because of bulk discounts and other agreements, may charge lower fees than if you were buying the fund on your own. However, despite this discount, the overall fees are higher for annuities. On the other hand, you are getting income for life plus insurance in a retirement plan.

Therefore, if you are not looking for income from the annuity and already have an insurance policy, you are better off investing in mutual funds on your own accord and saving on fees. An annuity is a viable retirement option for someone who wants to put away more than $2,000 per year (IRA maximum) into a retirement account and is not in a company offering a 401k. Often investors who are starting late in regard to saving for their retirement will buy an annuity contract and have a chance to catch up since they can put a higher amount of money into it.

If you are looking at buying an annuity, it is important to look at the investment options. Look at the insurance company and at the fund families offered. Some only offer their in-house investment vehicles. Most let you select from a well known fund from a fund family like Vanguard or Janus. Look at the track record of the investments, as you would if you were buying the mutual funds on your own. Too often people feel that because someone is in the position of account manager that they should make the selections. This person may very well help you in your selections, but, just like the 401k administrator in a corporation, they are not your financial advisors. It is best that you look at the selections and

Other Information on Annuities

While there are minimums for purchasing an annuity, which can be $2,500, $10,000, or more, there is no limit as to how much a person can put into an annuity while the money is in the accumulation phase. You should also look over fees and payout options very carefully. Once you reach retirement age, there are a number of ways you can receive a payout from a variable annuity.

You are getting insurance based on your investment, and the insurance is guaranteed not to be less than you have invested. In other words, an investment of $10,000 could drop to $7,500. But if the person who owns the annuity should die, the death benefit would be the $10,000. This will be more if the investments have gone up.

Generally, within an annuity, as within an IRA or company retirement plan, you can shift your allocations when necessary. Excessive transfers could result in additional fees in any of these areas.

For more information contact: Variable Annual Research & Data Service Large Reports (VARDS Reports) 1-770-998-5186. *www.navanet.org* for information from the National Association of Variable Annuities, also at 1-703-620-0674. Most of their information will be from ordering pamphlets. Also see *www.variableannuitiesonline.com* for more direct online information on annuities. They have information on types of annuities, explanations of annuities, a glossary of terms, top and bottom 25 returns in different categories (based on the funds they hold), and performance analysis.

Note that fixed annuities are entirely different; the insurance company does the investing for you in more conservative securities. They will offer you a rate, which will sometimes drop after the first year, so be forewarned. Variable annuities can see much higher returns, but the fees can cut into your returns in a big way. Look over the prospectus carefully.

decide for yourself. Keep in mind that if you do not see fund selections that you like, you can buy variable annuities from a vast number of other places. It is not easy to transfer from one company's variable annuity to another, so take your time and select carefully.

VARIABLE LIFE INSURANCE

There are more places today than ever where you can purchase a mutual fund. You can now buy variable life insurance, which is becoming a popular insurance favorite of the younger, investment-savvy set. This is a way of selecting investments, generally mutual funds, within your life insurance policy. Here you are paying a portion of the premium into the policy and a portion into your selected investments. This means that if the variable portion loses money, you will still get the full amount of insurance coverage you are paying for. By investing part of the premium, you are able to see your overall benefits grow much higher than in a traditional whole life portfolio. You can also borrow money from the account and set up a flexible premium payment schedule to fit your lifestyle.

As with annuities, you should look over your choice of investment options carefully. Other things to look for include:

- Flexibility to make adjustments within the account
- Flexibility to change the premium
- Flexibility to change the face value of the policy
- Any additional fees

Don't forget that life insurance policies will allow you to change the name of the beneficiary. **Don't forget this.** Sometimes, in the case of a divorce, people are busily building up their investment portfolio in their variable life insurance policy to leave to an ex-spouse whom they really no longer want to leave anything to, much less some great sum of money from an insurance policy.

Compare life insurance policies. Keep in mind that your mutual fund and the distributions are not taxed within your variable life insurance policy.

Also, some variable life insurance policies, usually by paying for a special rider, will insure your insurance, so to speak, by guaranteeing a death benefit amount even if the market drops. Some variable universal life insurance plans will also provide you with opportunities to withdraw money (under specifications) for special needs without penalties.

If you're buying life insurance, variable life is an option that lets you help your benefits grow by investing in a tax-deferred manner. Once again, look at fees, riders, and other areas of payment closely. And keep in mind that, even if you are investing in variable life insurance, this in no way impinges on your other mutual fund investments, including your retirement account. After all, you do want to take care of those you love after you are gone, but you also want to take care of them (and yourself) while you're still around.

Annuities: Governed by Whom?

State insurance departments and state laws as well as the SEC are all involved with licensing, registering, and overseeing annuities. Anyone selling annuities must be licensed.

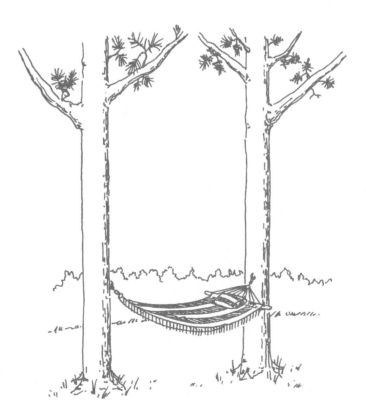

CHAPTER SIXTEEN

BUYING, HOLDING, AND SELLING YOUR MUTUAL FUND SHARES

Okay, you've carefully evaluated your financial situation, you've looked at your goals and both short- and long-term plans, you've done your research online, offline, in the newspapers, you've talked with friends, you've read the prospectus, you've familiarized yourself with the tax ramifications, and now you're ready to buy. Heck, you've even read this book! So, what comes next?

The next step is filling out the application form. This will usually be part of the package sent to you by the fund, either with the prospectus or separately. It may also be provided by your broker or possibly even your financial advisor. The early part of the form is fairly basic, name, address, and all of that easy stuff. You also need to indicate to which address you want the fund statements sent.

Next you'll need to check off the fund in which you are investing. (You must meet the minimum investment amount, which is usually listed.) Then you can decide whether to have dividends and capital gains reinvested or sent either to yourself or to your bank account by automatic deposit. Having the income reinvested will allow you to build up much greater long-term returns through compounding. However, if you want the dividends for income purposes, you may choose to have it forwarded into your money market account or bank account. You will also need to indicate whether the mutual fund investment is part of an IRA or other retirement account.

Then comes the slightly trickier part: signature(s) and ownership of the account. You must decide whether anyone else will own these shares along with you. You'll have some choices to consider in this area. You can have sole ownership, meaning you make all the decisions and pay all the taxes. You can select joint ownership, which can be in the form of joint tenancy with rights of survivorship. This means that any two people (related or not) can own the fund jointly and if one should die the ownership goes to the other person. There can be problems, however, when checks are sent out, as both parties generally need to sign them. Therefore, it may not be wise to make such a fund purchase with someone who is not easily accessible. Also, keep in mind you're in this together so that both of you will be in on the decision-making process unless you work something out in advance whereby one of you takes control of the fund responsibilities.

If you choose to own the fund under what is called "tenants in common," you are also sharing the fund, but unlike joint tenancy, you can own different amounts of shares. This frees up the ownership responsibilities so that either person may sell his or her shares. Married couples may also have joint ownership in other manners in which they must act as one owner. Accounts can also be community property in several states.

The signature(s) and ownership of the fund are important for tax purposes and for making allocation adjustments. Therefore, it may be worth talking to your tax advisor/accountant about whose name to put on the application/ownership form.

You can also open accounts under your children's names thanks to what is called the Uniform Gift to Minors Act or the Uniform Transfer to Minors Act. This can be beneficial because "kiddy taxes" (for 14 and under) are less than taxes assessed to adults. You have to follow the instructions and look at the effects of the different acts. Also keep in mind that when applying for federal assistance for college, the child's own assets are factored in heavily, which can work against them. Talk to your tax specialist about what is the best plan of action for your own individual circumstance. State tax changes in laws regarding taxes and minors, along with your own financial situation all need to be factored into the equation. Sometimes it's best saving money for your child under your own name, and other times it's advantageous to have money in their names.

There is also a place on most application forms where you can specify whether you want to link your fund to your bank account or any other such account. You can have money automatically deposited into your fund every week or every month if you sign up for an automatic investing program.

Some fund families will ask for other information. Some will offer you a lower commission if you have x number of dollars invested in other funds within that fund family. In other cases, if you intend to make a major lump sum investment, you may be eligible for a lower sales charge in a load fund. Some funds, primarily money market funds, come with check writing privileges that you can also sign up for.

Margin Accounts

Margin accounts are basically accounts whereby you are borrowing from the broker to invest. It's almost like having a credit card for buying funds. And, although you will pay back the loan with interest, most funds give you some time to pay back. If you have a fund at an NAV of 10 that is a "can't lose" proposition and you only have $10,000 invested, you can borrow another $5,000 so instead of having 1,000 shares, you'll have 1,500 shares. The problem is that if the fund loses money, you are losing both on the investment and by paying back your loan with interest on a bad investment. Needless to say, you can make or lose money a lot faster by investing using margin accounts. This is high-risk investing and should only be done if you know you have assets elsewhere to cover a potential loss.

When you sign up to open a brokerage account with a firm, you will be asked what type of fund you wish to open up. Besides the question of opening a single or joint account, you can open up a cash account, margin account, or discretionary account. Most common are the basic cash accounts. This way you will send a check when you open an account and have cash on hand from which to make your transactions. Whether you're dealing with an online broker like E*TRADE or a multipurpose full service brokerage company like Merrill Lynch, you will generally want to have the money easily on hand for transactions. This is generally where you can open up a money market account to handle the cash that funnels to and from other investments or use the account to move some of your assets into during a prolonged bear market. You can also move money into your money market when you need to send out checks.

You can also open a margin account, where you are essentially borrowing money to invest (and paying interest on the loan). This is extremely risky.

BUYING

Unlike a stock, where you can buy shares at $50 when the market opens and sell them at $55 a share when the market closes, your mutual fund will have one share price based on the NAV calculated from the close of the market each day. When you place an order, you will get the closing price for that day. If you then go online and check your price at noon the following day, don't be surprised if it's exactly the same. The new price won't appear until the market closes and the NAV is calculated. This calculation of the NAV (net asset value) for the fund is called forward pricing. A good time to check out your day to day fund activity is in the evening (all daily NAVs are due into the National Association of Securities Dealers by 5:30 P.M. Eastern Standard Time) when you're done with the business day and can get a few minutes on the PC between your teenagers chatting on the Internet and your younger children doing homework and playing computer games. Actually, if you're living on the

West Coast, you can get the NAV during the afternoon, past 2:30 P.M. Long-term investing, which is generally the category in which mutual funds fall, does not require such close day to day scrutiny. Spiders and diamonds are examples of new variations on the index fund theme that allow for day trading, meaning you can buy and sell them at any time since they appear on the stock listings (see Selecting Mutual Funds section).

When you buy your shares of a mutual fund, you are buying them at the fund's public offering price or asking price. This is the NAV plus the front-end load or commission charged. The public offering price or asking price will therefore be higher than the NAV. In a no-load fund, since there is no front-end load or commission, the public offering price and the NAV will be the same. Therefore, if you see two mutual funds with the same NAV of 50.00, and one is a no-load with a $50.00 asking price and the other has a load and an asking price of $52.50, you will get more shares for the same $5,000 investment with the no-load, since part of your money in the second fund is going to the load. If you bought 100 shares for $5,000, you would need $5,250 to get the same 100 shares in the load fund because of the higher asking price.

It's also important that when you have filled out the application, sent in the check, opened the account, and placed your order for a specific fund, that you follow up your hard work. Online trading will result in a confirmation of the opening of your account, sent to you by mail as well as e-mail. You will then receive e-mail confirmations, in most cases, from your online broker that your transaction has taken place. You should print out this information and periodic copies of your online portfolio. Funds bought via 800 numbers or any other manner send a statement that will include each transaction. No matter which manner you use to buy funds, you will always have a statement to look at to confirm the purchase. Look it over carefully and make sure that you:

- Bought the correct fund
- Paid the correct amount
- Received the number of shares you anticipated at the per share price after the load if there is one

Online Accounts and Patience

It's rather easy to go onto E*TRADE or Ameritrade to open an account. However, you can't jump right in and start trading until you have money in that account. Therefore, you'll have to be patient and wait until they have your funds. Once you open the account and the money is there, all else moves very quickly. Online accounts will show you how much is initially in your account, and once you start trading they'll give you the up to date balance in your account at any given time. Usually, it's a matter of a few business days to get your account started. Once you are notified that your account is set up (the money is in a cash account), you will be able to make trades and the commissions will be automatically factored into your ongoing account balance.

- Are not paying any fees that you did not anticipate or did not know about
- Have no additional transactions listed that you did not know about or authorize

It is always good practice to sit down with a statement and look it over carefully, just as you should look over your check before paying at a restaurant. You'd be surprised how many errors are made, despite modern computerized technology. Remember, despite the overused phrase "But the computer says," people are at the root of computers and incorrect information entered into the computer results in incorrect transactions coming out. The old phrase "Garbage in, garbage out" is still accurate.

BUYING ADDITIONAL SHARES

Once you have set up your account and are the proud owner of a mutual fund, you can either set up an automatic investment plan (described on p. 235) or buy more shares when your heart desires. You usually have the option of buying additional fund shares via telephone, online, or by wire.

When you buy additional share funds by mail, you will need to send a check specifying the fund in which you wish to purchase more shares. The shares will be bought at the price of the fund on the day the check is received. This is also why the phone method is far more popular. In fact, you should always establish a relationship by phone with the broker, including discount or deep-discount brokers. The latter will have less chance to discuss the transaction since they are buying and selling in a hurry, but this is how they best know what you want to do and when you want to do it. A full service broker who knows you will make the transaction and you can send a check within 3 business days. In general, with discount brokers, if you are going to make phone orders, you'll need to have money available in a cash or money market account or you'll have to wait until the broker gets your check. A broker or brokerage firm will generally have ways of verifying that you are who you say you are. After all, they can be held liable if someone

You Shouldn't Have to Ask

What happens when you send in money to invest in a fund that closes its doors to new investors? The money gets returned to you, the investor, right? Well, not always. One prominent fund group got a great deal of flack for taking the investors' money and putting it into money market funds, claiming that at least the investors were getting something back on their investment until the fund reopened or they chose a different one. Critics voiced their complaint loudly and explained that investors did not ask for a money market fund, but in fact asked for a specific type of mutual fund. If that fund decided they needed to close their doors to new investors, all of the money should have been returned to the investors so that they could decide what to do with their money.

What all of this brings up is a point that seemed fairly clear before this story but no longer is obvious. When you send in your money for a fund, you should ask, "What happens to the money if the fund closes before my money is invested?" The answer should be, "We'll give you the option of another fund or returning the money to you." The answer should not be, "We'll think for you and put the money in another fund that we think you'd like." Wrong answer.

Make sure you know where all the money you have at a brokerage house, online or otherwise, is at any given time. If you have assets that are not invested in a fund, are they in your money market account? Are they in a separate cash account? Are they lost somewhere in the system? It happens. One investor found that his extra money just happened to purchase a CD that he knew nothing about.

calls with fraudulent instructions, claiming to be you and sells your shares. It's been done! You can always wire them the money.

Companies will state in their literature that they will only carry out phone transactions that they believe to be genuine and accurate. They may ask for written confirmations to be faxed and check the signature against a signature card as is done at a bank. They also often tape phone conversations, which sounds intrusive at first, but is another way of having backup material to prove that you did indeed ask that a certain transaction be made or not.

The Internet works in a similar manner to the phone method. Passwords can be used to verify information, and your transactions are secured. It is easier on the Internet for the broker to verify who is making the transaction since you have pass-words, online I.D.s, and account numbers that you can enter.

Keep the following points in mind

- You need to specify dollar amounts, as opposed to share amounts, with most mutual funds.
- The time that the transaction actually takes place depends on the broker and the fund. Some brokers will let you make the transaction over the phone; others will not make the transaction until the check is received. The Internet, or a phone call, once you have funds already available in a money market or cash account, is generally the fastest method.
- The transaction can be rejected by the fund. This will only occur if there is either a problem with your account (or your check) or if the fund is closed to new investors.
- You should read the report of your transaction carefully and make sure everything is correct. You'll also be able to double check the number of shares that your $500, $1,000, or whatever amount you invested has actually purchased.

You should also keep your own records of all additional fund shares purchased. This will prove particularly important when it comes to doing your taxes so that you will know how many shares were purchased at which price.

AUTOMATIC REINVESTMENT

As mentioned earlier in the section about filling out the application, you can elect to have dividends and capital gains reinvested. This is a common choice since reinvestment is the way in which you can build up your savings in a much faster manner. Each capital gain or dividend reinvested means more shares owned by you. Most funds allow you to reinvest without any additional fees or loads for the privilege of building up your assets in this manner.

This is different from an automatic investment plan whereby you add additional money not generated by the fund to your mutual fund investment.

DOLLAR COST AVERAGING

Dollar cost averaging is a system whereby you invest the same amount into the fund (or into any investment) at regular intervals. Once you have bought shares in your initial investment you can then decide to put a certain dollar amount into the fund at a steady rate that fits your budget. You'd be surprised at how easy it is to put away an extra $100 or $200 a month. Perhaps it means one more meal at home and not in a restaurant or it means you wash and hang onto last year's winter jacket rather than buying a new one. It's usually a matter of small sacrifices to invest in your future—ones that you'll barely notice. Often there's money already sitting in an account you've practically forgotten about that's gaining a minimal rate of interest just above inflation. Even a steady income-producing, safe account such as a money market fund can provide you with interest income to put toward a long-term fund investment. An $8,000 safe and secure money market account producing a 5% interest will give you $1,200, which is $100 a month to put toward a stock mutual fund with a higher rate of return. Naturally, you have to decide whether you want to invest regularly.

Dollar cost averaging means that your money is going into the fund at a set date monthly or weekly even and you are investing at both the high points and the low points. Therefore, the share price or NAV you invest at averages out. Theoretically, you are investing equally when the stock or fund is up as when it's down. Naturally

Could Have and Should Have

All investors, even those who have had the good fortune to have selected the right mutual funds, find something to fret over. "I could have invested more in the fund or should have sold earlier" are the most commonly uttered phrases of those who like to kick themselves all the way to the bank. If this is you, always remind yourself that second guessing in the world of investments is an exercise in futility. When it comes to investing, "could have" and "should have" are time-wasting phrases. Just as past returns are not indicative of future results, past mistakes are also not indicative of the future; we learn and do things differently the next time. And, you know what? That still doesn't mean it will work out.

you hope the stock or fund will keep going up, but either way you continue to put in the same amount of money with the theory that despite the ups and downs, you are headed for a long-term positive gain. You are continually purchasing more shares—some at a higher price, meaning your $100 buys fewer shares, and some at a lower price, meaning your $100 buys more shares—depending on the NAV. The dollar cost averages out. *A lower share price means more buying power and less unrealized return on your current investment principal. A higher share price means less purchasing power and higher unrealized gains on your current investment principal.*

For example: You are putting $300 a month into your mutual fund using dollar cost averaging.

In January the NAV is 15, so you have purchased 20 shares.
In February the NAV jumped to 25, so you have purchased 12 shares.
In March the NAV is 15 again, so you have purchased 20 shares.
In April the NAV is 20, so you have purchased 15 shares.

In this example, at the 20 NAV, your $1,200 4-month investment gains 11.7% or $1,340. The 40 shares purchased at the 15 NAV are up $5 per share (to 20) and are worth an additional $200, while the 12 shares purchased at the NAV of 25 are worth –$60, a loss of $5 per share. The final 15 shares you just purchased at an NAV of 20 obviously haven't changed in value as the NAV is still at 20. Therefore, you are +$200 and –$60 for a gain of $140.

While you are buying at higher and lower costs, naturally you hope to buy more shares at the lower price as in the example, so that as the fund goes up you will have more shares benefiting from a greater increase in net asset value.

VALUE AVERAGING

Like dollar cost averaging, *value averaging* is a method whereby you invest regularly, only you do not invest the same amount consistently. Like value investing, you invest more money when the share price is low and is expected to rise and less money when the price is higher. You hope your fund will continue to rise, but there will almost always be peaks and valleys as it does. You are taking advantage of the valleys, using them as an opportunity to pick up additional shares. It's different than timing the market as you are not guessing when it's going to move, but following an ongoing pattern whereby you act accordingly when the fund makes a drop. From a psychological point of view, this can be a difficult investment plan to follow since it's hard to watch the fund drop and then decide to put in more money. However, as it climbs over the long term, you will (hopefully) see that the valleys over time are just bumps in the road to your overall goal—ones you can use to your advantage.

AUTOMATIC INVESTMENT PLANS

As mentioned earlier, you can sign up for automatic reinvestment of your dividends or interest. There is some logic behind this plan of action. Since it's psychologically not always easy to buy when the NAV drops and you're wondering why you're putting more into what is (at present) a sinking ship, you can do what millions of investors do and have automatic investment plans set up whereby the money goes from your bank account (or money market account) directly into the mutual fund or funds of choice at the regular intervals as you have stipulated. You generally have various options although monthly investment is most common. You will set up the date each month that you want to invest and the dollar amount (usually there is a minimum of at least $50, sometimes more). This will save you the trouble of remembering a schedule of when to write a check and send it to the fund. After a while, you'll never notice the difference. It's like the process many people use who have part of their paychecks automatically invested into their 401k plans and after a while never really miss it.

MARKET TIMING

Market timing, the idea of trying to strike when the market is about to go up and sell right before it drops, is considered by anyone but

Final and Other Transaction Statements

Even though you've sold off your shares and are no longer an investor in the fund, you should receive a transaction statement about your final transaction. If you don't get such paperwork, or any expected paperwork for that matter, contact the fund family. It's required that funds send you statements on all transactions.

most well versed investors (and even they blow it from time to time) to be a dangerous game, particularly with the incredible volatility of the market over the past year. Many people have tried it and done well for a brief period of time before blowing it all. While this may be an approach to stock investing, it is rarely used with mutual funds, which cannot be bought and sold for various prices throughout the trading day (stocks can be sold at different prices as the day commences). Funds are also generally long-term investments. In fact, most fund families put limitations and fees on excessive trading to limit such activity.

The market is too unpredictable to time effectively for 99% of investors, which is why, if you watch FNN and read the *Wall Street Journal, Barons*, and *Kipplingers* and follow the experts you'll notice that the one thing they agree on is that they do not agree on where the market is headed. It's not that one source or expert is more reliable than another, but that the success of an investment deals in the future and unless someone has a crystal ball, no one can be sure of what is to come. Breaking news, a change in a foreign market, a slight change in the rate of inflation, and certainly a change or even a hint of a change (if Alan Greenspan raises an eyebrow) can send the market plummeting or skyrocketing. Based on the past, however, long-term investing has always fared well, historically speaking. Although the many facts that support this do not ensure future success, they do point in a positive direction for long-term, buy and hold investors. Short-term investing, however, which is where market timing falls, historically points to good results one day, bad the next, good the next three days, bad the next two days, and so on. If you can make that scenario work for you, good luck. It's basically gambling.

LUMP SUM INVESTING

If you have $15,000 to put into a fund, why not make a lump sum investment? A sudden windfall from an inheritance, a bonus, selling an antique, a really really profitable garage sale, or perhaps hitting the jackpot on a game show can provide you with the

necessary money to jump right into the market with both feet and your eyes wide open.

While this is a way to get your portfolio off to a running start, most investors, even if they do land a lump sum of money, are not game to make a big jump into the market—any market. The amount that constitutes a lump sum payment is of course relative to the person investing. A multimillionaire does not consider $15,000 a major lump sum, but a daily investment. On the other hand, someone who knows that he or she can only invest $15,000 total can either put it all right in or invest it gradually, over time. If you do not have that kind of money on hand after paying all necessary expenses, then the decision is made for you.

People tend to jump into lump sum investing by putting *x* amount in one fund. While you have to start somewhere, you do not have to put it all in one place, or even one market. A lump sum of $15,000 may be best divided up among three funds to give you diversity and more efficiently allocate your assets across markets. This way if one market has a downturn, the other investments are not (or less) affected. One of those funds is often a money market fund for safekeeping (or a bank account, CD, or IRA).

Often people who come into a lump sum of money do their own sort of asset allocation that doesn't always involve stocks or mutual funds. Perhaps a few thousand dollars are going to build a backyard deck, which is a different kind of investment, in the value of your home. People may wish to take a much needed vacation, which is a quality of life investment.

The other way to go is to put the majority of your lump sum in a cash investment and slowly, but steadily, move it into funds and (if you're ready) stocks. This is essentially dollar cost averaging starting with a lump sum.

However you land a lump sum of money, you should consider:

- How to allocate your assets.
- Which investments are best for you.
- At what rate you want to put the money into your investments; this needs to be comfortable for you.

Good Times and Bad Times to Sell

It's a good time to sell if you have an aggressive fund that has outpaced its competitors and the category average by a significant amount. Don't get greedy. It's also a good time to sell if you have a sector fund and it appears that the sector has run its course. Get out before the roller coaster begins its rapid downward decent. It's a bad time to sell if you own a sector fund in a growing field or have to pay a back-end load and haven't had the fund long enough to see how well it might perform. It's also a bad time to sell if the market is showing typical volatility and you are following other investors who are in a panic.

FROM BUYER TO SHAREHOLDER

Once you have officially purchased your shares of a mutual fund and are in the daily or weekly routine of checking the NAV on the Internet or in the newspapers, you can also expect some privileges or services that come with being part of a fund family. Since competition for your investment dollar is fierce, as exemplified by 11,000+ mutual funds, most fund companies have put increased emphasis on customer service. If they haven't, they stand to lose your account. But along with quality of service, you will find other amenities to make your life easier as a fund holder. Many funds are trying to provide more simplified records and easier to read literature. There are fund profiles available, often on the Internet and fund news so you don't always have to wait for the semiannual report to know what's going on with your fund. While much of the information on the Internet is available to everyone, shareholders often have access to more detailed information and the ability to ask questions of fund representatives via the Internet. As a shareholder you will have access to and will receive all pertinent information about the fund in fund reports.

There are other perks and privileges offered in different funds. Remember that they are vying for more business so it's a good market in which to be a buyer. If there's something you're looking for, ask about it. Fund families are adding new features and services every day. As evidence, all you have to do is look at the fund family Web sites. What was once a place to simply promote a fund family is now an information center loaded with listings, statistics, and market news.

SELLING YOUR SHARES

"Show me the money!" That aging cliché may still hold the battle cry for selling shares of your mutual fund. It may be time for you to take those unrealized paper gains and make them realized gains to pay for your new house, your son's or daughter's college tuition, or your 9-month retirement trip around the world.

There are actually several good reasons to sell off, or redeem, your shares of a mutual fund. First, you may see your goals approaching in the near future and want to move your assets into a lower risk investment—perhaps into another mutual fund or into a money market fund. You may also have actually reached your goals. You might have a pressing need for the income or may simply be moving your assets out of a troubled market while you're still ahead. These are some good reasons to redeem your shares. Shares, by the way, are bought back by the fund company; you do not sell to another buyer as you would with a bond or a closed-end fund. On the other hand, you may be getting out because the fund "tanked," "stunk," "bombed," "sank," or any other way you wish to express the notion that it lost money or gained less than the rate of inflation. You should give your fund a fair amount of time before giving up.

Selling shares does not mean you need to sell off all of your shares. You can sell some but not all if you so choose. You need to contact the seller, which means calling the 800 no-load number or the broker, or brokerage house and letting them know you want to sell. Online trading means clicking on selling shares.

Redeeming your shares will result in one potential positive and two negatives. On the positive side (hopefully) the net asset value (NAV) will be significantly higher than that which you paid for the bulk of your shares and (with the help of reinvesting and that lovely word "compounding") you will see a substantial capital gain from selling the fund. On the negative side, you'll need to do a bit of paperwork to close the account, but, more significantly, you'll need to pay taxes on your substantial capital gains. There are several ways to calculate the taxes, as explained in Chapter 14.

Another negative that you may have to deal with is a back-end load, which is usually on a sliding scale that decreases the longer you own the fund shares. If you bought the fund for a long-term investment and held it more than 5 or 6 years, a back-end load will have disappeared. Otherwise, it will drop annually from generally around 5% the first years to 4%, then 3%, and so on as the years increase that you've held the fund. Shares that have been purchased through a reinvestment plan can be sold first (if you're only selling some of your shares) without the back-end load being applicable to those shares. While taxes and back-end loads can cut into your profits, the hope is that you have still been successful in reaching your initial goal.

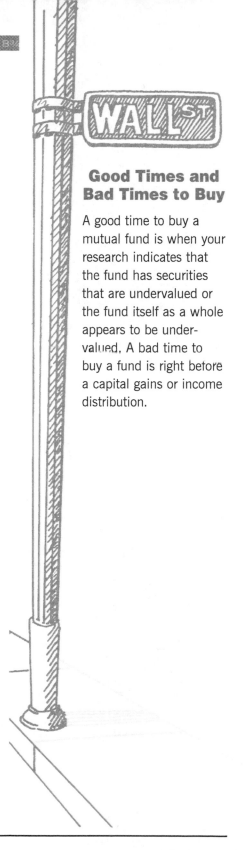

Good Times and Bad Times to Buy

A good time to buy a mutual fund is when your research indicates that the fund has securities that are undervalued or the fund itself as a whole appears to be under-valued. A bad time to buy a fund is right before a capital gains or income distribution.

If your intention is to reallocate your investment dollars into a different, perhaps lower risk fund, then you are often best staying in the same fund family to cut down on paperwork and fees. Often a fund family will not charge you a commission for "exchanging" or "transferring" from one fund to another similar one (in terms of type of load). There may be a lesser but applicable "exchange" or "transfer" fee that is still lower than if you went out and bought the fund elsewhere. The fund families want you to exchange and stay within their happy family. You may also be charged a redemption fee. This is not common, but it is a fee that is not a commission but money that goes back into the fund's asset. In essence, the fund is simply saying if you're redeeming your shares, you'll need to leave a small percentage behind. Try to avoid funds with such redemption fees. They are only taking money from your returns.

Keep in mind that an exchange or transfer is considered by the government to be selling one fund and buying another. Except in the case of tax-deferred plans, you will have to pay capital gains taxes in most cases when switching from one fund to another, unless you do not have gains.

Usually such transfers, exchanges, or laterals (if you're into football) from fund to fund are ways of reallocating your assets to coincide with either your goals or a changing market that has you looking for a safe haven. It is ill advised, and in some cases, not allowed by the fund family to do excessive shuffling between funds. Not only is this cumbersome from a paperwork standpoint, but it's tax ineffective in most cases.

When selling your shares, make sure you get a copy of the transaction and review it carefully. You want to make sure the right amount of shares were sold and that you received the price per share that you were expecting. If you specified which shares were to be sold, and the fund confirmed your request, you want to make sure that the fund sold those shares. You want to make sure you were not charged any fees that you did not know about.

Similar to buying shares, you can sell shares by letter, phone, Internet, or by wire. You will usually have to have authorized redemption privileges to sell shares by telephone. Not unlike buying shares, your fund company will need to take precautions to make sure you are who you say you are. This will mean positively identifying you as

the customer, taping conversations, or providing written confirmation of telephone redemptions. User passwords and ID will be necessary for online redemptions.

Try not to get frustrated following these procedures when redeeming shares. Fund companies are looking out for your best interests. Once a fund has all the information they require for proper validation, you should receive a check promptly, as they are mailed out within 1 business day after your redemption. This is about as liquid as an investment can get.

Your redemption amount will follow the policies of the fund. If the fund lets you sell your shares online, you will get the NAV at the end of the day you are selling. In another fund, however, you may not get the redemptions until the day all information is received by the fund, which could be after the closing of the market for the following day. Read the fund information, or ask customer service how this policy works.

SYSTEMATIC WITHDRAWALS

You can elect, should you desire, to withdraw your money from a fund in a steady, ongoing (systematic) manner. Sometimes people will elect to do this as a goal, such as tuition payments, is approaching. This is also a method often used by retirees. The money can either be transferred into a money market account, wired automatically to your bank account, or show up in the form of a check. Whichever way you take the money, you will be taxed on it as a capital gain. It is more dependent on what you are using the money for. If the money is earmarked for college tuition, you will more likely want to have it going into a bank or money market account where you have check writing privileges. If it is being used for day to day income, you might want to receive the checks. The choice is yours.

When withdrawing the money in this manner, you can elect to have the money withdrawn at fixed time and dollar intervals, such as x amount of dollars every 2 months, much in the manner you systematically build up your shares in the mutual fund. You can also elect to take out x number of shares on a fixed schedule. This

Service, Please

If you are an investor, or even a potential investor, you should be treated politely and courteously whenever you speak to anyone working at the mutual fund company. They should be able to provide you with information on the total return for the previous month, previous year, and so on. You should be able to receive information on the fund by mail, including a prospectus in a matter of a few business days. Once you are an investor in the fund, you are entitled to a prompt statement that is readable. Most important, you should be able to get your questions answered regarding the statement, the fund, its objectives, and management. Unreturned phone calls, unsatisfactory answers like "see our Web site," and misinformation are inexcusable.

Buyers and Sellers Beware!

Mutual funds make their own rules and establish their own policies regarding the buying, selling, and exchanging of fund shares. Read the literature carefully to understand the rules for each fund. For example, some funds will allow you to make a redemption based only on an amount of money you are looking to redeem and not by how many shares you are looking to sell. In other words, you will let the fund know that you want to redeem $5,000 worth of your investment and not 50 shares. If this is the case, you'll have fewer options of methods for calculating your taxes.

Some funds will limit how many transactions you can make in a given period of time; this avoids additional paperwork on the part of the fund and prevents investors from trying to market time the fund. This can also help keep the pool of assets steady.

Funds will have different requirements, and as businesses they are entitled to do so within the framework of the FCC. Some funds reserve certain rights. For example, a fund might say that for a large redemption, over $150,000, they have the right to pay you in marketable securities instead of cash. Read the prospectus and other literature about the fund. Also ask questions such as:

Are there any limits on how often I can make a transaction?

Is there a minimum amount I have to invest or withdraw when buying or redeeming shares after the initial investment?

How long will it take before I receive a check for redeeming shares?

Ask these and all other questions you can think of. Write them down ahead of time.

will result in inconsistent amounts being withdrawn based on the current NAV each time the distribution is made. Some funds won't allow you to do this; others will.

Planning carefully with your tax advisor, you can try to arrange it so that your systematic withdrawals won't bump you into a higher tax bracket. You can withdraw money over a course of 1 or several years. Generally, the more you spread out the withdrawal, the more you can benefit by not getting hit with a large tax bite at once and the longer the money that remains in the fund can continue to work for you. However, it is all dependent on your needs. If your needs are for steady income, you'll want to figure out what you need on a steady basis and then stretch out the withdrawals as long as possible.

ONLINE TRADING

The relative ease and accessibility to markets worldwide make online trading very inviting to anyone and everyone who is comfortable in front of their trusty PC. Online trading sites like Schwab or E*TRADE offer a great deal of information, as well as the option to make trades and look up quotes and prices. Little by little, all of the online sites are increasing their available information, making these discount brokers much more like full service brokers from a research and information vantage point. No, they generally won't provide individual advice or hand holding, but some do actually make suggestions. My own E*TRADE account e-mailed me that they had a mutual fund just right for me. Okay, perhaps that is more marketing than detailed financial planning. It does show that these Web sites are using their stored data to process information. It's only a matter of time before more detailed help is just a few clicks away. Some sites already offer online assistance for a fee.

The most important aspect of online trading, besides saving on commissions, is that it is user friendly and provides you with all the options you need. If a site allows you to easily select between numerous funds, stocks, bonds, and other securities, then it is serving you well for asset allocation. If you can make

transactions quickly, including selling and receiving a check in a matter of 3 business days, then liquidity is not a problem. If the site doesn't impose a whole bunch of additional fees (most do not), then you are okay in that respect as well. The site should also provide easy to download and print transaction statements and even send you via good old-fashioned mail, hard copies of your statements. These are all areas to keep in mind when trading online.

What sets online trading apart from other types of trading is that it is quick and convenient. There is a concern about security, however, when using the Internet. Ameritrade, E*TRADE, and all of their competitors would not stay in business if this was a major area of concern. But with some 100,000 of reported identity thefts in the past year (many over the Internet), people are concerned. For this reason, you go with the better known online brokers (see broker listings in Chapter 10), you double check mailed statements to make sure no other activity is going on in your account, and you keep an eye on your e-mails to make sure that no information you gave out to your online broker (or any e-commerce site with which you may have done business) shows up in the form of an e-mail from another company or individual. Naturally you tell no one your password. It's also not a good idea to log into your online account from other people's computers. You need to take the necessary precautions and you will usually be safe when dealing with major online brokers.

CHAPTER SEVENTEEN

ASSET ALLOCATION: SOME PLANS OF ACTION

Now that you're more familiar with the many types of mutual funds that you can choose from, it's time to consider asset allocation in more detail. The examples provided are just that, examples. They are no more rigid than any other investment philosophy or game plan. Always use model portfolios as rough guides when creating your own portfolio. Remember, no two persons' needs and financial situations are identical, and no one can confidently know the future outcome of any investment. Keep in mind that a portfolio does not have to be extensive. You do not need a dozen securities or types of investments, sometimes just a few diversified ones will do.

Nearly a decade ago the *Financial Analysts Journal* noted that only 7% of successful investing was dependent upon the selection of specific stocks, bonds, and mutual funds, while 93% hinged on selecting the right asset classes in which to be invested. Nonetheless, a great emphasis is placed on which funds to select without careful consideration given to where to put your money in a broader sense. Brokers, fund marketing, and periodicals will tell you which funds are great funds without telling you who should be buying them. After all, the fund management isn't concerned whether it's the right fund for your portfolio, and, unfortunately, neither are many brokers. Proper asset allocation can provide you with a better opportunity to meet your goals without being stymied by the effects of a single down market. Suffice to say, whether you're driving a Jaguar, a Volvo, or the old beat-up station wagon, if you're sitting in a major bottleneck. it doesn't matter which vehicle you're in. A downswing in a particular asset class or of a sector within an asset class is the same thing. Therefore, before determining which international stock fund to buy, determine how the international market is faring as a whole and if it serves a purpose in your portfolio. It may be a piece of the portfolio puzzle that doesn't fit or is covered by another piece or asset. Any fund you choose will follow the same course as the market it is part of, since investments in a particular asset class generally react similarly to the bigger investment picture. Therefore while one small-cap fund may be making great strides, if the market has not been good for small companies, the majority of small market funds will perform similarly. One of the reasons for the popularity of index funds has been to allocate across all sectors within a given asset class. This limits the need to allocate the stock fund part of your portfolio unless you then choose to play one sector more heavily or add a growth or income fund depending on your needs. Even with an index fund and a sector or growth fund giving you more strength in a certain area, your allocation is not complete. You then need to balance these investments with fixed asset investments and cash since the first two funds are both in the stock market.

Your asset allocation is contingent on several factors including:

1. Your own level of risk/tolerance. No matter who tells you which investments you *should* focus on, the only one you need to answer to is yourself. Go with your own level of comfort.

2. Your financial situation in regard to keeping money invested over time. Can you tie up $5,000 or $10,000 for *x* number of years? Long-term investing is the key to much greater success.

3. Your need for capital preservation. Just because you have $10,000 to invest doesn't mean you can afford to lose it. You need to assess how secure your assets and income are. Could the value of your home drop? Could you or your spouse be let go by your company? If you are self-employed, could you have a slow year? While mutual funds (open-end funds in particular) are generally liquid, your concern is having the full principal available should you need it. Should your $10,000 investment be down to $5,000 when you suddenly need it, you cannot recover the other $5,000. Therefore, you are only liquid at 50% of your investment.

4. Your potential goals. As discussed earlier, other than tuition, you should be flexible with your goals since life will change and other goals and needs may arise. Also your financial situation can change and alter your plans for better or for worse.

5. Your available time and ability to follow your investments. The more widespread your assets are, the more time it

Real World Philosophy

It's easy for someone on Wall Street who is earning $500,000 a year to tell you to invest aggressively. You, however, know that a $10,000 loss is far more significant for your family than the Wall Streeter. The average family income in the United States as of 2000 is around $50,000. Therefore real world philosophy is to follow the route that makes you feel comfortable, not the Wall Street execs and big ticket financial advisors.

will take you to keep tabs on them. If you don't have time to follow the results of nine mutual funds, buy two or three. If you don't have time to follow two or three, get an index fund!

6. Your age and current needs. Do you need income now? Are you retired and not concerned about long-term investing but just living comfortably? Are you 25, with a good paying job, a decent-sized apartment for a single person, and have this extra money to put somewhere that you don't need at present?

7. Your tax situation. Sure, you can own a technology fund and see higher rewards, but if Uncle Sam is going to take most of them, you might need to look at some tax-free funds before April 15th begins looking like D-day.

Asset allocation is much more than a goal in the future, it's a way of creating a sound investment plan that will bring you substantial returns while providing the proper level of safety. It's a plan designed by you. Following are some sample plans.

THE CONSERVATIVE ALLOCATION ROUTE

You've heard about the great success others are having with investments and thought you'd join the fun. Although you have some money to invest, you are not in a position where you can afford to take any great loss to your principal investment. Perhaps you have a goal that is only 2 or 3 years away or are seeking current income now. These are reasons you may be looking at building a more conservative portfolio whereby:

Plan A You might allocate 60% to bond funds, 20% to a large-cap stock fund or an S&P 500 fund, and 20% into a money market mutual fund that yields about 6%. Of the 60% bond funds, look at short- to intermediate-term bonds, which provide income and are not as volatile as long-term bond funds.

Plan B   You take the same allocation as listed above, except if you are in a high tax bracket take 50% of the 60% in bond funds (or 30% overall) and put it in tax-free municipal bond funds.

Plan C   You might also want to have some income generated from the stock portion of the portfolio as well as the bond portion, so you might look for growth and income stock funds with the 20%.

Notes on conservative investing:

1. Quite often more aggressive investors will switch to one of these plans as a longer term goal becomes a short-term goal. They start out more aggressively and then become increasingly more conservative as their time frame grows shorter and certainly after they retire.

2. There are those investors, however, who go against the grain and start out very conservatively, build up their initial investment from $5,000 to $10,000 in a safe manner and then take the $5,000 they have gained and go into the aggressive funds with the theory that they are now investing found money. Then, once that money grows, they recoup the $5,000 back into the safe portion of the portfolio, or reallocate into the conservative plan.

3. The conservative allocation plan (or plans) is preached as the way to go for retirees. This theory is starting to erode as retirees are living longer and want to keep on playing the market. With 401k plans, pension plans, and IRAs coming due, coupled with social security, a paid-off mortgage, and investments that have built up for years, many retirees are more than comfortable and have fewer financial obligations. They want to enjoy the fruits of investing. On the contrary, many young investors who are supposed to be going after the trendy, hot funds take a more conservative, slow and steady route. There's nothing wrong with slow and steady.

4. If you are investing conservatively, you will generally see conservative returns. This is fine, and these can build over time. However, it is important to keep an eye on inflation so that you continue to beat the rate of inflation.

Float It!

It's not uncommon for investors to have much of their assets in secure long-term places, such as 40% in stock funds, 20% in bond funds, and 10% in cash. But what about the other 30%? This is the part that you move around when the market looks to be making its moves or shifts. Not that you should run and panic when the market has a bad day or two, but you should shift with major trends. For example, if growth investing is in favor for several years, the 30% is in growth stocks, if value stocks now take over for the next 2 years, that same 30% is in value stocks. If the market becomes a bear market for 6 months, that 30% is in bonds and in your money market fund. A core allocation and a portion of money to move at the right times (not timing the market) is very important to successful asset allocation.

Allocating by Goals

Planners will tell you that if you have at least 20 years to go until you retire, put nearly all your money into stocks and stock funds. If the market takes a dive, you'll have plenty of time to recover. Sure, why not jump into the ocean and have plenty of time to swim to shore before a shark gets you. The point is, you don't want to spend too much time swimming back to where you started even if you will end up ahead in the end. During each downturn in the market you lose liquidity if your stock funds have lost value. What good is a paper loss that should someday be a gain if you suddenly need the money now? Furthermore, if you've had gains, you are still paying capital gains taxes while you are fighting to get back to where you started. Regardless of the one retirement goal, you may have tuition, home buying, car buying, and even some business you hope to open up someday. Therefore you need to allocate accordingly for each of these areas with mutual funds and other investments.

If you are starting with $20,000 and want to reach each of your goals in approximately 3, 5, 8, 10, and 20 years, you may be best served looking at approximately how much you are looking to gain to achieve each goal individually. Naturally buying a car in 3 years is a lot less to build toward than college tuition for two children in 8 and 10 years. Therefore, you might look at each goal as a separate plan. Often people are doing this to some degree by having a 401k for retirement and a separate portfolio of two or three mutual funds for college tuition. You can spread it out farther if you choose. Then it's not as risky to be more aggressive in one area. For example, if you are looking at 15 years until retirement and you put $5,000 toward that goal, you can go for the highest growth you can find while not jeopardizing the more immediate need to be conservative as you get close to needing the down payment for that new house. That money can be moved into a short-term income-generating bond fund, while the funds for the other goals stay on their respective tracks.

Don't let a planner talk you into investing the bulk of your money toward your retirement. Divide up your investments into goal-oriented plans, then invest accordingly, taking into consideration time frame, risk/tolerance, and all that other good stuff talked about throughout this book.

5. A conservative approach to investing can also mean simply starting small and building. You may have some aggressive growth investments or may be buying some stocks on your own in small amounts. A conservative approach is to start with a small amount and build slowly from that point keeping in mind your budget and comfort level.

THE MIDDLE OF THE ROAD ALLOCATION ROUTE

You've got kids in middle school heading for college in 5 to 7 years. You're working hard and want to benefit from good investments but can't afford to take great risks. Perhaps you're a newly married couple, looking forward to a family someday. You're just establishing your career and between the two of you have some money to put aside. You're new to investing but know it's important to start putting some money away toward your future. Or you may be an investor who has already taken the more aggressive route and built up some savings and now as your goals are approaching in the shorter term you want to head in a more conservative direction. For numerous reasons, investors often take a middle of the road approach whereby:

Plan D   You start with a 60, 35, 5 split, with 60% in stock funds, 35% in a bond fund, and 5% in a money market mutual fund. The stock portion should be divided up to cover different segments of the market. You might seek out a growth fund and a value fund, leaning more heavily in the direction of which is in favor at the moment—growth or value. You might choose a sector fund in a hot, growing sector for a smaller amount of your allocation. The market trends change often. In 1999 you would want to dump a large portion of the stock allocation into any fund holding a great deal of technology stocks. If in doubt as to which direction the market is heading (value or growth?), you might be safe going more heavily with the blue chip stocks as they will almost always remain a good place to be over time. The stock funds should cover the bases, giving you diversity as well as protection against a

Time Is the Key

Money grows over time. Even if you invest only $1,000 a year, thanks to reinvestment and compounding, over 40 years in a rather safe fund yielding a 9% return (don't forget a total return over a span of 40 years isn't going to be some tremendous number like 40%) you would reach a total of $337,000 if you were to retire at age 65, and at 10% you'd top $440,000. And this is a conservative investment below the 11% return the stock market sees annually!

down industry or segment of the market. You'll also want to be covering the large- and small-cap companies with your funds, thus exposing you to both sides. The bond fund will help balance the risks and add potential income. You'll mix intermediate- and short-term bond funds and consider municipal funds if you're in a high tax bracket.

Plan E You use the same allocation percentages as Plan D, only you go entirely with index funds. You could take a fund like the Vanguard Total Index Fund that mirrors the Wilshire 5000 (covering nearly the entire stock market), and an international index fund for the stock portion, or divide it up between an S&P 500 index fund and a small-cap index fund. Use bond index funds as well, except, of course, if you're in a high tax bracket and go with some municipal bond funds as well.

Notes on middle of the road investing:

1. Middle of the road investing is often the route taken by people with multiple goals, some short term and some long term. Since retirement, tuition, a new home, and other goals are not mutually exclusive, you may have all of them on your plate at once. Therefore, you cannot commit to a more conservative or aggressive plan in hopes of reaching all of your goals and plans.

2. The middle of the road stance is also a solid position from which to switch gears and move in another direction should the market take an up or down turn or should you feel more confident in your abilities as an investor. You can maintain much of your portfolio and let the long-term advantages take effect, while fine tuning in the direction you want to go by reallocating 20% in either direction. A middle of the road portfolio is by no means saying that you expect to break even. It simply means you are looking for good returns but have enough safety nets set up so a downturn in the market or an unexpected change in your own life plans or goals will not mean rethinking and subsequently shifting your entire portfolio.

THE AGGRESSIVE ALLOCATION ROUTE

You're in your early 30s, single, and making a good living. You figure now is the time to build up your assets before you settle into greater financial responsibilities. Perhaps you're married with toddlers, you have both been setting money aside for the past few years in safe cash accounts. Even though the children are in diapers now, you know in 15 or 16 years they'll be ready for college and the costs by that time . . . well, you don't even want to think about it. You could also be a hard-working couple with children in grade school. Sadly, one of your close relatives passes away. It is certainly not how you wanted to come into money, but you now have a $25,000 inheritance beyond that which you have already been putting into middle of the road or conservative investment vehicles.

There are a number of scenarios that warrant more aggressive investing, provided you are comfortable with the greater risks involved. If you are ready to invest more aggressively, you might allocate your portfolio whereby:

Plan F You tuck 10% away in a money market fund, put 10% in a short-term bond fund, and put 80% into your stock fund portfolio. You then spread the 80% around within a combination of sector funds, growth funds, value funds, small-cap funds, and international funds.

Plan G Go with Plan F except put 60% into the hot industries (such as tech and telecommunications in the late '90s) and 20% into big, safe blue chippers, just in case the hot industries go south. Be ready to switch your funds around after a really great year . . . chances are two in a row will be unlikely. Don't get greedy.

Notes on aggressive investing:

1. Remember, don't go with last year's super hot funds, as they are likely not to be this year's winners.
2. Aggressive investing does not mean market timing. It means going after bigger returns with potentially greater risks. Such

returns can be over time and not simply a fund that is going to have a hot year. Yes, you'd love to have that sector fund that gains 186%, but you'd also like to have the funds that gain 40% over 3 years.

3. The theory that you start out aggressively over the long term is a fine one to follow. However, be sure you have a safety net of money tucked away in safe places.

4. Aggressive doesn't mean foolhardy. Cocky investors often get big returns and then forget that such returns don't last forever and that they come from doing research on the fund and not just diving in with an "I'm on a winning streak" attitude.

All of these strategies assume you are allocating a portion of your investing dollar to mutual funds. You certainly need not put 100% of your investments into mutual funds. You should have cash accounts that do not earn a great deal but keep your money safe and sound and liquid. Short-term investing is important for the here and now. CDs, T-bills, and bank accounts are still viable means of investing so that you have your money working for you but available at present. After all, your ATM machine isn't going to give you $500 from your mutual fund. More significantly, you need to deal with ongoing living expenses and short-term investments work for that reason.

There is also the added level of safety from certain surefire investments. U.S. savings bonds or Treasury bills are not exciting investments, but they are the safest investments around.

On the other hand, you can invest more aggressively outside of funds by allocating some money directly into stocks in companies that you believe in. Buying through places like E*TRADE or Ameritrade makes it very simple to buy stocks for a very low commission. Nowhere does it say that only fund managers can select the right stocks for you. Chart a stock price for a while, review the com-

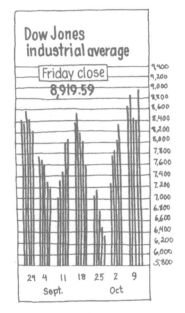

Too Many Funds in the Old Portfolio?

What's the magic number for mutual funds in your portfolio? The magic number is how many mutual funds you can keep track of and get solid returns from without spreading your investing dollars too thin.

All right, all right, the number is around five, counting your safety valve money market mutual fund. Once you start getting beyond that, you will start duplicating too many of the holdings in the funds you already own. Many investors are more than content with three funds, one being an S&P or Wilshire index fund, plus a money market fund and a bond fund. Sometimes four funds lets you cover the various categories more thoroughly, large-cap growth, small-cap value, a bond fund, plus the money market fund.

It's also worth noting that since mutual funds generally have minimum investments, sometimes as low as $1,000 and other times as high as $15,000 or $20,000, the more funds you buy, the more money you may have to invest to get into the funds you want.

The number of funds should usually correlate with your investment goals and strategies. If you are lacking in one aspect of your portfolio or need to balance out other fund investments, then you may be looking to fill in that portion of your portfolio with another fund.

The "Rule Of Thumb" Age Range Philosophy

While this is a basic asset allocation philosophy and serves as a general investing guideline in regard to age, the problem with this rule of thumb is that it doesn't account for personal situations, personal goals, individual attitudes regarding risk, peak earning years (which could now be anywhere from 25 to 65), and people living and working longer.

Nonetheless, in a broad sense this is the general breakdown by ages, assuming you start out working steadily in your 20s with enough money to invest.

Late 20s and 30s: 75% in stocks and stock funds, 25% in bonds, bond funds, and money market funds.

40s: 65% in stocks and stock funds, 35 % in bonds, bond funds, and money market funds.

50s: 50% to 60% in stocks and stock funds, 40% to 50% in bonds, bond funds, and money market funds.

60s: 40% in stocks and stock funds, 60% in bonds, bond funds, and money market funds.

70s: 20% in stocks and stock funds, 80% in bonds, bond funds, and money market funds.

The needs of people in their 40s and 50s vary greatly as some people are sending kids to college, while others are looking toward an early retirement. Some are also in peak earning years, while others are looking at a second career following a midlife crisis. The point is that these are probably the most diverse age categories.

Keep in mind that there are other options besides money market funds, such as CDs or T-bills, depending on the current interest rates. Also remember to reallocate your assets even in a defined contribution plan.

Finally, remember that your investing style is part of your overall personality. In other words, you'll find 29-year-old conservative investors and 59-year-old aggressive investors.

pany, read up on it, feel confident about the product or service provided by this company, and you can start playing the market on your own. In fact, equity investors can create their own mutual fund of sorts by purchasing several stocks and making corrections when necessary. Believe it or not, as of early 2000 there were still more individual stock investors than mutual fund investors even though there are more mutual funds.

While investing for the future is advised, the problem with long-term investing is that while it always has paid off, the past still does not mean for sure that it always will pay off in the future. When the market suddenly drops for a few months, the hearts of long-term investors drop with it. Yes, you can read all the papers that say it is only temporary, but it's hard to sit by patiently and weather the storm.

Since you're allocating with a long-term plan in mind, it's best to look at 5- and 10-year annualized returns. You are generally hoping to have the money in place for mid- to long-range goals, and you want to have funds that have performed over a span of time. The 1-year wonder funds that bring in 190% are marvelous if you have the right one, but the wrong one can hurt you. If a fund has a 1-year total return of 100% and a 5-year total return of 40%, that means it is not consistent, but at least over time it has still paid off. It has around a 25% return over the other 4 years (assets in the fund may have been higher or lower in those years, so it's not an exact mathematical equation). Nonetheless, a 5-year 25% return is still better than the average return. However, if you see that in 1 year a mutual fund's returns were disproportionately higher than over 5 years, you are dealing with a very volatile fund that has had its down years as well. For example, a 1-year total of 180% and a 5-year total of 20% means the fund is at around −20% in each of the other 4 years. Therefore, you have only a 20% chance (one in five) of hitting that big year with a fund that has had this type of past performance.

Stocking up for Retirement

Even as you approach retirement, you can still keep a substantial amount of your assets in stocks and stock funds. But what about current income? You can go with some of the big companies that pay dividends such as IBM or Johnson & Johnson. What about cash now for an emergency? For liquidity, you can always sell off a stock or a stock fund. You can always move money into a money market mutual if the market is experiencing a downturn. It's a matter of feeling comfortable. A 60% stock fund, 30% bond fund, 10% money market fund portfolio is not out of the question for a retiree if he or she is living comfortably. Many retirees also want to accumulate something to leave their heirs and not deplete all of their savings on living expenses.

FYI

No one is investing to lose money. In fact, people are usually not investing to prevent losing money but are safeguarding themselves by proper asset allocation. People still wonder, what if the bottom fell out completely, would I lose it all? Well, it's quite unlikely. Even if you went with only large-cap stocks and sank $50,000 into them, the worst you would come out, based on history, after 5 years, is with $43,650. This is based on the fact that since 1926, over any 5-year span, large-cap companies have never been down more than 12.7%. Therefore, suffice it to say: Yes, long-term investing can have its pitfalls, but, no, you shouldn't lose everything unless you buy a fund investing in swamp land in Florida or just invest in swamp land in Florida, or perhaps eight-track tapes (*for those old enough to remember them*).

ASSET ALLOCATION—A FINAL WORD

When allocating the stock portion of your portfolio, look to balance your assets to protect your investment but also to lean toward profitability. In other words, value and growth funds generally perform in opposite manners, large- and small-cap funds also generally see a similar contrast. You want to invest more assets into the one that is in favor at the time you are investing and reallocate if and when the tide turns. International funds, like sectors, go in and out of favor based on the global markets and numerous other factors. Yours is not to question the reasons that categories of funds go in and out of favor as much as to determine how much to play these funds. Do you need to invest in a sector, or does your growth fund have it pretty well covered? The same holds true with international funds. Do you need one or are you getting 5% exposure to the international market from your existing funds? Remember, you don't want to play the market timing game on an ongoing basis where you're trying to time when to buy and sell regularly. But you do have to try to decide if, from an overall standpoint, these markets are worthwhile and to what degree. There are marvelous times for international investing and for each of the various sectors, you need to determine whether this is the time to go in heavily, lightly (just to have some presence in the category), or not at all.

Keep in mind that an index fund, or a couple of index funds, allocates assets between large- and small-cap companies and can be a good place for much of the stock portion of your portfolio. Then you need to decide where to go from there. One thing you need to avoid is buying funds that are too similar, which will make you too heavily weighted in one area. You don't want much overlap in your asset allocation, particularly when it comes to stock funds.

ASSET ALLOCATION

You can use the worksheet below to start mapping out how much money to allocate into each asset class and then how to allocate the assets (in broad terms) within that asset class.

Investment goal(s) _____

Amount of time to reaching goal(s)

_____ More than 6 months

_____ More than 1 year

_____ More than 3 years

_____ More than 5 years

_____ More than 7 years

_____ More than 10 years

_____ More than 15 years

Amount of money to invest: $_____

Amount of above investment to put into stock funds $_____   _____%

Amount of above investment to put into bond funds $_____   _____%

Amount of above investment to put into money market fund $_____   _____%

Amount of above investment to put into other cash investments $_____   _____%

Amount of stock fund investment above in higher yield, higher $_____   _____%
   risk stock funds. This would include aggressive growth funds,
   sector funds and international funds.

Amount of stock fund investment above in less risky stock funds. This $_____   _____%
   would include large-cap blue chip funds, growth and income funds, and
   index funds.

Amount of bond fund investments in high-yield (junk bond) high-risk funds. $_____   _____%
   You could also include international bond funds in this riskier category
   for different reasons.

Amount of money in high-grade corporate, government, or municipal $_____   _____%
   bond funds.

CHAPTER EIGHTEEN

CONCLUSION:
SOME POSITIVES AND
NEGATIVES

So, there you have it, mutual fund investing, all the basics. It's hard to say that everyone should go out and buy a mutual fund or three since it's an individual decision based on an individual's financial situation and goals. Over the past decade, funds have grown in popularity because the hype has proven to be valid. Many funds have produced good returns for investors. It hasn't hurt any that the 1990s were a bull economy almost from start to finish and that the technology and media have made great strides in making information accessible.

Throughout the book we've explored everything about mutual funds without delving into specific best funds since today's best fund pick isn't tomorrow's. There have been many reasons discussed that explain why you should purchase mutual funds. Here is a brief reminder of what you need to keep in mind as a potential fund investor. Also included in this final chapter is a look at the downside of mutual funds, including common complaints.

ALL THAT GLITTERS ISN'T GOLD!

Mutual funds are the rage. But does that mean they are flawless? Do they have imperfections?

Mutual funds have played a significant role in the financial success of millions of people worldwide. They have also been a source of disappointment for others. Marketing, hype, and profiles of extremely successful fund managers can present the wrong impressions. Yes, there are 32-year-old multimillionaire fund geniuses out there. We get the point. However, for every one of the 11,000 or so fund managers (some doing better than others), there are thousands of investors, many of whom own funds that are helping them slowly build up a nest egg for their retirement.

Problems ensue when there are unrealistic expectations—thanks to hype and marketing. If you believe you will see instant riches, you are not looking at funds in the right perspective. It's not hard, however, to see things out of perspective when following the media. How many people were disappointed when Mark McGwire only hit 65 home runs the year after his record-setting 70 home run season? The American ideal of being the best and setting new standards is something that can create great joy but also disillusionment. Look at how many people are conned into get rich quick schemes because everything points to instant riches. How many people have bought the latest and greatest new product only to find it was inferior to what they had?

That's why it's quite understandable when we see people invest and expect immediate rewards. The fastest way to riches is exciting and sells newspapers and magazines. Likewise, hot funds and big returns are big ticket, front-page stories. Naturally, you don't see the funds gaining a mere 10% return making the front pages of the top financial magazines. Too many investors got caught up with the glowing results of the top tech funds. Hence the misconception that you will retire a millionaire from a mutual fund investment. Just sit back and watch the money come pouring in! Most tech funds, however, are not the basis by which the slow and steady route to retirement is really made. The hot sector, tech, or aggressive mutual funds can work wonders in the short term but you will need to reallocate your assets from time to time.

Another misconception is that funds are a sure thing. This is far from true. Many funds have seen great success over recent years, while others have had their ups and downs. Over time, however, there is a better likelihood of seeing positive returns than seeing a loss to your principal investment. This does not negate the fact that mutual funds come with fees, expenses, commissions, and taxes accompanying them. All of these factors may make for more modest realistic returns when all is said and done. Yes, you still have to go out and go to work, your funds are not the answer to all your financial worries.

Like any investment, there are risks associated with buying a stock or bond mutual fund. If you want to strictly maintain the lowest level of risk, look to money market mutual funds and bond funds, but then understand that you are investing with the "I don't want to lose" philosophy overshadowing the "I want to make a killing" philosophy. This is not a bad thing as long as you understand the conservative manner in which you are investing.

Bad Bull

A bull market is generally a good thing. Everyone is making money and everyone is happy! However, here are a few notes of caution.

1. Bull markets don't last forever.
2. Bull markets make fund managers look better than they really are.
3. Bull markets make typical investors a little too sure of themselves.
4. Bull markets can make people forget about allocating assets into safer places like fixed income funds.
5. Bull markets lead people to believe money is practically falling from the sky, so they go out and overindulge.

Remember that good things don't last forever. Enjoy the bull, but be safeguarded against the bear!

The bottom line is that, as wonderful as funds can be, there are pitfalls, many of which are created by the fact that people want more than a fund can provide. All expectations aside, funds also receive common complaints, and those are valid and also worthy of some attention. Next we look at some of the common complaints about mutual funds and provide some answers.

COMMON COMPLAINTS ABOUT MUTUAL FUNDS

Complaint: There are so many funds out there, it's just overwhelming trying to select one or two.

Answer: True. But, if you narrow down the field it will make selecting much easier. First determine your own goals and needs. Determine how much risk you are willing to take and how much money you can comfortably invest. Between this book, online Web sites from financial institutions, and financial magazines, you should be able to match your investment plans to that of a type of fund. Once you know that you will be comfortable with a growth fund, or you know that you want income from a growth and income fund, you should be ready to narrow your field and look for funds in different families that fit the category. Like anything else, it's a matter of focusing on what you are looking for and then comparing the few favorites that meet your needs. Look at a few fund families and you will usually start to see similarities within the same type of fund. If this is the case, you can stop after looking at growth funds in five or six mutual fund families and assume all others will be relatively similar. Compare expense ratios, loads, and no-loads, and other factors such as additional fees and turnover rate. It's like buying a car. There are thousands of models, but if you're looking for a four-door family car in a certain price range, that will narrow your search. Then you'll compare possible deals, including extras and extra costs.

Complaint: There seem to be a lot of hidden taxes that sort of sneak up on you when you own a mutual fund.

Answer: True again, only they're not really hidden once you understand that mutual funds are assuming capital gains by their

Top 10 Things to Remember
When Investing in a Mutual Fund

In case you haven't been paying attention:

1. Invest in the funds that are best suited for *your* needs, not the needs of the friend, neighbor, business associate, golfing buddy, party clown, or cab driver who offers advice.
2. Unlike the New York Yankees, last year's winners may not be this year's winners.
3. Despite the jargon, read the prospectus carefully and slowly enough to actually understand most of it.
4. Steer clear of funds hawked by phone callers no matter how good the sales pitch. Remember, if the fund is so great, why is he or she harassing you? Why doesn't the caller just invest in the fund and retire?
5. If you have to mortgage your house to pay the fund fees, then they are too high. Watch the expense ratio and the fees carefully.
6. Remember, you're investing so that you can see more money, not send more to Uncle Sam. Keep the tax bite in mind and watch for funds with excessive turnover and high capital gains.
7. If you don't want to leave American soil, then stay put! Don't let someone else talk you into international funds. Buy them if they fit your personal portfolio.
8. Don't buy tax exempt funds in your tax-free retirement account. That's paying no tax on something you're already not paying tax on, or investment redundancy.
9. Variety is the spice of fund investing. Diversify!
10. If you need more than just your fingers to count up your funds, then you have too many. Don't overindulge, no matter how tempting.

trading activities and that you are responsible for
the taxes on those gains. Naturally the fund companies have tried to keep this quiet, since it's not
their strongest selling point, but of late there has
been widespread reform starting with Schwab,
whereby funds are now publishing their tax-
adjusted returns. Although taxes can knock as
much as 3% off your returns, you won't be too
upset if the return is dropping from 35% to 32%,
which is much better than you'll get in a bank account.
Just watch to see that a fund isn't going to be a greater tax burden
than it is worth.

Paying taxes is the unpleasant part of owning mutual funds,
unless you select tax-free municipal bond funds or have your mutual
fund in a tax-deferred retirement plan. You can also minimize the tax
bite by placing the funds with higher turnover rates or a greater difference between their returns and tax-adjusted returns into your tax-
deferred retirement account.

As the tax-adjusted returns on mutual funds become more out in
the open, taxes on gains will seem less hidden and more acceptable.
Just as real estate taxes won't stop you from buying the home you
really love, paying taxes won't stop you from a good investment.

Complaint: I own a fund, but I don't know what they're investing in.
Answer: That is a problem with mutual funds that does disturb
some investors while others shrug it off. There is a listing of the top
holdings of the fund in the prospectus. For some investors this is sufficient, since it's unlikely that they're going to know many of the "less
well known" companies the fund owns shares of. Morningstar fund profiles often have a little more detail. The annual or semiannual report
should list the securities held by the fund. The problem is that this is
published, as the name indicates, annually or semiannually, which
means there is lag time in which a fund with high turnover may no
longer be holding several of the funds listed. Fund managers don't want
their success duplicated elsewhere, so it's often next to impossible to
get an up to the minute listing of what is being held by the fund. It is
a good idea to look over the annual or semiannual report though, so
you can get an idea of what the holdings are and see if any trend is

forming other than that set forth in the objective of the fund. Also you can notice if you have the same holdings in more than one of your funds. This can be good if it's a big winner. However, if there's a lot of overlap, you'll want greater diversification between your funds.

One way to have a pretty clear picture of what securities are in your fund, or funds, at any given time is to buy an index fund and get hold of the list of stocks on the particular benchmark index. I know, that's a cop-out, but otherwise the problem does indeed remain that you do not always know what stocks you are invested in.

Complaint: I bought the fund that had 189% returns last year, and now it's doing nothing. Why was it so highly touted?

Answer: It was touted as one of last year's winners, not one of the winners for this year. Just as the Yankees will win the pennant in one season, someone else may (doubtfully) win it the following year. One-year wonders generally do not repeat in the financial world. Look for long-term winners over 3, 5, and 10 years. Ignore hype and go with solid research on your part.

Complaint: There seem to be a lot of little fees and expenses eating away at my returns. What can I do about that?

Answer: Once you are ready to invest in a fund, you'll be playing by their rules when it comes to expense payments. The longer you stay, however, the lower a back-end load or commission will become. In time, like 5 years, it will disappear completely. Other fees, however, are spelled out in the prospectus. It's boring, dry, and all in all like sitting through your neighbors' home movies of their trip to the Grand Canyon, but it's still important to *read the prospectus,* or at least the key parts like "Fees and Expenses."

The first fee so many people are advocating to avoid is the "load." No-loads are very popular, and if you know what you want and don't need anyone to help you buy it, then do it yourself by calling the 800 number.

While investors aren't big fans of paying fees to mutual funds, the reality is that any kind of investment will have a price attached. Even if you buy individual stocks on E*TRADE, you'll pay a commission— granted a low commission—but a commission nonetheless. If, however, you are finding funds with too many fees attached, look elsewhere.

Stocks Do Go Up

While it is certainly possible to pick a losing stock fund, it's less likely that a stock fund will continue to fall if you hold onto it longer. Despite the four significant bear markets over the past 71 years, the market has generally gone up. Stocks have finished up in 54 of the past 74 years. It is also calculated that if you hold a stock for 10 years, 90% of the time you will make money. Thus, over time a stock fund should be profitable; however, there are no guarantees.

Complaint: Why does everyone push mutual funds on me when I'd prefer to buy stocks and bonds?

Answer: Because it's the in thing and because many people have done very well with them. However, a great deal of the assets in mutual funds are through retirement plans. In actuality there are still more individual stockholders than mutual fund holders. The choice is totally up to you. If there's a stock you believe in, or several (diversify), by all means buy them and follow them. Be patient, as stocks can be volatile. There's nothing wrong with buying bonds if you can afford to. In, fact, if you are approaching a short-term goal, zero coupon bonds are an excellent way to go, and no, you don't need a mutual fund to do this investing. What funds do is to give many people who are worried about buying one single stock or may not have $10,000 to plunk down on a bond (and wait for it to mature or try the daunting task of trying to sell it on the market) the opportunity to own small pieces of many stocks or bonds or both. They are a way to diversify and build up your savings for the future. They are certainly not the only way, and a vast number of fund owners also own stocks and, or, bonds besides. Stock funds, in a time of a strong (yet volatile) market, have helped cushion the blow of volatile stocks that go up one day and down the next on the roller coaster known as investing. Funds are volatile too, but not always as volatile. There's a sense of security knowing that you own 200 stocks and not just one; it's a safety in numbers kind of thing.

CONCLUSION

Just as mutual funds are the rage, following money market funds, which followed CDs, there will probably be a new spin-off of mutual funds in the near future (perhaps spiders and diamonds are hinting at a combination index fund/stock). The reality is that newer, wider reaching, bigger, and better investment opportunities will always come along. As they said in *Star Wars,* "There's always a bigger fish."

The bottom line is that whatever makes you feel comfortable and secure as a well educated investor is the right path to follow. No matter which route you choose—stocks, bonds, mutual funds, collectibles or anything else—learn before you leap. An educated investor is a good investor whether or not he or she makes money—no one can predict the future. With that in mind, good luck in any funds or other investments you choose.

MAKE YOUR OWN FUND PROFILE WORKSHEET

Name of fund _____

Fund family _____

Fund objective _____

Category (small-cap stocks, high-grade corporate bonds, etc.)_____

Assets _____

Expense ratio _____

Load (if applicable) _____   Redemption fee (if applicable)_____

Minimum investment $ _____

Beta (volatility ranking) _____

Current NAV_____

Fund performance history _____   > (percentage gained or lost) previous year _____   3 yrs. _____
5 yrs. _____   10 yrs. _____   Since inception _____

Load-adjusted return (if applicable)   > 1 year _____

Tax adjusted return _____   > 1 year _____

Rate of turnover _____

Fund manager _____

Sector breakdown (i.e., Technology 41%, Health 23%, Communications 12%, and so on.) _____

_____

_____

Top 10 Holdings:

_____   _____

_____   _____

_____   _____

_____   _____

_____   _____

Percentage of international holdings (or domestic holdings if global fund) _____

We Have EVERYTHING!®

Available wherever books are sold!

Everything® **After College Book**
$12.95, 1-55850-847-3

Everything® **Astrology Book**
$12.95, 1-58062-062-0

Everything® **Baby Names Book**
$12.95, 1-55850-655-1

Everything® **Baby Shower Book**
$12.95, 1-58062-305-0

Everything® **Barbeque Cookbook**
$12.95, 1-58062-316-6

Everything® **Bartender's Book**
$9.95, 1-55850-536-9

Everything® **Bedtime Story Book**
$12.95, 1-58062-147-3

Everything® **Beer Book**
$12.95, 1-55850-843-0

Everything® **Bicycle Book**
$12.95, 1-55850-706-X

Everything® **Build Your Own Home Page**
$12.95, 1-58062-339-5

Everything® **Casino Gambling Book**
$12.95, 1-55850-762-0

Everything® **Cat Book**
$12.95, 1-55850-710-8

Everything® **Christmas Book**
$15.00, 1-55850-697-7

Everything® **College Survival Book**
$12.95, 1-55850-720-5

Everything® **Cover Letter Book**
$12.95, 1-58062-312-3

Everything® **Crossword and Puzzle Book**
$12.95, 1-55850-764-7

Everything® **Dating Book**
$12.95, 1-58062-185-6

Everything® **Dessert Book**
$12.95, 1-55850-717-5

Everything® **Dog Book**
$12.95, 1-58062-144-9

Everything® **Dreams Book**
$12.95, 1-55850-806-6

Everything® **Etiquette Book**
$12.95, 1-55850-807-4

Everything® **Family Tree Book**
$12.95, 1-55850-763-9

Everything® **Fly-Fishing Book**
$12.95, 1-58062-148-1

Everything® **Games Book**
$12.95, 1-55850-643-8

Everything® **Get-a-Job Book**
$12.95, 1-58062-223-2

The ultimate reference for couples planning their wedding!

- Scheduling, budgeting, etiquette, hiring caterers, florists, and photographers
- Ceremony & reception ideas
- Over 100 forms and checklists
- And much, much more!

$12.95, 384 pages, 8" x 9¼"

Personal finance made easy—and fun!

- Create a budget you can live with
- Manage your credit cards
- Set up investment plans
- Money-saving tax strategies
- And much, much more!

$12.95, 288 pages, 8" x 9¼"

For more information, or to order, call 800-872-5627
or visit www.adamsmedia.com/everything

Adams Media Corporation, 260 Center Street, Holbrook, MA 02343

Everything® **Get Published Book**
$12.95, 1-58062-315-8

Everything® **Get Ready For Baby Book**
$12.95, 1-55850-844-9

Everything® **Golf Book**
$12.95, 1-55850-814-7

Everything® **Guide to New York City**
$12.95, 1-58062-314-X

Everything® **Guide to Walt Disney World®, Universal Studios®, and Greater Orlando**
$12.95, 1-58062-404-9

Everything® **Guide to Washington D.C.**
$12.95, 1-58062-313-1

Everything® **Herbal Remedies Book**
$12.95, 1-58062-331-X

Everything® **Homeselling Book**
$12.95, 1-58062-304-2

Everything® **Homebuying Book**
$12.95, 1 58062-074-4

Everything® **Home Improvement Book**
$12.95, 1-55850-718-3

Everything® **Internet Book**
$12.95, 1-58062-073-6

Everything® **Investing Book**
$12.95, 1-58062-149-X

Everything® **Jewish Wedding Book**
$12.95, 1-55850-801-5

Everything® **Kids' Money Book**
$9.95, 1-58062-322-0

Everything® **Kids' Nature Book**
$9.95, 1-58062-321-2

Everything® **Kids' Puzzle Book**
$9.95, 1-58062-323-9

Everything® **Low-Fat High-Flavor Cookbook**
$12.95, 1-55850-802-3

Everything® **Microsoft® Word 2000 Book**
$12.95, 1-58062-306-9

Everything® **Money Book**
$12.95, 1-58062-145-7

Everything® **One-Pot Cookbook**
$12.95, 1-58062-186-4

Everything® **Online Business Book**
$12.95, 1-58062-320-4

Everything® **Online Investing Book**
$12.95, 1-58062-338-7

Everything® **Pasta Book**
$12.95, 1-55850-719-1

Everything® **Pregnancy Book**
$12.95, 1-58062-146-5

Everything® **Pregnancy Organizer**
$15.00, 1-55850-336-0

Everything® **Resume Book**
$12.95, 1-58062-311-5

Everything® **Sailing Book**
$12.95, 1-58062-187-2

Everything® **Selling Book**
$12.95, 1-58062-319-0

Everything® **Study Book**
$12.95, 1-55850-615-2

Everything® **Tarot Book**
$12.95, 1-58062-191-0

Everything® **Toasts Book**
$12.95, 1-58062-189-9

Everything® **Total Fitness Book**
$12.95, 1-58062-318-2

Everything® **Trivia Book**
$12.95, 1-58062-143-0

Everything® **Tropical Fish Book**
$12.95, 1-58062-343-3

Everything® **Wedding Book, 2nd Edition**
$12.95, 1-58062-190-2

Everything® **Wedding Checklist**
$7.95, 1-55850-278-5

Everything® **Wedding Etiquette Book**
$7.95, 1-55850-550-4

Everything® **Wedding Organizer**
$15.00, 1-55850-828-7

Everything® **Wedding Shower Book**
$7.95, 1-58062-188-0

Everything® **Wedding Vows Book**
$7.95, 1-55850-364-1

Everything® **Wine Book**
$12.95, 1-55850-808-2

Everything® is a registered trademark of Adams Media Corporation

OVER **TWO MILLION** EVERYTHING BOOKS SOLD

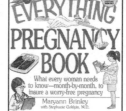

Your friends and family will be amazed with what you can do!

- Tutorials on the most popular programs
- Simple instructions to get your home page started
- Maintenance routines to keep your site fresh
- And much, much more!

$12.95, 304 pages, 8" x 9 1/4"

A pregnancy book that really does have everything!

- Extensive medical evaluation of what's happening to your body
- Exercise and diet tips
- 40-week pregnancy calendar
- And much, much more!

$12.95, 320 pages, 8" x 9 1/4"

EVERYTHING KIDS'® Now Available! Only $9.95 each

For more information, or to order, call 800-872-5627 or visit www.adamsmedia.com/everything
Adams Media Corporation, 260 Center Street, Holbrook, MA 02343